MY EGYPT

VORACIOUS

Voracious
Little, Brown and Company
New York Boston London

MY EGYPT

Cooking from My Roots

MICHAEL MINA

with Adam Sobel & Kate Leahy / photography by John Lee

Hachette Book Group supports the right to free expression
and the value of copyright. The purpose of copyright is to
encourage writers and artists to produce the creative works
that enrich our culture.

The scanning, uploading, and distribution of this book without
permission is a theft of the author's intellectual property. If you
would like permission to use material from the book (other than
for review purposes), please contact permissions@hbgusa.com.
Thank you for your support of the author's rights.

Voracious / Little, Brown and Company
Hachette Book Group
1290 Avenue of the Americas, New York, NY 10104
voraciousbooks.com

First Edition: October 2024

Voracious is an imprint of Little, Brown and Company, a division
of Hachette Book Group, Inc. The Voracious name and logo are
trademarks of Hachette Book Group, Inc.

The publisher is not responsible for websites (or their content)
that are not owned by the publisher.

The Hachette Speakers Bureau provides a wide range
of authors for speaking events. To find out more, go to
hachettespeakersbureau.com or email
HachetteSpeakers@hbgusa.com.

Little, Brown and Company books may be purchased in bulk for
business, educational, or promotional use. For information,
please contact your local bookseller or the Hachette Book Group
Special Markets Department at special.markets@hbgusa.com.

Design by Alice Chau
Food styling by Lillian Kang
Prop styling by Glenn Jenkins

ISBN 9780316429788
Library of Congress Control Number: 2023949961

10 9 8 7 6 5 4 3 2 1

RRD-APS

Printed in China

For my parents, Minerva and Ezzat,
who kept Egypt alive at home

And for my wife, Diane, and sons, Sammy and Anthony,
for supporting me through all my long hours
at work and travel far from home

CONTENTS

Introduction 22

About the Recipes 29

Start Here: Cooking
From This Book 34

The Middle'Terranea Pantry 35

WELCOME DRINKS

Limeade 46

Tangerine Carrot Juice
with Aleppo Sugar 46

Hibiscus Pomegranate Juice 48

Cucumber Honeydew Juice 49

SETTING THE TABLE

Tahina 52

Black Tahina 52

Pumpkin Seed Tahina 53

Tzatziki 53

Hummus 54

Smoked Beet Cream 55

Fresh Fava Bean Bessara 56

Smoky Baba Ghanoush 59

Ful Medames 60

Crispy Chickpeas 70

Mixed Pickles 73

Pickled Eggplant 74

Breads

    Baladi Bread 78

    Dukkah Flatbread 84

    Feteer with Ishta 87

APPETIZERS

Ta'ameya 92

Ahi Crudo on Ta'ameya 97

Steak Fries with a Trio of Dips 98

Za'atar-Cured Salmon
with Tzatziki and Salmon Roe 101

Kataifi-Wrapped Shrimp
with Mango Chile Sauce 108

Lobster Mango Salad 111

Grilled Octopus with Ful Medames 118

Turkey Hawawshi 121

Pumpkin Red Lentil Soup 122

Hummus with Cauliflower,
Pomegranate, and Foie Gras 125

SALADS AND VEGETABLES

Salata Baladi 129

Halloumi and Watermelon Salad 130

Middle Eastern Waldorf 133

Okra with Shallots and Chile 134

Harissa Ratatouille 136

Mashed Dukkah Cauliflower 137

Lemon Potatoes 139

Saffron Fingerling Potatoes 140

Roasted White Sweet Potatoes
with Mixed Herbs 142

Zucchini Mahshi 143

Roasted Squash Steak with Brussels
Sprouts and Onion Labne 146

RICE, GRAINS, AND PASTA

Freekeh Tabbouli 150

Lemon Saffron Couscous 152

Everyday Egyptian Rice 152

Sayadeya Rice 153

Koshari 156

Lamb Meatballs with Ricotta
Dumplings and Date Chutney 159

One-Pot Toasted Orzo
with Duck Ragù 162

Macaroni Béchamel
with Mushroom Bolognese 165

SEAFOOD

Sizzling Prawns 170

Molokhia Bouillabaisse 172

Grilled Swordfish
with Nigella Seeds, Preserved
Lemon, and Green Onions 175

Alexandria Fish Fry 178

Samak Singari 184

Salt-Baked Whole Fish
with Zucchini and Lemon 188

Tomato-Ginger Glazed Salmon 192

Phyllo-Crusted Sole
with Dukkah Beurre Blanc
and Golden Raisins 195

POULTRY AND MEAT

Grilled Sesame Quail
with Black Tahina 200

Roasted Squab
with Farro and Rice 203

Baharat Chicken in Grape Leaves
with Tangerine Labne 206

Feta-Brined Spatchcock Chicken
with Mint and Green Onions 208

Alexandria Steak Sandwiches 217

Beef Tenderloin Kebabs
with Egyptian Pepper Sauce 218

Grilled Lamb Kofta
with Chile Labne 222

Black Harissa Lamb Chops
with Fava Beans, Peas, Mint,
and Dried Lime Yogurt 228

Spiced Tomato-Braised
Lamb Shanks 231

Braised Oxtails with Potatoes
and Shaved Carrots 234

DESSERTS

Minerva's Fayesh 241

Lime Popsicles with Mint
and White Peach 243

Cardamom Candied Pistachios 243

Raspberry Rose Water Granita 244

Labne Frozen Yogurt
with Stone Fruit 247

Kataifi-Wrapped
Caramelized Bananas 248

Carob Ice Cream 251

Rice Pudding with Figs 252

Om Ali 255

Ma'amoul 256

Baklava Napoleon 259

Mango Basbousa 262

BASICS

Baharat 266

"Dukkah" Spice 266

Smoked Dukkah 267

Middle Eastern Vegetable Stock 269

Mushroom Stock 270

Chicken Stock 271

Roasted Tomatoes
with Smoked Dukkah 273

Blistered Cherry Tomatoes 273

Tomato-Braised Fennel 274

Labne 274

Vanilla-Roasted Figs 277

Crispy Onions 278

Date Chutney 279

Chile Oil 279

Acknowledgments 281

Index 282

INTRODUCTION

At 9 a.m., Old Cairo is still waking up. Vendors set out their wares in front of shops while young delivery guys zip past on bikes balancing racks of aish baladi, local flatbread, on their heads. Imposing gates punctuate the walls surrounding the neighborhood; during the Middle Ages, the sultan ordered them closed to keep the Crusaders out. But these days, the gates to the ancient core of the city stay open to all. At this hour, the sun isn't too strong, and traffic hasn't yet reached peak chaos. So I go with my chef buddy Moustafa Elrefaey to hit up one of our favorite ful carts.

Cairo runs on ful medames, Egypt's breakfast of champions. Cook dried fava beans for hours in a tall pot that resembles an amphora, ladle them into a bowl, and top them with onions, pickles, cilantro. That's how you stay fueled for hours.

The ful cart we visit also makes ta'ameya, Egyptian falafel. My mom cooked them for my siblings and me when we were growing up, and hers were always light, almost delicate, in texture. Her secret is passing the beans through a meat grinder and frying the patties in a skillet, not a deep fryer. My mom's ta'ameya has always been the standard against which I judge every falafel. But this ful cart takes ta'ameya to a new level. When we arrive, the owner leads us into a small, semisubterranean kitchen behind the cart. In the corner, a block of marble holds a piece of kitchen machinery unlike any I've seen. A paddle shaped like a cupped hand spins around a bowl embedded into the marble, whipping the soaked favas and herbs into a mint-green paste. The result—the lightest ta'ameya I've had—is a revelation. So is the rest of our meal: aish baladi, arugula, pickles, and bowls of ful, crowding our table set at the edge of this narrow street.

Even though I've run restaurants for decades, this hole-in-the-wall place fascinates me, an operation that would be impossible to replicate anywhere else. And I wouldn't want to. Instead, I look to it—and places like it in Egypt—

to ground me in my heritage. I was born here, and even though I've cooked professionally since high school, it's only in the past decade that I've explored Egypt as a chef.

* * *

In 1969, when I was two years old, my family moved from Cairo to Ellensburg, an agricultural town in the center of Washington State best known for Central Washington University and a rodeo, the second largest in the country. I was too young to remember anything about our life in Cairo, but now that I'm a husband and father, I appreciate how brave my parents were to relocate so far from family, friends, and community. "We didn't immigrate for the money or the career," my dad says now. "We immigrated for the children."

My parents are opposites in many ways. My dad, Ezzat, is calm and quiet, and my mom, Minerva, is the outgoing, social one. They had a solid middle-class life in Cairo, and if the country's politics in the 1960s had been more stable, they would have stayed. But my family is Coptic Christian, and though Copts and Muslims have lived side by side in Egypt for centuries, the political situation in the mid-twentieth century made it harder for families like ours to feel secure there. We had relatives in Washington State, and my parents decided it was better to take a chance on an unfamiliar country than to wait out political turmoil and hope for the best. A few weeks after we arrived, my dad took a job at the university, and we settled into life in a town of cowboys and academics, the lone family who spoke Arabic at home and ate food that no one else knew anything about.

At the beginning of every school year, I looked around my classroom to confirm that I was, once again, the only one who looked different. Kids were merciless, calling me slurs that I won't repeat here. I learned not to walk down certain hallways at school to avoid fights. The hazing continued after school in organized

sports, even with coaches. Because they were older, my brother, Magid, and sister, Mennel, had it worse. Back then no one talked about racial tension. I just knew that our family was different, and standing out gave me tremendous anxiety.

My name had a lot to do with it. My first name is Ashraf. But when I was eight years old and our family got our US citizenship, I was asked to choose a middle name. I picked Michael, the name of my best friend at the time. It could have been Kevin or Brian, that's how arbitrary the decision was. As I got older, however, the name took on more importance. I thought about what it would be like to be called Michael instead of Ashraf, to introduce myself and not have to explain where my family was from. But in a small town, it didn't feel possible to tell everyone to call me something else, so I waited until I left home.

The food my mom cooked also set us apart. We didn't have hamburgers or spaghetti for dinner, and because our food smelled different, I never felt comfortable having friends over for fear they'd make fun of it. So I made excuses, telling friends that I'd rather eat at their houses than have them over to mine. When I started working in restaurants in high school, I went out of my way to learn how to cook everything *but* Middle Eastern food.

Despite pushing part of myself down to fit in, it was in restaurant work that I found solace as I learned how to cook, do payroll, and place orders for ingredients. I liked the adrenaline of cooking on the line, of being in control. In kitchens, it didn't matter what you looked like or what your name was—it mattered how you performed. I knew I wanted to become a chef when I graduated from high school. All I had to do was convince my parents that cooking could be a viable career.

In some families, this could have been easy. But not with mine. When we moved to Ellensburg, my mom had weighed whether to continue toward a PhD in chemistry, the track she'd been on as a highly regarded teacher back in Cairo, or stay home and run the household. She crunched the numbers and figured she'd at best break even if she also had to pay someone to take care of me and my siblings. So she gave up her chemistry dreams and threw everything into raising us. I say this so you understand what happened when I got up the courage to tell my parents that I wanted to be a chef.

"It was like a funeral," my mom recounts. In a middle-class Egyptian household, parents expect their kids to grow up to be doctors or engineers, not cooks. My parents made huge sacrifices to give our family a better life in America. In their eyes, I was throwing away every advantage they had provided to pursue a lowly profession. "How can you support a family on a cook's salary?" my dad asked, while my mom dropped to her knees and began to pray.

After many discussions, my parents realized I wasn't going to change my mind, so they insisted that I get a good education. It was at my dream school— the Culinary Institute of America in Hyde Park, New York—that I began introducing myself as Michael instead of Ashraf and my name became one less thing to be anxious about. But what I never set aside was my palate, my secret weapon. Growing up with Middle Eastern food gave me an exposure to a broad range of flavors and an innate understanding of how to cook with spices and use acidity to amp up dishes.

In culinary school and in my first jobs after, I concentrated on learning technique. In my early career, I didn't want to get pigeonholed as only cooking Middle Eastern cuisine simply because of my heritage. Instead, Middle Eastern food had a much more subtle impact on how I cooked. With the Mina Group, the company I launched in 2002, I created menus with spinach-garlic soup and spot prawns accented with cumin oil, and crusted fish in phyllo. I also started to see connections to other food traditions, recognizing, for example, that sesame oil—an ingredient primarily associated with Asian cuisine—echoed the flavor of tahini used in Egyptian cooking. Occasionally, I unfurled dishes inspired by my childhood, like my mom's ta'ameya and a rice dish inspired by koshari. Yet, for the most part, my Egyptian side sat at the margins of my cooking until a decade ago.

* * *

In a way my journey to this book started when I began traveling to the Middle East for work and found myself extending trips to research local food. When I'd return to California after each trip, I couldn't get the flavors from my travels out of my head. I wanted to go deeper. In 2016, I began experimenting with new recipes, playing with flavors and ingredients, with Mina Group's corporate executive chef, Adam Sobel. Fired up from our travels, we created a pop-up restaurant called Middle'Terranea, serving za'atar-cured salmon with flatbread and elegant lime popsicles with cubes of white peach. I even incorporated my full name, Ashraf Michael Mina, into the logo. And it was packed every night.

It felt right to push further into my heritage. In 2018, Adam, chef Raj Dixit, and I overhauled the menu at the Michael Mina restaurant in San Francisco, infusing it with my personal Middle Eastern perspective. It was the first time my Egyptian roots were front and center on a fine dining menu, featuring ingredients I had grown up with in entirely different ways. For example, we wrapped kataifi, a pastry usually used for dessert, around prawns, and grape leaves around chicken. Spice blends from the spice purveyor Lior Lev Sercarz of La Boîte became the heart of the menu. Bringing together what had once felt like separate parts of myself—technique-driven California cooking and Egyptian heritage—led me to look back to what got me excited about food in the first place. Although the pandemic disrupted what we were doing in San Francisco, we revamped the space, turning it into Ornos, a restaurant inspired by the Mediterranean. Today, we continue to bring these influences to menus across the country. This book is a culmination of the explorations that have highlighted my family's Egyptian table.

When I was a kid, all my aunts, uncles, and cousins who lived within a 150-mile radius descended frequently on our house for barbecues. There would be at least forty people, and it would go on all day. Before anyone showed up, food was on the table—dips, spreads, maybe some stuffed grape leaves. There were also bowls of dried fruits, nuts, and cookies set around the house for snacking. Later, the hot food came out, from macaroni béchamel to grilled lamb and chicken and stuffed vegetables. There was always a card game in play—mostly thirty-one, a variation of blackjack that's popular in the Middle East—which could go on well past midnight. At the end of these barbecues, my mom and aunts would bring out trays of basbousa and baklava, along with more nuts and fruit to snack on.

And that's what it was all about: food on the table, all day long, all of us spending time together. People would cry, fight, laugh, joke, all in the same day, dramatic scenes that ended in hugs and plans for the next barbecue. It was the one time when I never had to worry about feeling different from everyone else. When I met my wife, Diane, she fit right in. She is half Italian, half Puerto Rican, and she grew up going to big family gatherings every weekend, too. (The difference is she likes being in the center of the party while I prefer to be off to the side—or in the kitchen.) Today our sons, Anthony and Sammy, have embraced their multicultural heritage wholeheartedly. And they love my mom's ta'ameya just like I do.

* * *

On one of our last days in Cairo, I bring Adam to shop for kitchen gear with Moustafa and his right-hand man, Yasser Ramadan. Yasser grew up a stone's throw from the Great Sphinx of Giza, and we joke that he is Moustafa's body double, at least when you see them from the back. They're about the same height, have shaved heads, and wear the same jeans and t-shirts. The giveaway, though, is that Yasser always has two or three

Michael Mina and wife, Diane Mina

cell phones shoved in his back pockets. Sometimes he talks into two phones at once, one against each ear.

We enter Old Cairo at Bab al-Futuh gate, where a bulldozer is leveling a building, sending clouds of dust everywhere. Yasser—who can charm anyone—asks the guy to stop for a minute so we can walk by. Farther down the street, a woman sells lemons and limes while olives cure in the sun. Moustafa guides us down a narrow road lined with cookware shops. We pick out tabletop grilling items and kettles and teacups and pass stacks of the tall ful pots. We pick up corers for hollowing out zucchini and eggplant to make mahshi, stuffed vegetables. To cool off, we stop at a juice stand and choose between freshly squeezed sugarcane and pomegranate. A block away, we reach the complex of Sultan al-Mansour Qalawun, which dates to the thirteenth century. It's a stunning construction of marble, granite, and stained glass, built when Cairo was growing into a medieval metropolis.

When I started traveling to Egypt, it was to get to know the food—learning how a pickled vegetable can transform a dish, or how a restaurant creates balance between spice, acidity, and salt. Sometimes I'd see the original version of something my mom cooked in Washington using the ingredients she had. I began to understand why my dad always charred anything he grilled; in Egypt, smoky char acts as a seasoning for grilled kofta and poultry.

Now I go to Egypt to be around other Egyptians. As soon as I'm off the plane, I light up when I start to hear the joking, badgering, complaining, bartering. We Egyptians can dish it out and take it. You see a lot of heartbreak, people who are barely getting by. But you also see joy, generosity, and superhuman abilities to laugh even in tough times. Visiting cities like Alexandria or Faiyum, or spending time on a friend's backyard farm, it's like being at the table playing thirty-one with my family again, joking and eating and protesting to your hosts that you are way too full to eat anything else. (Good luck: in true Egyptian fashion, they keep the food coming anyway.)

At the center of it all, there's this generous, deeply hospitable heart of gold. That's my heritage, my Egypt.

ABOUT THE RECIPES

In this book, I weave together cooking techniques and classic flavors from a part of the world I love. Some are from my family, some from my travels, and most from ideas that I've been kicking around for years learning and cooking and eating in the Middle East, the Mediterranean, and North Africa. Rather than a comprehensive or definitive collection of Egyptian dishes, it's a collection of recipes that represent Egypt through my lens.

At my restaurants, I'm a big believer in teamwork. Menus come together through collaborations with my chefs, and we push each other to generate new ideas. The following recipes came together in a similar way. I worked closely with Adam Sobel, our corporate executive chef who has traveled with me in the Middle East, on many of the recipes, while I iterated on Middle Eastern desserts with Veronica Arroyo, our corporate pastry chef. I would get it in my head that mangos—a beloved fruit in Egypt—belonged in basbousa, say, or lobster salad, and I'd work with my chefs until we figured out how to make the flavors and textures come together like I imagined. Beyond the restaurant kitchens, I also bring in recipes from the Mina family archives, like my mom's Fayesh (page 241), a savory, biscotti-like biscuit my dad likes to eat with tea, and—of course—her Ta'ameya (page 92).

Michael with his mom, Minerva, and dad, Ezzat Mina

OUR CHEF GUIDE

My friend Moustafa Elrefaey is the chef and cofounder of Zooba, a growing restaurant concept in Cairo and New York where he takes Egyptian street-food classics and recasts them using the best ingredients and techniques. I call him a "chef guide" because that's what chefs do—if we're visiting a place and we want to eat well, we network with other chefs to make sure we're hitting the best spots. In Egypt, Moustafa is my guy. In truth, Moustafa and I should have met in 2004, when he was working as a chef in Detroit and I was opening what ended up being a short-lived restaurant in the same city. But our paths never crossed, something that I now regret.

In the States, Moustafa proudly shared Egypt's culinary heritage with non-Egyptian friends. But when he returned to Egypt in 2009, he was frustrated by how much Egyptians seemed to love every cuisine in the world except their own. He wanted to help Egyptian people understand their food legacy, which prompted him to travel around the country, seek out traditional recipes, and teach Egyptian food traditions. And this is how we connected. In 2019, when looking for local chefs to help me better understand the food of my heritage, I reached out, and he happily agreed to share what he knew. The first time we met, he started by taking me to the ful cart in Old Cairo, and we've been friends ever since. Today, Moustafa is less like a guide, and more like a brother.

Eating at Zooba

START HERE: COOKING FROM THIS BOOK

I hope this book encourages you to mix and match recipes. Some recipes include a "serve with" suggestion, which is often what's pictured in an accompanying photo. But the suggestion is just that—a suggestion—and I hope you will experiment and follow your own instincts just as often.

The foundational part of this book is the second recipe chapter, Setting the Table. Here you'll find the dips, pickles, and breads that are omnipresent at Egyptian meals any time of day. It is the longest chapter but also the simplest, filled with recipes that work with nearly every meal cooked from this book.

While it's not typical in Egypt to have appetizer courses, I have an appetizer section to reflect the meals I serve at my restaurants. The recipes in that chapter lean more "restaurant style," but, in many cases, you can modify the method to suit your taste. For instance, you can serve the ful medames shown with octopus on page 118 with a poached egg but no octopus, or vice versa.

Some chapters are a mix of restaurant dishes and simpler, homier recipes, with notes to offer guidance along the way.

Just about any meal from this book can be served with a side of Everyday Egyptian Rice (page 152) and Baladi Bread (page 78) or good-quality store-bought pita or flatbread. Simple sides from the salad and vegetables chapter, like Salata Baladi (page 129), Harissa Ratatouille (page 136), or Lemon Potatoes (page 139), also round out any meal.

Any time there's an ingredient to explain, a detail on where to find a specific product or piece of equipment, or an alternate method, I call it out in a note.

For pantry recipes, the kinds of things you'll like to have around no matter what you're cooking (think stocks, spice blends, and so forth), see the Basics chapter starting on page 264.

Finally, while it is really easy to skip, please read the Middle'Terranea Pantry (pages 35–43) before you cook from the book. It includes notes on the salt used in the recipes as well as useful tips, such as how many tablespoons of juice you can expect to extract from an average lemon.

COOKING FOR FRIENDS AND FAMILY

All Egyptian households run on unspoken rules of Arabic hospitality. To my mind, it means treating your home like the most welcoming restaurant in the world. Here's the standard operating procedure: First, wait to sit down at the table until everyone has arrived. Otherwise, it feels like an incomplete restaurant reservation. While waiting, offer friends and family something to drink (like one of my welcome drinks starting on page 46). When the feast begins, keep the food coming. Start with the dips and pickles (with recipes starting on page 52), then bring out the rest family style, making sure everyone has what they need to feel content at the table. Finally, before the last bite of basbousa or baklava is eaten, start making plans for the next meal together.

COOKING WITH SPICES

Many spices have a tendency to burn in the pan when sprinkled on fish or meat before searing. Often, the spices scorch before the meat or fish is seared. While there are some exceptions in the world, for the purposes of this book I recommend seasoning only with salt before searing any protein, then waiting until afterward to add any spices, even ground black pepper.

THE MIDDLE'TERRANEA PANTRY

I inherited my mom's knack of packing assertive flavors—acid, salt, spice—into the meals she prepared when I was growing up. Egyptians like food with punch, and this point of view filters into how I season, whether I'm cooking classic French dishes or recipes I picked up on my travels. I call it my "Middle'Terranea" approach, with nods to Greece and Italy as well as North Africa and the Middle East. This isn't so different from how Egyptians cook at home. After all, Egypt is a cultural melting pot. The country has African heritage, Mediterranean heritage, and Arab heritage. Tourists have come to the Pyramids of Giza since the time of the Ancient Greeks and Romans, and they've all influenced the national cuisine. Here are the ingredients that I turn to often in this book.

SEASONINGS

Salt

Kosher salt isn't used in Egypt, so in this cookbook, I mostly call for fine sea salt. Not only is it the most common salt in Egypt, but it also has the advantage of being relatively consistent in salinity. (In comparison, kosher salt brands vary.) When kosher salt is important for a particular dish (such as the salt-baked fish on page 188), it's indicated in the recipe. If you prefer kosher salt as your go-to, you may want to add a pinch or two more salt to the recipes, but trust your judgment. By volume, Diamond Crystal kosher will taste a little less salty than fine sea salt. In addition to salt used for cooking, I like to finish dishes with flaky sea salt, like Maldon. It dissolves on your tongue and is light enough to never make things taste too salty.

Vegeta

This Croatian all-purpose vegetarian seasoning mix, first developed in the mid-twentieth century, is very popular in the Middle East. The classic blend contains MSG, but they do make an MSG-free version, too. I like it in vegetable stock or any vegetable-forward dish that needs a savory note separate from salt. Find it at specialty grocery shops or online.

Spices

Walking through the spice markets in Old Cairo gives you a sense of how central spices are to the Egyptian kitchen. Burlap bags sit waist-high, opened to show each shop's bounty, while the most valuable spices are held in the back close to the counter. Except for coriander and fenugreek, which grow in Egypt, most spices come from farther east, along the west coast of India, for instance. Egypt has long been the center of the spice trade, with spices flowing to the Red Sea before landing in Luxor and traveling north down the Nile to Cairo and Alexandria.

Here is a list of spices I call for frequently in this book and that I saw on my travels.

Core spices:

- Black pepper, freshly ground
- Coriander seeds, used crushed or ground
- Cumin seeds, mostly used ground
- Ground red pepper (sweet or hot paprika or cayenne can be used)
- Ground turmeric

Also important:

- Cardamom (it's common to add smashed pods to ghee when cooking rice)
- Ground cinnamon (mostly for desserts, and sometimes in kofta)
- Nigella seeds (lending a subtle onion flavor)
- Sumac (I like how the tart spice adds another layer of acidity)
- Fenugreek seeds (often steeped in tea and milk)

Chiles / Red Peppers

Ground red pepper: Egyptian ground red pepper has a mellower burn than cayenne but a higher level of heat than paprika. Still, for the purposes of this book, either cayenne or paprika can be used for any inclusion of a ground red pepper, depending on the level of heat you want. Aleppo and Urfa peppers are less common in Egypt, though in our kitchens my team uses them quite a bit. Urfa tends to be more savory than Aleppo, and it has a deep purple-black color. If either is out of reach, experiment with Korean gochugaru or red pepper flakes, though you may want to start with a smaller amount, taste, and add more if you need it.

Harissa paste: For a quick hit of heat in a marinade or sauce, a spoonful of harissa paste will do the trick. The brand DEA, which comes in a tube, is reliable and widely available.

TOASTING, GRINDING, AND STORING SPICES

Ground spices have a shorter shelf life than whole spices—as soon as they are ground, they begin to lose their punch. When making spice blends, start with the whole spice, then toast it gently for a couple of minutes in a dry skillet over medium heat until you wake up its aroma but not so long that it starts to darken. Grind in a spice grinder. It's best to grind only what you need in the short term. Store all spices, whole or ground, in a sealed container away from sunlight.

ACID AND CITRUS

Vinegar

Egyptian cooking is all about layering acidity and spices, and vinegar is one key way to punch things up. White distilled vinegar is the most common, but verjus, the juice of unripe grapes, is also used to cut through richness. For this book white distilled vinegar, white wine vinegar, or red wine vinegar will work in most cases. Or experiment with verjus in place of white wine vinegar. (Always refrigerate verjus after opening to prevent it from fermenting.)

Citrus

Limes and lemons: Citrus is a central component of Egyptian cooking, and limes are more common than lemons. Egyptian limes have thin skins and are ideal for making limeade using the whole fruit. In North America, Mexican limes come the closest, though go with whatever limes you find at the store. In general, one lemon yields about ¼ cup (60ml) juice and one lime provides about 2 tablespoons (30ml) juice. In this book, I also call for a lot of zest. To finely zest citrus for our recipes, use a rasp grater (such as a Microplane). Scrub citrus well before zesting.

Preserved citrus: Egyptian cooks cure limes in salt and lime juice, setting them in a jug at room temperature (which in Egypt is warm) for a week. The process softens the rind and tempers the acidity, creating a complex, salty, sour flavor with a bit less bite than fresh juice. I also use preserved lemons, which are ready to go out of the jar from brands such as Les Moulins Mahjoub.

Dried limes / Omani limes: Originally from Persia, dried limes look like shrunken dark brown-black balls and have an evocative, earthy flavor. They can be firm enough to grate with a rasp grater, though some crumble easily with your hands. Use them in Black Harissa Lamb Chops with Fava Beans, Peas, Mint, and Dried Lime Yogurt (page 228).

EDIBLE FLOWERS AND FLOWER WATERS

I often add edible flowers to dishes for color and texture. There are many to choose from, including marigolds and cosmos, but the best bet is to use the flowers from flowering herbs such as cilantro or tarragon. Another way to add a floral note is with rose water or orange blossom water. A little goes a long way. Store rose and orange blossom waters in the refrigerator once opened.

COOKING OILS AND FATS

Neutral oil, such as grapeseed, sunflower, or canola: These oils have higher smoke points than olive oil, which means they are less likely to burn and introduce

37

acrid flavors, so they're good for searing and roasting. I sometimes use a blend of canola and olive oil for a neutral oil with a touch more personality. Flaxseed oil is traditional in Egypt, but sunflower oil is quickly becoming more popular for its versatility.

Olive oil: Olive trees grow along Egypt's Mediterranean coast and in the Siwa and Faiyum oases, but even so, olive oil is too expensive for most Egyptians to use regularly. I love finishing dishes with extra-virgin olive oil. For cooking, I often blend olive oil with a neutral oil, such as canola or sunflower, because olive oil alone has a low smoke point.

Lemon olive oil: This is olive oil made by pressing olives with lemon rinds, and it's a great way to add citrus flavor without extra acidity. Use it as a finishing oil on a dish, not an oil to cook with.

Ghee and clarified butter: While I cook more with olive oil and neutral oils, ghee (also called samna) is a common cooking fat in Egypt. Sometimes nothing else will achieve the same rich flavor or texture. Ghee is easier than ever to find at grocery stores (look on the shelf near the oils and vinegars; refrigerate it once opened). A lot of ghee is also labeled clarified butter now, and while they are slightly different, they can be used interchangeably in this book (taste it first; some ghee is strong in flavor).

Make your own clarified butter by slowly melting butter in a small saucepan without stirring, then removing the butter from the heat and letting it rest for about 5 minutes to let the milk solids fall to the bottom of the saucepan. Skim any of the solids from the top of the melted butter, then strain through cheesecloth, being careful not to pour in the milk solids from the base of the pan. Clarified butter is essential for my Phyllo-Crusted Sole with Dukkah Beurre Blanc and Golden Raisins (page 195). It is also important for making Kataifi-Wrapped Caramelized Bananas (page 248), though store-bought ghee works for both recipes.

DAIRY

Labne (also spelled labneh): Thicker, creamier, and tangier than yogurt (it's strained, making it denser than regular yogurt), labne is one of my go-to ingredients when making a quick dip. Just drizzle olive oil on top, sprinkle it with za'atar or dukkah, and it's ready to go. It's easier than ever to buy tubs of labne at grocery stores these days, but see the recipe on page 274 for how to make it. In a pinch, whole-milk plain Greek yogurt is a fine substitute.

Cheese: Cheese in Egypt is most frequently eaten with bread for breakfast or dinner. The cheese can be made with everything from cow's milk to sheep's milk to buffalo milk. Many of the cheeses served in Egypt are hard to find in North America—one of them is aged on a roof for five years, then reconstituted—but some are more common, like feta and Halloumi. Save feta brine for brining chicken (page 208); you can freeze it until you have enough.

Ishta: This cream is like English clotted cream, with the same spreadable texture. In Egypt, it's served with pieces of feteer (page 42), where you break off pieces of the bread, add a dollop of cream, and then eat it with a drizzle of honey or molasses. Whipping up crème fraîche or cream cheese with a splash of heavy cream gets close to the tangy taste and texture of Egyptian ishta.

BEANS AND LENTILS

Lentils (brown, red): There's proof in the tombs of ancient Egyptians that lentils have been eaten along the Nile for more than three thousand years. Today, red lentils are cooked in soup while brown lentils top Koshari (page 156).

Fava beans (dried and fresh): Egyptians probably consume more fava beans than almost anyone else in the world. It's crucial in Ful Medames (page 60) and Ta'ameya (page 92). Dr. Mennat-Allah El Dorry, a Cairo-based archeologist, says favas likely didn't become widespread in Egypt until after the Greco-Roman

period, when Lower Egypt (the northern part of the country) became part of the Greek and Roman empires.

Chickpeas: Found in small quantities in the tombs of ancient Egyptians, chickpeas are one of many toppings in Koshari (page 156), a favorite comfort food. Along the Nile, vendors sell chickpeas in broth seasoned with lime, cumin, salt, pepper, and cayenne. The point is to drink the broth as well as eat the chickpeas.

RICE, GRAINS, PASTA

Freekeh/fireek: This traditional grain (called fireek in Egypt and freekeh in North America) is made by harvesting wheat while still green, then roasting and drying it before peeling and crushing it. It's the classic grain for stuffed pigeon (squab) and also makes an excellent base for Tabbouli (page 150).

Rice: Egypt produces high-quality, medium-grain rice, though it is hard to find abroad. The closest in North America is Calrose rice.

Wheat berries: You can find wheat berries served as a savory side dish in Egypt, but it's more common to eat as a dessert or breakfast, cooked with milk and sugar or honey and topped with cinnamon, nuts, raisins, and/or coconut flakes.

Couscous: Egyptians use couscous much like wheat berries—cooked sweet with milk. The couscous used is the finer grain, standard kind, not pearl (sometimes called Israeli) couscous. As a savory side, I cook it with saffron (page 152) to dress it up.

Flour: The ancient Egyptians grew a range of grains, such as emmer and barley, which were ground in simple mills. Today, whole wheat flour is the base of Baladi Bread (page 78). In this book, recipes were tested with King Arthur all-purpose flour and whole wheat flour. Use the sweep-and-level technique for measuring cups of flour (as opposed to when you spoon the flour into a measuring cup, then level it off). One cup measured this way is about 140 grams (4.9 ounces).

When in doubt, use a kitchen scale and follow the weight measurements in recipes that call for flour.

ALLIUMS, HERBS, AND GREENS

Onions and garlic: Along with spices, these form the foundation for nearly every Egyptian savory recipe. Crispy fried onions are essential for topping Koshari (page 156). I like using a rasp grater to grate garlic, making it easy to incorporate garlic into a marinade or labne.

Herbs: Cilantro, dill, and parsley (often mixed together) are the main herbs in Egyptian meals. If you have on hand only one or two of the herbs called for in a recipe, don't worry. Use the herbs you have, but don't reduce the quantity of herbs called for in the recipe. Mint is mostly used for drinks and tea, and sometimes blended with limes for limeade.

Arugula: Unlike the small, curly arugula sold in plastic bags at the grocery store, Egyptian arugula is big and leafy and always served directly on the table. The idea is you can pick up a couple of leaves and wrap them in bread with a dip such as Fresh Fava Bean Bessara (page 56) or Hummus (page 54).

NUTS AND SEEDS

Cashews, hazelnuts, and peanuts: Toasted and seasoned with salt and spices, these are all eaten as snacks. They can also be blended into Egypt's signature spice blend, dukkah (see page 266).

Sesame seeds: Sesame is an integral flavor across the Middle East and parts of Africa. Egyptians prefer tahini (a paste made of sesame seeds) from seeds grown in Ethiopia and Sudan because they have more fat. Sesame seeds grown in Egypt are leaner and are typically used in desserts instead of in tahini.

Tahini vs. tahina: Tahini paste is either white, black, or (rarely) red and is used in countless ways in the Egyptian kitchen. Tahina (page 52), the dip made from tahini, is a classic Egyptian condiment.

SWEETENERS AND DATES

Molasses, sugar, and honey are the most common sweeteners I encounter in Egypt, while dates are ever-present on the table. Egyptian molasses isn't as dark as blackstrap molasses, but lighter and more golden, like sorghum syrup. Use it to make a dip for bread by mixing equal parts tahini and molasses with a spoonful of nigella and sesame seeds.

Dates are grown and used extensively in Egypt, as an ingredient and as a snack. There are endless varieties. Some, like the prized medjool, taste like candy while others are tart and tannic and not sweet at all.

Carob molasses: In Egypt, carob is used in juices, and carob molasses is its concentrated form, with mellow coffee-chocolate-toffee notes. Look for it in Middle Eastern grocery stores and try it in ice cream (page 251).

Fruit molasses: Pomegranate, cherry, and grape molasses are used often across the Middle East. Pomegranate and cherry are the most versatile, allowing for a pleasant tangy flavor in place of citrus juice or vinegar. Use pomegranate molasses in Roasted Squab with Farro and Rice (page 203).

EQUIPMENT

Most of the recipes in this book don't require special equipment. I'll assume you already have a couple of sharp knives, some mixing bowls, and a large skillet (I like having both cast-iron and stainless steel skillets on hand). Additionally, I recommend a large Dutch oven or heavy-bottomed pot, tongs, spatulas, a box grater, a vegetable peeler, and a rasp grater (the brand Microplane is the most common). A blender and food processer will also come in handy. Any time I call for a sheet pan, I mean a rimmed 13- by 18-inch (33 by 46cm) baking pan. (In restaurant kitchens, we call these half-sheet pans.) I line sheet pans with parchment paper, but reusable nonstick silicone baking mats (such as Silpats) are useful, too.

In general, when I call for a baking dish, I am referring to a glass or ceramic vessel and when I say baking pan, I'm referring to a metal pan. For baking, a stand mixer, such as a KitchenAid, is useful for making bread and some of the desserts in this book. Fine-mesh strainers are important for straining stock and draining yogurt to make labne. I like to have a few on hand, including small ones for lemon juice and larger ones for straining liquids. I use a colander for draining pasta or vegetables. When a recipe benefits from a specific or unique piece of equipment, it is mentioned at the top of the recipe.

Finally, you'll notice I've included gram measurements for some of the ingredients in this book. When cooking in restaurants, weighing ingredients by the gram helps ensure consistency, especially when baking or preparing desserts. It also is easier to put something on a scale than to shove it into a measuring cup. You can toggle from ounces to grams on most scales, and I prefer grams. When the exact weight is not important (¼ cup chopped pistachios to sprinkle on top of a dish, for instance), the gram measurement is not included.

EGYPTIAN CLASSICS

Since this cookbook detours away from traditional Egyptian cooking, here is more context for my sources of inspiration.

TA'AMEYA

Think of ta'ameya as Egyptian falafel, made with dried split fava beans, not chickpeas. (See recipe, page 92.) In her book *Feast: Food of the Islamic World*, food writer and historian Anissa Helou writes that falafel were originally from Egypt.

BESSARA

Picture hummus made with fava beans and you have bessara. It can be made with dried split favas, or fresh favas, which is my preference. Either way, it's seasoned with cilantro, garlic, and tahini. (See recipe, page 56.)

KOSHARI

This starchy vegetarian dish of lentils, rice, vermicelli, and macaroni is my ultimate comfort food. Although popular throughout the country, it's only been eaten in Egypt since the 1800s, evolving from Indian khichdi. (See recipe, page 156.)

FUL MEDAMES

Ful medames is the most common breakfast in Egypt, whether you're rich, poor, or in between. Beans are soaked for hours and then cooked overnight in a ful pot (qidra), which is tall and narrow at the top to minimize evaporation. Red lentils added at the end add texture and color. (See recipe, page 60.)

BALADI BREAD

Whether you're eating ful, bessara, or anything else that requires dipping, aish baladi, a flat pocket bread made with whole wheat flour, is your utensil. Tear off a piece, make a shape like a cat's ear, and drag it through the dip for the perfect bite. (See recipe, page 78.)

MOLOKHIA

Molokhia is one of Egypt's most iconic and oldest dishes. Called a stew, a soup, or a sauce, it is built on a leafy green also called molokhia (as well as jute leaves or mallow). Once cooked, it takes on its signature gelatinous texture. (See recipe, page 172.)

MACARONI BÉCHAMEL

This popular dish is noodle casserole the Egyptian way: mix cooked macaroni with béchamel, top it with ground meat sauce, and bake it. (See Egypt's *Joy of Cooking*, opposite page.)

HAMAM MAHSHI

Pigeon (usually called squab in North America) is one of the most beloved birds to eat in Egypt, and many places specialize in serving the birds stuffed with grains (rice or freekeh). The birds are then grilled or roasted and served whole. (See recipe, page 203.)

FETEER

This multilayered, buttery flatbread is one of the first things I seek out on a trip to Egypt, especially so I can eat it with ishta—Egyptian clotted cream—and honey. In some touristy parts of Old Cairo, it's called Egyptian pancakes, but I don't see the resemblance. In the countryside, cooks bake large wheels of it. I make it into mini versions that work as a vehicle for caviar. (See recipe, page 87.)

OM ALI

Think of this dessert as Egypt's version of bread pudding, studded with raisins, nuts, and sometimes coconut. (See recipe, page 255.)

EGYPT'S JOY OF COOKING

My mom made macaroni béchamel from the classic cookbook *Ossol Al Tahey* (Fundamentals of Cooking), by Naziera Nicolla and Baheya Othman, though most Egyptian home cooks call it Abla Nazira's book ("abla" is a term of affection). Abla Nazira was Egypt's best-known twentieth-century food writer, and the book became the Egyptian equivalent of *Joy of Cooking*. My mom even cooked from her copy when we moved to America, but unfortunately no one in my family knows what happened to it.

While Abla Nazira's book was published in 1941, the recipe for macaroni béchamel is older. In the first part of the twentieth century, Greek restaurants became trendy in Cairo and Alexandria, and Egyptians got into eating pastitsio, a Greek dish made by mixing white sauce with a hollow-noodle pasta similar to bucatini. The story goes that pastitsio comes from the Italian word pasticcio, the name for elaborate stuffed pastries filled with pasta and meat. Ferrara, a city in Italy, has been making pasticcio di maccheroni, a pastry filled with pasta in white sauce, for centuries. Once the recipe made it to Egypt, it was renamed "macaroni béchamel."

My own version of the dish on page 165 is an homage to the elaborate pastas of Italy and the homey dish I grew up eating.

WELCOME DRINKS

When my wife and I entertain, we always start by offering our guests something to drink. In Egypt, hosts show the same kind of hospitality. But while I may pour cocktails, restaurants in Egypt go all out with nonalcoholic drinks, like juices and tea. (Egypt is 90 percent Muslim, so most people don't drink alcohol.) Spice shops sell balls of tamarind pulp, ready to be reconstituted into tangy tamarind juice, while hibiscus leaves are sold to steep, sweeten, and turn into iced tea. When eating out, servers will bring three or four bottles of juice to the table at the beginning of the meal—standards such as limeade and tangerine juice as well as sweetened coconut milk, iced hibiscus tea, or carob juice. I call these welcome drinks, the kind of refreshers to serve friends as soon as they come through the door. Since my family isn't Muslim, I offer suggestions on how to turn these drinks into cocktails, but I'll let you decide if you want to veer in that direction.

Limes are much more common in Egypt than lemons, and what makes Egyptian limeade stand out is the intensity of the lime flavor. Whole limes are blended with sugar before being diluted with water and lime juice. Because Egyptian limes have thin skins, the pith never tastes bitter. The closest limes in North America are Mexican limes, though use whatever juicy limes you can find.

LIMEADE

Active Time: 10 minutes

Equipment: A blender

MAKES 5¼ CUPS (1.3L), SERVES 4

6 limes (about 1¼ pounds / 560g), divided

½ cup plus 2 tablespoons (130g) granulated sugar

4 cups (960ml) cold water

1 tablespoon chopped mint (optional)

Trim off the stem end from 1 lime, then cut it into 8 pieces and add to a blender. Add the sugar and blend until the lime is well blended in the sugar, about 1 minute in a high-speed blender. Squeeze out the juice of the 5 remaining limes (about 10 tablespoons / 150ml) and add to the blender with the water and the mint, if desired. Blend to combine. Serve the limeade over ice or refrigerate until ready to serve. For a pulp-free juice, strain before chilling and serving.

Freshly squeezed tangerine juice is a favorite in Egypt. This drink is a nod to that juice, with a few twists to enhance its deep orange color. Enjoyed from a glass rimmed with a mix of sugar and Aleppo pepper (or paprika), it's also savory and spicy. Serve it over ice as is, or add 1½ ounces (45ml) of tequila to 4 ounces (118ml) juice if you want to turn it into a cocktail.

TANGERINE CARROT JUICE
WITH ALEPPO SUGAR

Active Time: 5 minutes

MAKES 8 CUPS (2L), SERVES 6 TO 8

1 tablespoon granulated sugar

2 teaspoons Aleppo pepper

1 lime wedge

6 cups (1.4L) tangerine juice

2 cups (480ml) carrot juice

1. In a wide, shallow bowl or plate, stir the sugar and Aleppo pepper together. Rub a lime wedge along the rim of 6 to 8 glasses, then dip the rim of the glass in the bowl to coat the lip with the spiced sugar. Fill the glasses with ice.

2. In a pitcher, stir together the tangerine juice and carrot juice. Pour into the rimmed glasses and serve immediately.

Packed with vitamin C and antioxidants, hibiscus tea is made all over Africa by steeping the flowers of the hibiscus plant in water. (You may know it as agua de jamaica.) In Cairo, I had it chilled and lightly sweetened, which is the inspiration for this drink. Fresh pomegranate juice brings even more tang and color, while lime juice gives it zip. To turn this drink into a cocktail, fill a glass with ice, pour in 4 ounces (118ml) juice and 1½ ounces (45ml) vodka or gin, and give it a good stir. Or, for a flavored seltzer, top with sparkling water. You can find dried hibiscus flowers at specialty shops, online, and increasingly in larger supermarkets (check the tea aisle).

HIBISCUS POMEGRAN- ATE JUICE

Active Time: 10 minutes

Plan Ahead: The hibiscus tea can be made up to 5 days ahead of serving the drink.

MAKES ABOUT 8 CUPS (2L), SERVES 6 TO 8

1 cup (50g) dried whole hibiscus flowers

4¾ cups (1.12L) water

½ cup (100g) granulated sugar

4 cups (960ml) pomegranate juice, chilled

Juice of 2 limes

½ cup (118ml) Simple Syrup, or to taste (recipe on page 49)

Sparkling water (optional)

1. To make the hibiscus tea, rinse the flowers and add enough room-temperature water to cover. Soak for up to 30 minutes to soften. Drain well, discarding the soaking water, then put the flowers in a pot and add the 4¾ cups (1.12L) water and the sugar. Bring to a simmer over medium-high heat and cook until the color and flavor of the hibiscus petals have been extracted and the tea is tart, about 10 minutes. Turn off the heat and let sit for 5 minutes, then strain the tea and chill. (You'll have about 3½ cups / 840 ml.) Ensure the tea is cold before adding the pomegranate juice.

2. In a 2-quart (2L) or larger pitcher, mix the cold hibiscus tea with the pomegranate juice and lime juice. Stir in ½ cup (118ml) simple syrup and taste, adding more to your liking. (The tea should taste concentrated so it won't be diluted when served over ice.) Add ice to the pitcher, or put ice in glasses and pour in the juice. Top with a splash of sparkling water if desired.

This drink is all about peak summer refreshment, when melons and cucumbers are both at the farmers' market in abundance. It's not something I have had on my own travels in the Middle East, but the flavors work—and it really cools you down during the heat of the day. Using simple syrup infused with lemon verbena or thyme adds a nice fragrant note to the melon and cucumber, but it's optional. The drink is smoothie consistency, though it thins as the ice melts.

CUCUMBER HONEYDEW JUICE

Active Time: 15 minutes

Equipment: A blender; a juicer is optional

MAKES ABOUT 4 CUPS (960ML). SERVES 3 TO 4

4 Persian cucumbers

3 cups diced honeydew (about ¼ large honeydew, seeded, peeled, and cut into chunks)

2 cups (285g) ice

¼ cup Simple Syrup (60ml), preferably infused with lemon verbena leaves, plus additional to taste

1. Peel 3 cucumbers and leave 1 with the skin on (this gives the juice more color). If using a juicer, run the cucumbers through the juicer. If using a blender, dice the cucumbers small enough so they will blend easily, then puree and strain through a fine-mesh strainer. (You will have a scant 1 cup / 225 ml.) Refrigerate until cold, at least 30 minutes, or put the juice in a bowl and chill over an ice bath.

2. Puree the honeydew chunks in a blender. Add the ice and blend again until smooth. Add the cucumber juice and blend briefly to combine. Pour into a pitcher, stir in ¼ cup (60ml) simple syrup, then taste, adding more as desired. Serve over ice.

SIMPLE SYRUP

You can have this on hand for sweetening drinks to your liking. Simple syrup keeps, refrigerated, for a week. Adding lemon verbena leaves or thyme is especially good with Cucumber Honeydew Juice, though you can keep it plain to use with a range of other drinks.

MAKES A SCANT 1½ CUPS (360ML)

1 cup (200g) granulated sugar

1 cup (240ml) water

6 lemon verbena leaves, fresh or dried, or 3 thyme sprigs (optional)

In a small saucepan, stir together the sugar and water. Bring to a simmer over medium heat, then remove from heat. If infusing with lemon verbena or thyme, add them at this point. Let the syrup cool completely at room temperature, with the herbs if using. Refrigerate until needed. The simple syrup keeps for a week.

SETTING
THE TABLE

When family came over when I was growing up, the table was filled with food long before anyone sat down to eat. It was all about abundance, and showing hospitality as soon as guests stepped in the door. Dips, pickles, snacks, bread, something to drink—these are omnipresent, on every table, part of every Egyptian meal. That's why I call this chapter "setting the table." It's longer than other chapters, but my hope is that this is the chapter you turn to again and again, the place to ground you in true Egyptian hospitality.

If Egypt had American-style diners, the ketchup bottle would be swapped out for tahina, the dip made from tahini paste (see Tahini vs. tahina on page 40). In Alexandria, this sesame-rich dip is always served with fish. It's also the condiment of choice with ta'ameya. Easy and quick to make, it's worth stirring together a batch for any meal you serve from this book. For more than four people, double the recipe.

TAHINA

Active Time: 10 minutes

MAKES ABOUT 1 CUP (240ML), SERVES 4 TO 6

½ cup (120g) tahini, well stirred

⅓ cup (85ml) ice water

2 tablespoons freshly squeezed lemon juice, plus more if desired

1 garlic clove, minced

¼ teaspoon fine sea salt, plus more if desired

Pinch of ground cumin (optional)

In a small bowl, whisk together the tahini, water, lemon juice, garlic, and salt until smooth and creamy. Taste, adding cumin or more salt and lemon juice if desired. Store extra tahina in the refrigerator for up to 5 days. It will thicken over time, but stirring in a splash of water will loosen it up.

Made by grinding toasted black sesame seeds, black tahini takes regular tahini in a deeper, smokier direction, a perfect companion to anything with a bit of char, from Grilled Sesame Quail (page 200) to grilled eggplant. Black tahini is harder to find, but Japanese black sesame paste (called neri goma) works, too. Stir it well before using, as it can sometimes be thinner than white sesame tahini.

BLACK TAHINA

Active Time: 10 minutes

MAKES JUST UNDER 1 CUP (180ML), SERVES 4 TO 5

½ cup (123g) black sesame paste, well stirred

¼ cup (60ml) ice water

1 tablespoon freshly squeezed lemon juice, plus more if desired

¼ teaspoon fine sea salt, plus more if desired

In a small bowl, whisk together the sesame paste, water, lemon juice, and salt until smooth and creamy (this will take a few minutes). Taste, adding more salt and lemon juice if desired. Store extra tahina in the refrigerator for up to 5 days. It will thicken over time, but stirring in a splash of water will loosen it up.

This isn't a traditional tahina—no sesame here. Instead, pumpkin seeds (pepitas) take the place of sesame. The seeds themselves do not have as much natural oil as sesame seeds (which makes adding oil essential to the blend), but they have a distinct nutty flavor. If the dip is too thick, stir in a splash of water to loosen it up.

Serve with Pumpkin and Red Lentil Soup (page 122) or Turkey Hawawshi (page 121).

PUMPKIN SEED TAHINA

Active Time: 15 minutes

Equipment: A blender

MAKES ABOUT 1¾ CUPS (420ML), SERVES 6

1 cup (150g) shelled raw pumpkin seeds

1 cup (25g) lightly packed cilantro leaves

2 teaspoons ground coriander

¼ cup (180ml) neutral oil, such as grapeseed or canola

½ jalapeño, sliced

3 tablespoons freshly squeezed lime juice

¼ cup (60ml) warm water

¼ teaspoon fine sea salt, plus more if desired

1. Preheat the oven to 350°F (180°C). Spread the pumpkin seeds on a rimmed baking sheet and bake for 5 minutes or until evenly toasted.

2. In a blender, blend together all the ingredients until smooth. Taste, adding more salt if desired. For a thinner tahina, add a splash of water. Pumpkin tahina keeps about 1 week in the refrigerator. It will thicken over time, but stirring in a splash of water will loosen it up.

Cooling, refreshing, and classic, tzatziki is a popular Greek export for a reason. I've found it works very well with Egyptian meals. I like it as a dip with Baladi Bread (page 78) or with anything off the grill. Use it right away or refrigerate in a sealed container for up to five days.

Serve with Za'atar-Cured Salmon with Tzatziki and Salmon Roe (page 101).

TZATZIKI

Active Time: 10 minutes

MAKES 1¾ CUPS (420ML), SERVES 4 TO 5

1 Persian cucumber

1 garlic clove, grated with a rasp grater

1 tablespoon extra-virgin olive oil

2 teaspoons red wine vinegar

½ teaspoon fine sea salt

1½ cups (360ml) plain whole-milk Greek yogurt

1. Use the large holes of a box grater to grate the cucumber. Lay out a clean kitchen towel or a few layers of paper towels and put the cucumber on top. Roll up and squeeze out the extra water.

2. In a small bowl, stir the garlic, oil, vinegar, and salt together. Stir in the yogurt, then stir in the cucumbers until evenly mixed in.

In the canon of beans and pulses mixed with tahini, Fava Bean Bessara (page 56) is the most uniquely Egyptian. Still, it's hard to deny hummus its role as a favorite dip throughout the Middle East and Mediterranean, including Egypt. Serve it alongside a larger meal or to eat as a quick bite with flatbread. See the note for shortcuts if you don't have time to soak the chickpeas.

Serve as part of Hummus with Cauliflower, Pomegranate, and Foie Gras (page 125).

HUMMUS

Active Time: 20 minutes

Plan Ahead: Soak the chickpeas overnight before making the hummus. You will need 60 to 90 minutes to simmer the chickpeas after soaking.

Equipment: A food processor

MAKES 4½ CUPS (1L), SERVES 6 TO 8

1½ cups (300g) dried chickpeas (see Chickpea Options below)

½ cup (120g) tahini, well-stirred

¾ cup (180ml) cold water, divided

⅓ cup (80ml) freshly squeezed lemon juice

3 garlic cloves, coarsely chopped

2½ teaspoons fine sea salt, divided

½ teaspoon ground cumin

Extra-virgin olive oil

1. Put the chickpeas in a large pot or bowl and cover with at least 2 inches (5cm) of water. Let soak at room temperature for at least 8 hours or up to 24.

2. Drain the chickpeas and rinse. Put the chickpeas in a medium pot and cover with about 2 inches (5cm) of water. Bring the chickpeas to a boil over high heat, reduce the heat to medium, and let simmer until quite soft, 1 to 1½ hours, adding more water as needed to ensure they stay submerged.

3. Drain the chickpeas, saving the liquid for Middle Eastern Vegetable Stock (page 269) if desired. Transfer the chickpeas to a food processor and pulse briefly to combine. Add the tahini, ¼ cup (60ml) water, lemon juice, garlic, 2 teaspoons salt, and cumin, and blend until creamy, about 1 minute, stopping to scrape down the sides of the food processor with a flexible spatula if necessary. With the processor running, drizzle in the remaining ½ cup (120ml) water and blend until very smooth and creamy, about 2 minutes. Taste, adding the remaining ½ teaspoon salt if desired. Serve at room temperature with olive oil drizzled on top.

CHICKPEA OPTIONS

If you have a pressure cooker, you can skip the soaking step for the chickpeas and cook the chickpeas according to the pressure cooker instructions. Alternatively, make this hummus with 2 (15-ounce / 425g) cans of chickpeas. Drain and rinse, then proceed with step 3.

One of the signature flavors throughout Egypt is smoke from a grill or fire, which makes everything taste more savory and meaty, even vegetables. Barbecues featuring Egyptian fare were always part of family reunions in Washington State, something that linked my family to our heritage. This recipe takes the idea of smoke as a seasoning and applies it to a bright, creamy dip.

Serve with Roasted Squab with Farro and Rice (page 203).

SMOKED BEET CREAM

Active Time: 45 minutes

Plan Ahead: The beets take at least 45 minutes to cook, and you can do it ahead of smoking. If you're planning to grill that day, smoke the beets while you are grilling other things. The sauce can be made up to 5 days ahead.

Equipment: A blender for pureeing and wood chips for smoking the beets. Look for wood chips at hardware stores. Alternatively, if you have a pellet grill, you can follow the grill's instructions on smoking vegetables with wood pellets.

MAKES 4½ CUPS (1L), SERVES 6 TO 8

1¾ pounds (795g) medium-sized red beets (about 5)

1 tablespoon extra-virgin olive oil

¼ cup plus 1 tablespoon (60ml plus 15ml) red wine vinegar, divided

1 teaspoon fine sea salt, plus more if desired

1 cup (60g) applewood or mesquite wood chips

2 tablespoons extra-virgin olive oil or ghee

2 cups (480ml) heavy cream

¼ teaspoon freshly ground black pepper

1. Preheat the oven to 400°F (200°C). In a 9- by 5-inch (23 by 12cm) loaf pan, use your hands to coat the beets with the oil, 1 tablespoon (15ml) vinegar, and ½ teaspoon salt. Cover the dish with aluminum foil and roast until tender when pierced with a knife, 1 to 1¼ hours, depending on the size of the beets. Let cool, uncovered, until just warm, about 20 minutes, then peel. (If there are any stubborn patches of skin, rub them off with a damp paper towel.) Slice into wedges about ½ inch (12mm) thick.

2. Heat a gas grill to high heat or build a fire in a charcoal grill for direct-heat cooking. Cut two 9-inch (23cm) long rectangles of foil and crimp the edges, creating two makeshift trays. Put one foil tray on the grill, put the wood chips on top, and cover the grill. In the other foil tray, arrange the beets in an even layer. Once you can smell the smoke (after about 3 minutes), put the foil tray with the beets on the grill. Cover and smoke the beets for 10 minutes. Uncover and transfer the beets to a sheet pan. Let the wood chips cool completely on the grill and discard as you would for used charcoal.

3. In a medium saucepan, add 2 tablespoons oil or ghee. Stir in the beets to coat, then pour in the cream and remaining ¼ cup (60ml) vinegar. Stir in the remaining ½ teaspoon salt and the pepper and cook over medium-low heat, stirring occasionally, until the cream has reduced by half, about 15 minutes.

4. Ladle the beets and cream into a blender and blend until creamy. Taste, adding more salt if desired.

The easiest way to think about bessara is to imagine hummus made with fava beans instead of chickpeas. The traditional way to make bessara is with dried split fava beans, but fresh or frozen fava beans give the dip a bright color. Blanching the beans and herbs, then quickly shocking them in ice water, enhances that color even more. To serve it like they do at Zooba, my friend Moustafa Elrefaey's chain of restaurants in Cairo, top the bowl with crispy onions (page 278).

Serve with Black Harissa Lamb Chops with Fava Beans, Peas, Mint, and Dried Lime Yogurt (page 228).

FRESH FAVA BEAN BESSARA

Active Time: 15 minutes

Plan Ahead: Bessara keeps in the refrigerator for up to 7 days.

Equipment: A blender or food processor

MAKES ABOUT 2¾ CUPS (650ML), SERVES 3 TO 6

2¼ cups (340g) shelled and peeled fava beans, frozen or fresh (see Sourcing and Prepping Fava Beans to the right)

4 garlic cloves, peeled and smashed

1 packed cup (20g) cilantro leaves

1 packed cup (20g) flat-leaf parsley leaves

¼ cup (60g) tahini, well stirred

¼ cup (60ml) water

2 tablespoons freshly squeezed lemon juice

1½ teaspoons fine sea salt, plus more if desired

¼ cup (60ml) extra-virgin olive oil

1. Bring a pot of water to a boil and fill a bowl large enough to fit a colander with ice water. When the pot reaches a rolling boil, add the fava beans, garlic, cilantro, and parsley to the pot and boil over high heat for 90 seconds. Drain the pot into a colander and then plunge the colander into the ice water to chill the ingredients.

2. Drain the ingredients, shaking off excess water, and transfer to a blender or food processor. (If using a food processor, pulse briefly to combine.) Add the tahini, water, lemon juice, and salt and blend until creamy, about 1 minute, stopping to scrape down the sides of the blender or food processor with a flexible spatula if necessary. With the blender running on medium speed or processor running, drizzle in the oil and blend until very smooth and creamy, about 1½ minutes. Taste, adding more salt if desired. Serve at room temperature.

SOURCING AND PREPPING FAVA BEANS

Frozen fava beans are already parcooked and peeled and work great for this recipe. Look for them in the freezer section in Middle Eastern markets and well-stocked grocery stores (Goya sells them). If you are working with fresh fava beans, get a pot of salted water boiling and have a bowl of ice water handy. Pop the beans out of their pods, then blanch them briefly in the boiling water. Small beans will be done in under a minute while larger beans may need 4 minutes. (If you're not sure, remove one, peel it, and taste to see if it's cooked through.) Once cooked, plunge the beans in the ice water, then peel away the whitish outer layer. One pound (454g) fava beans in the pod yields about ½ cup. If using fresh fava beans prepared this way, you can omit them from step 1 in the recipe and add them directly to the food processor.

There is a reason that baba ghanoush is made all over the Eastern Mediterranean and Middle East: it's hearty and versatile, and makes a perfect dip for bread. The key to the smoky flavor is charring the eggplant on gas burners or a hot grill. If you don't have access to either, slice the eggplant in half lengthwise and broil on a sheet pan with the skin side up until the flesh is well charred and soft, though note that the smoke flavor won't be as strong using this method. Baba ghanoush keeps for up to five days in the refrigerator.

Serve with Grilled Swordfish with Nigella Seeds, Preserved Lemon, and Green Onions (page 175).

SMOKY BABA GHANOUSH

Active Time: 20 minutes

Equipment: A food processor or blender

MAKES 2½ CUPS, SERVES 4 TO 5

2 small globe eggplants (1½ pounds / 680g)

½ cup (120g) tahini, well stirred

2 garlic cloves, coarsely chopped

1 teaspoon fine sea salt, plus more if desired

½ teaspoon ground cumin

3 tablespoons freshly squeezed lemon juice, plus more if desired

2 tablespoons extra-virgin olive oil, plus more if desired

1. Pierce the eggplants a few times with the prongs of a fork. Place each eggplant directly on a gas burner and turn the heat to medium-high. Char the eggplants, using tongs to turn every 2 to 3 minutes, until the skin has blackened evenly on all sides and looks wrinkled and the eggplant feels soft when pressed, with some liquid coming out, about 11 minutes total. (Alternatively, char the eggplants on a gas or charcoal grill.) Put the eggplants in a heatproof bowl and cover with plastic wrap to steam further, about 15 minutes. When cool enough to handle, peel away the skin while holding the eggplant over the bowl to catch any liquid. (It's okay if some charred pieces remain on the eggplant and get in the liquid.) Reserve 2 tablespoons of the liquid.

2. Transfer the eggplants to a blender or food processor. Add the reserved liquid along with the tahini, garlic, salt, and cumin and blend until smooth, about 30 seconds, scraping down the sides of the blender or food processor if needed. With the blender or processor running, drizzle in the lemon juice and oil and continue to blend until silky smooth, about 1 minute. Taste, adding more salt, lemon juice, or oil as desired. If you want a looser consistency, add a splash of water or more oil. For the best flavor, serve at room temperature.

An importer who brings in fava beans to supply Egypt's unending demand told me that Egypt is the top consumer of fava beans in the world. After touring his factory as tons of dried fava beans poured off delivery trucks and were sorted and bagged (and after eating favas at nearly every meal I had in the country), I have no reason to doubt this claim. One of the reasons is this dish. Rich or poor, office worker or farmer, Egyptians eat ful medames, but everyone dresses up their ful differently. Vendors offer tahina, lime wedges, and little bowls with ground chiles, cumin, black pepper, and salt. In Alexandria, you'll see sliced peppers, garlic, and olive oil. Some cooks even stew the beans with tomatoes and tomato paste. This recipe takes highlights of many samples I've tried and weaves them together in one bowl.

Serve with Grilled Octopus (page 118).

FUL MEDAMES

Active Time: 30 minutes

Plan Ahead: Ful can be made ahead and reheated with a splash of water. If you want to cook it with dried fava beans instead of canned, see Canned Fava Beans vs. Dried Fava Beans.

Equipment: A food mill or potato masher

MAKES ABOUT 4 CUPS (960ML), SERVES 4 TO 6

2 (16-ounce / 454g) cans fava beans, drained and rinsed

½ cup (90g) dried red lentils

3 cups (700ml) water

1½ teaspoons fine sea salt, divided, plus more if desired

½ teaspoon ground cumin

½ teaspoon Aleppo pepper, plus extra for garnish

¼ teaspoon ground turmeric

¼ teaspoon freshly ground black pepper

2 tablespoons extra-virgin olive oil, plus more if desired

¼ medium yellow onion, finely diced

5 garlic cloves, minced

To serve:

2 limes, cut into 6 wedges each

Chopped cilantro or parsley

2 Roma tomatoes, seeded and diced

Aleppo pepper

¼ cup (65g) tahini, well stirred (optional)

Extra-virgin olive oil (optional)

Baladi Bread (page 78) or store-bought pita

Mixed Pickles (page 73) or Pickled Eggplant (page 74)

Arugula leaves (optional)

1. Drain the canned fava beans and rinse. Put the beans in a heavy-bottomed pot or Dutch oven with the lentils, water, and 1 teaspoon salt. Bring to a simmer over high heat, then lower to medium and cook, stirring occasionally, until the lentils are falling apart, about 18 minutes. Pass the beans through a food mill, which will remove some of their skins and make the ful more uniform in texture. (If you don't have a food mill, or prefer a more rustic approach, you can smash the beans with a potato masher.)

2. Put the cumin, Aleppo pepper, turmeric, and black pepper in a small bowl. In a medium skillet, heat the oil over medium heat. Add the onion and a pinch of salt and cook until softened, about 3 minutes. Stir in the garlic and cook for 30 seconds. Remove the pan from the heat, stir in the spices, then pour the contents of the pan into the pot, scraping to make sure all the oil and spices are added. Stir well, adding ½ cup (118ml) more water if the pot looks dry. Taste, seasoning with salt as needed, and simmer 5 more minutes to meld the flavors.

3. Spoon the ful into bowls and let everyone season their bowl as they'd like with lime juice, cilantro or parsley, tomatoes, and/or Aleppo pepper, with tahini and/or olive oil drizzled on top if desired. Serve with plenty of baladi bread for dipping and, if desired, with mixed pickles or pickled eggplant and arugula leaves on the side.

CANNED FAVA BEANS VS. DRIED FAVA BEANS

Canned fava beans are cooked from dried, skin-on fava beans (not peeled, split dried favas). Some cans are even labeled "ful medames." Can size varies from 14 to 20 ounces (400 to 570g), but this recipe is easy to adjust with more or less seasoning (no need to change the amount of red lentils, onion, garlic, or spices).

To use dried fava beans in place of canned, soak 2 cups (300g) dried large, unpeeled fava beans overnight in plenty of water. Drain them the next day, then cover with 1 to 2 inches (2.5 to 5cm) of fresh water, cover, and cook until tender, at least 3 hours. Add more water to the pot as needed to keep the beans submerged. Once cooked, season the beans with 1 teaspoon salt and allow time for the salt to soak in. Use 3½ cups (840ml) cooked favas for this recipe.

THE FELUCCA RIDE

The Nile is the heart of Cairo, coursing through the center of the city and its surrounding satellites. From its source in the highlands of Ethiopia, the river runs from south to north, so the ancient Egyptians divided their realm into "upper" and "lower" Egypt, following the river's path. Upper Egypt is the southern part of the country, where my dad grew up, while Lower Egypt is in the north, where Cairo is.

From the banks of the river in the city's Garden District, our crew gets on a felucca—a traditional river sailing boat— just before sunset. The canvas roof has been rolled back so we can take in the city view unobstructed.

As the sun sinks, the bridges that span the Nile fill with food stalls selling sprouted fenugreek and chickpeas spiked with cumin. Meanwhile, the island of Zamalek lights up, and so does the Cairo Tower. Built in the mid-twentieth century, it was once the tallest tower in Africa. The Sofitel Hotel, a pink tube of a building, anchors the southern tip of Zamalek, and we're told it was once a destination for celebrities and diplomats. A fountain in the middle of the Nile goes off, and all at once we have a water show.

The ride is a lazy loop, just long enough to snack on chickpeas and tiger nuts as we admire the sunset. Soon it's time to dock the felucca and return to the hectic streets of the city.

The traditional way for street food vendors to serve chickpeas is as a simple snack, scooping them into cups with their cooking water so you can eat them with a spoon and also sip the cooking water, spiced with cumin and chile. This recipe is an homage to that experience, but in a more snackable way, with the sumac adding acidity to balance the savory spices. Or try them scattered over a braise or stew for an extra layer of texture. Extra chickpeas can be refrigerated for up to five days and reheated in a dry skillet over medium heat.

Serve with Braised Oxtails with Potatoes and Shaved Carrots (page 234).

CRISPY CHICKPEAS

Active Time: 15 minutes

MAKES ABOUT 1½ CUPS (360ML)

1 (15.5-ounce / 439g) can chickpeas, rinsed and drained well

1½ teaspoons ground sumac

1 teaspoon ground cumin

1 teaspoon onion powder

½ teaspoon garlic powder

1 teaspoon fine sea salt

Pinch of granulated sugar (optional)

¼ cup (60ml) vegetable oil

1. Lay the chickpeas on a clean kitchen towel in a single layer and thoroughly pat dry.

2. In a medium bowl, mix together the sumac, cumin, onion powder, garlic powder, salt, and sugar (if using).

3. Have a tray lined with paper towels ready. Heat the oil in a 10-inch skillet over medium-high heat until it shimmers. Add the chickpeas and pan-fry, stirring occasionally, until they are deep golden brown all over, 5 to 6 minutes. Using a slotted spoon, scoop the chickpeas out of the skillet and scatter on the paper towels to absorb excess oil.

4. While still warm, transfer the chickpeas to the bowl with the spices and mix well. Serve at room temperature.

There is always a mixed pickle on the table in Egypt, whether it's breakfast, lunch, or dinner. Pickles in Egypt are tart and punchy; the most common acid used in pickle brine is white distilled vinegar. The ful cart I like to visit in Old Cairo has pickle jars lined up on top of the cart, the perfect refreshing complement to a rich bowl of Ful Medames (page 60). This recipe, with cauliflower, carrot, and onion, is made in that spirit.

MIXED PICKLES

Active Time: 20 minutes

Plan Ahead: The vegetables sit for 1 hour in salt before being pickled. If you have kosher salt, use it in place of the fine sea salt; it's easier to coat the vegetables with kosher salt. For best results, make the pickles a day or two before serving so the brine can properly fully infuse the vegetables. The pickles keep in the refrigerator for up to 1 month.

Equipment: 1 quart jar or similar heatproof container

MAKES ABOUT 1 QUART (960ML), SERVES 4 TO 6

2 cups (200g) cauliflower florets, cut into 1-inch (2.5cm) pieces (about ½ small head cauliflower)

1 large carrot, peeled and cut crosswise at an angle in ½-inch (12mm) pieces

½ medium yellow onion, sliced into ¼-inch (6mm) wedges

2 tablespoons (30g) fine sea salt or ¼ cup (30g) kosher salt

1½ cups (360ml) water

1 cup (240ml) white distilled vinegar

1 tablespoon granulated sugar

1. In a large bowl, mix together the cauliflower, carrot, and onion with the salt, ensuring all pieces are evenly coated. Place the vegetables in a colander, scraping any salt left in the bowl onto the vegetables, and then set the colander over the bowl. Let sit for 1 hour.

2. After 1 hour, a little water will have collected in the base of the bowl, and the vegetables will be softer. Rinse them well, then let drain for a few minutes longer.

3. Pack the vegetables into a quart jar or heatproof container, pressing them to fit if necessary. In a small saucepan over high heat, bring the water, vinegar, and sugar to a rolling boil until the sugar has dissolved. Pour the hot brine over the vegetables, ensuring they are fully submerged (top up with water if necessary), and let the vegetables sit, uncovered, until they reach room temperature, 2 to 3 hours. Cap the jar or cover the vegetables and refrigerate until needed.

This pickle is a staple at Egyptian ful carts. Some versions are more like a side dish, made by frying small eggplants and then tossing them with chiles, lime juice, vinegar, and salt. This version pays homage to that idea, but instead "cooks" the eggplant in hot brine. Extra goodies—carrot, jalapeño, shallots, and spices—add dimension. Use it on the side or try mincing it up and adding it as an aromatic accent to stir-fries and stews. Pickled eggplant keeps for up to 1 month in the refrigerator. See Making Quick Pickles for ways to make pickles with other vegetables.

PICKLED EGGPLANT

Active Time: 30 minutes

Plan Ahead: The pickle should sit for 2 hours at room temperature before being refrigerated. For best results, brine at least 1 day before eating so the spices infuse into the eggplant.

MAKES JUST OVER 1 QUART (960ML), SERVES 4 TO 6

1 Japanese or Chinese eggplant, sliced crosswise into ½-inch (12mm) rounds

1 celery stalk, sliced into ¼-inch (6mm) pieces

½ cup finely diced carrot (about 1 medium carrot)

½ Fresno chile or red jalapeño, thinly sliced crosswise, seeds removed for less heat

⅓ cup diced shallots (about 1 large)

1½ tablespoons minced garlic

1 tablespoon granulated sugar

1 teaspoon fine sea salt

1 teaspoon black peppercorns

1 teaspoon crushed coriander seeds

1 teaspoon fennel seeds

1 teaspoon black or brown mustard seeds

¼ teaspoon ground turmeric

1½ cups (360ml) water

⅔ cup (160ml) distilled white vinegar

1. Lay the eggplant pieces in an even layer in an 8-inch (20cm) square baking dish.

2. In a medium saucepan, combine the celery, carrot, chile, shallots, garlic, sugar, salt, and spices. Pour in the water and vinegar and bring to a boil over high heat. Lower the heat to medium and simmer for 2 minutes.

3. Pour the contents of the saucepan over the eggplant, spreading the vegetables out in an even layer. Cover with plastic wrap and let sit for 2 hours to soak up the seasonings and cool to a warm room temperature.

4. Uncover, pack the eggplant into wide-mouth pickling jars or other storage vessels, then ladle the brine on top. If needed, top up with water to ensure the eggplant is fully submerged.

MAKING QUICK PICKLES

Use this brine to pickle other vegetables, especially carrots, peppers, radishes, and cauliflower, shown right. To streamline, skip most of the seasonings above and focus on water, vinegar, and one or two spices.

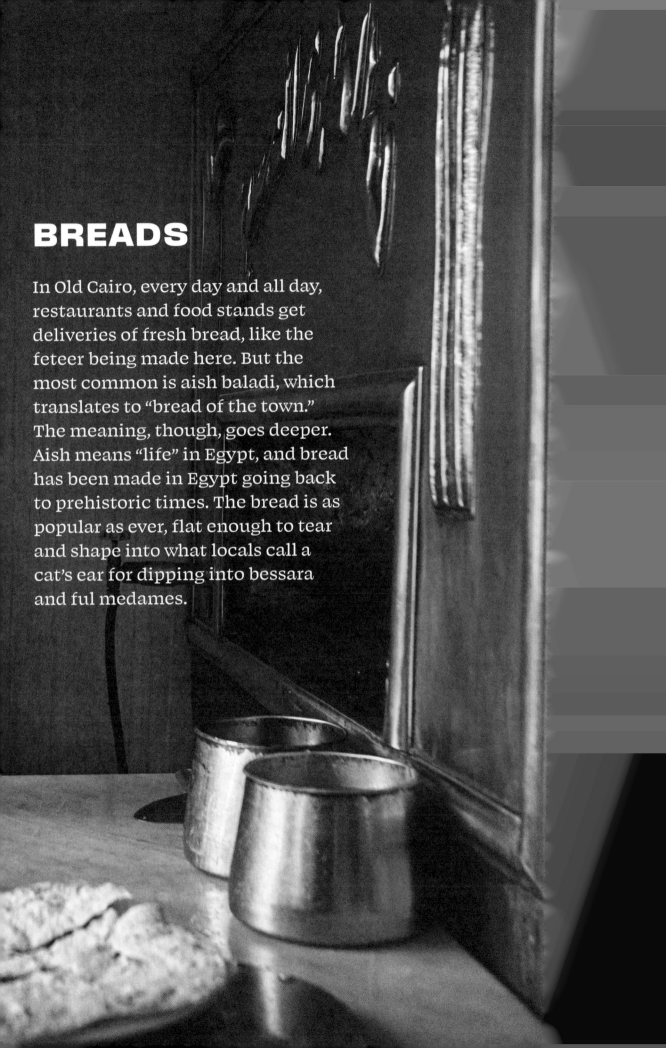

BREADS

In Old Cairo, every day and all day, restaurants and food stands get deliveries of fresh bread, like the feteer being made here. But the most common is aish baladi, which translates to "bread of the town." The meaning, though, goes deeper. Aish means "life" in Egypt, and bread has been made in Egypt going back to prehistoric times. The bread is as popular as ever, flat enough to tear and shape into what locals call a cat's ear for dipping into bessara and ful medames.

What differentiates baladi bread from pita bread made in other parts of the Middle East is the flour. Baladi bread is always made with whole wheat, a habit that goes back to an era when it was much harder for mills to separate wheat from the chaff. Even today, in many Egyptian bakeries, the whole wheat kernel is used in the bread-making process, with the balls of dough resting on a bed of untoasted wheat bran before being shaped and baked. In this version, I blend whole wheat with all-purpose flour for a dough that is easier to handle.

The biggest challenge with making baladi bread at home is handling the dough. People who have mastered shaping and baking the bread use a 90 percent hydration dough—meaning a dough that is very wet and unforgiving if you don't know what you're doing. To shape it, they bounce a portion on the palm of their hand until it spreads out into a round. They make it look easy but this skill takes practice. For this recipe, the dough is a little drier and easier to handle. It also uses a preferment (some flour, water, and yeast mixed together ahead of time) to help with structure. Be sure to get the oven as hot as possible, so the bread puffs up while it bakes. Baladi bread is best when it is still warm. To store for more than a day, let it cool completely, then freeze in resealable bags. Reheat from frozen in a toaster oven or oven set to 400°F (200°C) until hot all the way through.

BALADI BREAD

Active Time: 1½ hours

Plan Ahead: If you start in the morning, you'll have finished baladi bread by dinnertime. Or make the preferment the day before and refrigerate it, taking it out 30 minutes before starting to make the bread. You can also complete the recipe through step 4, refrigerate the dough overnight, and take it out an hour before shaping and baking.

Equipment: A stand mixer for mixing the dough and a pizza stone for baking the bread (though an overturned sheet pan works, too). Have a bench scraper or kitchen knife for portioning dough.

MAKES 10 INDIVIDUAL BALADI BREAD

Preferment:
Vegetable oil
⅓ cup (50g) whole wheat flour
⅓ cup (85ml) water, at room temperature
¼ teaspoon instant yeast (such as Fleischmann's RapidRise)

Main Dough:
1⅓ cups (325ml) water, at room temperature
2 tablespoons extra-virgin olive oil
1⅓ cups (175g) whole wheat flour
2 cups (280g) all-purpose flour, plus more for dusting
2 teaspoons fine sea salt
Nonstick cooking spray

1. To make the preferment, lightly oil a container (such as a deli pint container). In a small bowl with a fork or spatula, stir together the flour, water, and yeast until a sticky paste forms. Transfer to the oiled container, cover, and leave at room temperature for 1½ hours or until the paste has puffed up, is bubbly on top, and has nearly doubled in volume.

2. To make the dough, transfer the preferment to the bowl of a stand mixer fitted with the paddle attachment and add the water. Use your hands to squish the preferment with the water, breaking it up into pieces. Add the oil and whole wheat flour to the bowl. Mix on low speed to incorporate the water and flour until the dough looks like a sticky batter, about 30 seconds. Add the all-purpose flour and mix on low speed until incorporated, about 30 seconds. Remove the paddle attachment, scraping off any bits of dough and adding it back to the bowl. Cover the bowl with a clean kitchen towel and let rest for 20 to 30 minutes so the flours can hydrate.

3. Remove the towel from the bowl and attach the dough hook to the mixer. Mix on medium speed for about 3 minutes, repositioning the dough if it balls up too much on one side. Sprinkle the dough with the salt, then mix again until the dough releases from the side of the bowl without sticking and feels smooth, about 3 more minutes. (Adding the salt will cause the dough to tighten up.)

4. Lightly coat a large bowl with cooking spray. Add the dough, cover with plastic wrap, and let it rise until puffed but not quite doubled, about 3 hours.

5. Dust a work surface generously with all-purpose flour. Put the dough on top and dust the top. It will feel sticky. Using a bench scraper or knife, cut the dough into 10 even pieces. (The easiest way is to cut the dough in half first, then cut each half into 5 pieces. Each portion will weigh around 90g.)

6. Lightly coat a sheet pan with cooking spray. Roll the pieces into balls, cupping your hand over each piece and rolling quickly clockwise or counterclockwise until round and smooth, rinsing your hands if needed to keep the dough from sticking to them. Place the balls on the pan, giving them an inch (2.5cm) or so of space without touching. Lightly coat one side of a couple of sheets of plastic wrap with cooking spray and cover the tray with the oiled side touching the dough (the oil prevents the dough from sticking to the plastic). Let rest for 1½ hours or until puffy.

7. About 30 minutes before baking, put a baking stone on the bottom rack of the oven and remove the middle rack. (If you don't have a baking stone, you can put an overturned sheet pan in the oven 5 minutes before baking instead.) Preheat the oven to 500°F (260°C) or to its highest bake (not broil) setting.

8. Dust a work surface generously with all-purpose flour. Working with one round of dough at a time, pat it into a circle using the tips of your fingers. Then, using a flour-dusted rolling pin, roll into a 6- to 7-inch (15 to 17cm) round. Dust a pizza peel or overturned sheet pan with flour and place 1 or 2 rounds of dough on it (you can start with one to get the hang of it, then double up for the next batch). Slip the dough onto the hot pizza stone and bake until puffed and blistered in places, 7 to 8 minutes. Remove to a wire rack and repeat with the remaining rounds of dough.

MEASURING FLOUR BY VOLUME VS. WEIGHT

When measuring flour using cups instead of a scale, use the scoop-and-sweep method, where you drag a cup through a bin of flour and level off the top. It results in more weight per cup than the method where you spoon flour into a cup and then level it off. One cup of all-purpose flour measured this way is 140 grams, while the spoon-and-level method can vary from 125 to 132 grams, a big difference when baking. (When using a scale, I always default to using gram measurements.)

THE BAKERS OF KAFR EL DAWWAR

On our way to Alexandria, Moustafa Elrefaey has us stop at Kafr El Dawwar, a town known for its women-run bakeries. Ten years ago, one woman started selling bread, and business took off. Soon, she hired other women to help her bake, and now there are multiple bakeries on both sides of a main road, and Egyptians drive from all over to buy their bread here.

These are busy operations, with multiple ovens going at once. At one, a baker dips a small broom in water, then brushes it over the hearth before loading up the oven with different doughs, which puff on contact. Another baker is making feteer, a flaky pastry (see right). She stretches dough over a large, round, oiled table before pressing and folding it into what looks like an enormous deep-dish pizza pan. She then slides the tray into the blistering hot oven.

The shop is also stocked with ma'amoul, cookies filled with dates, and fayesh, a turmeric-yellow biscuit that my mom also makes. Piles of crackers and other types of flatbread fill the rest of the space, and the sheer variety is hard to absorb all at once. Before we get on our way, one of the bakers tears off pieces of warm feteer, loading each with ishta, a thick clotted cream, and offering us a piece. A quick stop for bread became a long one, demonstrating the generosity I've encountered time and time again in Egypt.

Making feteer in Kafr El Dawwar

My team and I created this flatbread for Middle'Terranea, our Middle Eastern pop-up that ran in San Francisco. It proved to be a versatile, near-foolproof recipe. Brushed with olive oil and sprinkled with smoked dukkah, it makes a great cracker-like flatbread to serve with dips. But if you grill it briefly (just until it puffs), it is pliable and can be used as a wrap. Dukkah bread is best right after it's baked. To store for more than a day, let it cool completely, then freeze in resealable bags for up to a month. Reheat from frozen in a toaster oven or oven set to 400°F (200°C) until hot all the way through.

DUKKAH FLATBREAD

Active Time: 1½ hours

Plan Ahead: The dough needs 2½ hours to rest for the first rise and 1 hour to rest for the second rise. You can also refrigerate the dough overnight for the first or second rise (it will rise much more slowly in there). Be sure to bring it to room temperature before baking.

Equipment: A stand mixer for mixing the dough, a pizza stone for baking the bread (though an overturned sheet pan works, too), and parchment paper. Have a bench scraper or kitchen knife for portioning dough.

MAKES 8 FLATBREADS

Dough:
2 cups (280g) all-purpose flour, plus extra for dusting

1¾ cups plus 2 tablespoons (256g) bread flour

2 teaspoons instant yeast (such as Fleischmann's RapidRise)

2 teaspoons granulated sugar

1½ cups (375ml) water, at room temperature

2 tablespoons extra-virgin olive oil

2 teaspoons fine sea salt

Nonstick cooking spray

Topping:
¼ cup (60ml) extra-virgin olive oil

½ cup (60g) Smoked Dukkah (page 267)

1. In the bowl of a stand mixer fitted with the paddle attachment, mix together the flours, yeast, and sugar on low speed. Add the water and mix on low speed to incorporate until a sticky dough forms, about 30 seconds. Remove the paddle attachment, scraping off any bits of dough and adding them back to the bowl. Cover the bowl with a clean kitchen towel and let rest for 20 to 30 minutes so the flours can hydrate.

2. Remove the towel from the bowl and attach the dough hook to the mixer. Add the oil and salt. Mix on medium speed for about 4 minutes, repositioning the dough if it balls up too much on one side, until the oil and salt are incorporated and the dough feels smooth and pulls cleanly from the side and bottom of the bowl. If the dough feels sticky, mix in about 1 tablespoon of all-purpose flour until slightly tacky but workable.

3. Lightly coat a large bowl with cooking spray and add the dough. Lightly coat one side of a sheet of plastic wrap with cooking spray and cover the bowl with the oiled side. Let it rise until puffed but not quite doubled, about 2½ hours. (Alternatively, let it rise overnight in the refrigerator.)

4. Dust a work surface generously with all-purpose flour. Punch the dough down in the bowl to deflate it, then transfer to the floured surface and dust the top. It will feel sticky. Using a bench scraper or knife, cut the dough into 8 even pieces. (The easiest way is to cut the dough in half first, then cut each half into 4 pieces.)

5. Roll the pieces into balls, cupping your hand over each and rolling clockwise or counterclockwise until round and smooth, washing your hands if needed to keep the dough from sticking to them. Lightly coat a sheet pan with cooking spray and place the balls on the pan, giving them an inch (2.5cm) or so of space to rise without touching. Lightly coat one side of a couple of sheets of plastic wrap with cooking spray and cover the tray with the oiled side touching the dough (the oil prevents the dough from sticking to the plastic). Let rest for 1 hour or until puffy. (Alternatively, let it rise overnight in the refrigerator.)

6. About 30 minutes before baking, put a baking stone on the bottom rack of the oven and remove any racks above it. (If you don't have a baking stone, you can put an overturned sheet pan in the oven 5 minutes before baking instead.) Preheat the oven to 500°F (260°C) or to its highest bake (not broil) setting.

7. For each round of dough, place it in the center of a piece of parchment paper. Using your fingers, press it into a rough rectangle shape, then dust a rolling pin and roll the dough into a rectangle about 10 inches (25cm) long and 9 inches (23cm) wide. Brush with the olive oil and sprinkle with 1 tablespoon dukkah, gently adhering the dukkah to the dough with your fingertips.

8. Slip the parchment paper and dough onto the baking stone and bake until puffed and crisp in places, about 8 minutes. Transfer the bread and parchment to a wire rack and repeat with the remaining dough, using a new sheet of parchment for each piece.

There's no one way to eat this flaky, buttery flatbread, but one of my favorites is ripping off a piece and dabbing it in ishta, which tastes like a cross between clotted cream and crème fraîche. I've tried feteer other ways, too, like at tourist spots (where it's called "Egyptian pancake") and in the Faiyum oasis, where I ate it while sitting on blankets, to the roadside bakeries just outside Alexandria. At my restaurants, I love to use it as a play on blinis and caviar. The professional way to make feteer takes time to master: Bakers flip and flick the dough out onto a large oiled surface until it's paper-thin, then they drizzle the layers with ghee and fold it over again while stretching it on a large round table.

This recipe takes the spirit of feteer and makes it approachable without having to stretch the dough like a pro. Cream cheese blended with heavy cream is easier to find than ishta, and I enjoy its tanginess with the rich flatbread. I like to dress it up with chives and caviar, but the same recipe can be served with honey for something sweet. For the best results, weigh the flour. (If you are using cup measurements, first read Measuring Flour by Volume vs. Weight on page 79.) If the dough feels very wet in step 1, you may need to add a tablespoon or two of flour. In the recipe that follows, the flatbread is baked. An alternative approach is to complete steps 1 to 6, then flatten the dough as much as you can with your hands until it's about the size of a flour tortilla and griddle it in a hot cast-iron pan until it is crisp and brown on both sides. To store for more than a day, let cool completely, then freeze in resealable bags for up to a month. Reheat from frozen in an oven or toaster oven set to 350°F (180°C) for 15 minutes or until hot all the way through.

FETEER
WITH ISHTA

Active Time: 1 hour

Plan Ahead: Factor in 50 minutes of downtime. You can also make the dough up to step 5 and refrigerate it overnight.

Equipment: A stand mixer and a cast-iron griddle or large saute pan

MAKES 3 SMALLISH FETEER

2 cups (280g) all-purpose flour

1 tablespoon granulated sugar

1 teaspoon fine sea salt

¾ cup (180ml) water, at room temperature

2 tablespoons vegetable oil, divided

2 tablespoons unsalted butter, melted

To serve:

½ cup (120g) cream cheese, at room temperature

2 tablespoons heavy cream

2 tablespoons chopped chives (optional, for savory feteer)

2 tablespoons honey (optional, for sweet feteer)

Caviar (optional, for savory feteer)

1. Put the flour, sugar, and salt in the bowl of a stand mixer fitted with the dough hook attachment. Add the water and mix on medium-low speed until the dough pulls away from the side of the bowl, about 2 minutes. Remove the dough hook, cover the bowl with a clean kitchen towel, and let the dough rest for 20 minutes.

2. Remove the towel from the bowl and place the dough on a dry, nonporous work surface (no need to dust it with flour first). Divide into 3 even pieces (about 5.5 ounces / 155g), then roll into balls, cupping your hand over each piece and rolling clockwise or counterclockwise until round.

3. Put 1 tablespoon oil in a mixing bowl. Put the balls of dough in the bowl with the oil, coating them on all sides so they don't stick together. Cover the bowl and let the oiled dough rest for 30 minutes.

4. Preheat the oven to 450°F (230°C). Line a sheet pan with parchment paper.

Continued

5. Mix the remaining 1 tablespoon oil with the melted butter. Oil your hands with the oil remaining in the mixing bowl and smear a layer of oil on the same nonporous work surface. Put the dough on top. For each piece, dip your fingertips into the butter-oil blend and pat and stretch the dough into a thin oval at least 10 inches (25cm) in length. If the dough resists stretching, let it rest and start working on another piece. Don't worry if it tears in places. Once stretched, dip your fingers again in the butter-oil blend and smear the surface of the dough.

6. When the dough is stretched and oiled, working in a clockwise direction, fold about 2 inches (5cm) of sides into the center as though making a freeform pie or galette. Smear with the butter-oil blend, using any drips from the work surface as well, then continue to fold the dough toward the center until you have a layered ball that resembles the size and height of a buttermilk biscuit, about 3 inches (7.5cm) wide and 2 inches (5cm) thick. Coat the ball with the butter-oil blend.

7. Place the dough portions on the lined pan spaced out enough that they aren't touching and press down to flatten slightly and even out the surface (they don't have to be identical or look perfect). Bake for 30 minutes or until the outside is golden and crisp and the center is flaky.

8. While the feteer bakes, in a small bowl whisk together the cream cheese and cream until soft and easily spreadable. Serve the feteer warm with dollops of the cream cheese, topped with the chives and caviar, if desired. Or serve sweet with the cream cheese and honey.

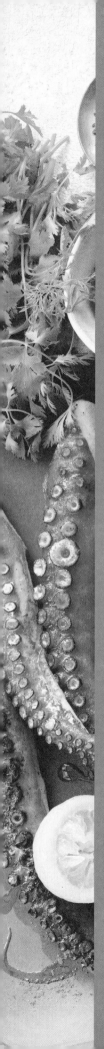

APPETIZERS

The recipes in this chapter combine my experience as a chef with the flavors and ingredients inspired by my travels. The first recipe, my mom's ta'ameya, was the first Egyptian dish I put on a menu. When my mom came to try them, she said the ta'ameya was good, but it was definitely not her recipe. The difference was how we cooked it at the restaurant, making it firm enough to hold up in the deep fryer. She liked hers a little more crumbly, which you can only get away with if you pan-fry them. So we started to cook them on the stove, just like she does. And she was right—they were better. And that's a big part of being a chef, figuring out the way to cook well and accurately while also maintaining the soul of a dish. This chapter bears some similarity to the Setting the Table chapter (page 50), though here the recipes are put together in a way that would work as a first course in a restaurant. Sure, they're a little more composed in concept and presentation, but you can mix and match and plate these in whatever way suits your own table.

In Alexandria, this fried snack is often called falafel, but for most Egyptians it's ta'ameya. No matter the name, it's always made with split dried fava beans—not chickpeas—soaked overnight, giving it an airy texture and vibrant green interior. My mom used a hand grinder to make hers, but you can use a food processor. My buddy Moustafa Elrefaey says the key is the order in which you add the ingredients. Start with the aromatics—onions, garlic—then add the drained soaked beans. Only add the herbs, spices, and salt at the end. Some say that the wealthier you are, the more sesame seeds you use to coat the ta'ameya before frying. If you're poor, you use only coriander seeds. I use a blend of both. Extra ta'ameya can be frozen for up to a month and reheated from frozen for 20 minutes.

Serve with Ahi Crudo (page 97).

TA'AMEYA

Active Time: 1 hour

Plan Ahead: Soak the dried fava beans for 8 hours or overnight. You can blend all the ta'ameya ingredients and refrigerate for 30 minutes before rolling and frying.

Equipment: A food processor, an instant-read thermometer for testing the temperature of the oil, and a spider skimmer

MAKES 24 TA'AMEYA, SERVES 6 TO 8

3 cups (300g) split dried fava beans

¼ medium yellow onion, chopped

5 garlic cloves, smashed

1 cup packed (25g) flat-leaf parsley leaves, coarsely chopped

1 cup packed (25g) cilantro leaves and stems, coarsely chopped

1½ teaspoons ground cumin

½ teaspoon ground coriander

¼ teaspoon cayenne

2 teaspoons fine sea salt

For coating and frying:

⅓ cup (25g) crushed coriander seeds

¼ cup (30g) white sesame seeds

6 cups (1.4L) vegetable oil, for frying

Flaky sea salt, such as Maldon (optional)

Serve with:

Tahina (page 52)

Baladi Bread (page 78) or store-bought pita

1. Rinse the fava beans, then transfer to a bowl and top with enough cold water to cover by about 2 inches (5cm). Let sit at room temperature for 8 hours or overnight to let the beans plump up. Drain, rinse, and leave in the strainer to continue draining until needed.

2. In a food processor, pulse together the onion, garlic, parsley, and cilantro until evenly blended but not completely smooth, about 10 (1-second) pulses. Add the fava beans and pulse until the largest pieces of fava are no bigger than a peppercorn, about 40 (1-second) pulses, scraping down the sides now and again for even blending. Pulse in the cumin, coriander, cayenne, and salt and blend until you have a cohesive mass that holds together and can be formed into balls without crumbling much.

3. For frying, have a large Dutch oven and spider skimmer or slotted spoon handy and line a sheet pan with paper towels. In a shallow plate or bowl, combine the crushed coriander seeds and sesame seeds. Shape the blend into 24 balls about 2 tablespoons each and set on a separate pan or plate in a single layer.

4. Heat 1½ inches (4cm) of oil in the Dutch oven over medium-high heat until an instant-read thermometer registers nearly 350°F (180°C) or when bubbles form around a wooden spoon placed in the oil. Gently roll the balls, then press into the coriander-sesame mix to flatten into ½-inch (12mm) thick, 2-inch (5cm) wide patties. In batches of 6, carefully lower the ta'ameya into the oil and fry, turning once or twice, until dark brown on the outside, about 3 minutes total. Transfer the ta'ameya to the paper towels to drain. Sprinkle with flaky salt, if desired. Skim the oil as needed to get rid of stray pieces of sesame seeds and coriander. Check the temperature, adjusting the heat as necessary to maintain 350°F (180°C) before frying the next batch.

5. Serve warm with tahina sauce and baladi bread. Ta'ameya can also be eaten at room temperature or reheated in a 350°F (180°C) oven for 10 minutes.

Making ta'ameya in Old Cairo

I've been making some version of tuna tartare in my restaurants for at least thirty years. The first iteration took the idea of beef tartare but replaced raw beef with ahi tuna. I mixed it with Asian pear, chiles, sesame oil, mint, and garlic and topped it with a quail egg. I've made that dish so many times I could make it in my sleep, but it was much later that I started to think about how these flavors—sweet, salty, and tart—echo flavors in Middle Eastern cooking. That's how I realized that my mom's ta'ameya, which is crusted with coriander and sesame seeds, goes great with raw ahi tuna.

AHI CRUDO
ON TA'AMEYA

Active Time: 25 minutes

Plan Ahead: You can make the ta'ameya ahead and either refrigerate or freeze it according to the instructions in that recipe.

SERVES 6

12 cooked Ta'ameya (page 92)

1 ripe tomato, seeded and finely diced

1 Persian cucumber, peeled and finely diced

1 tablespoon minced yellow onion

1 tablespoon chopped dill,
plus extra sprigs for garnish

Flaky sea salt, such as Maldon

1 lemon, cut into 8 wedges

1 tablespoon extra-virgin olive oil,
plus extra for brushing

6 ounces (170g) ahi tuna, chilled
(see Buying Raw Tuna)

¼ cup (60ml) Tahina (page 52)

Flat-leaf parsley sprigs (optional)

Pinch of Aleppo pepper (optional)

1. Preheat the oven to 350°F (180°C). Heat the ta'ameya until hot all the way through, about 10 minutes if chilled or 20 if frozen. While the ta'ameya are heating up, mix together the tomato, cucumber, onion, dill, and a few pinches of flaky salt in a small bowl. Squeeze in the juice from 2 lemon wedges and add the olive oil, then mix until evenly coated. Taste, adding more lemon or salt if desired.

2. Using your sharpest knife, slice the tuna across the grain into ¼-inch (6mm) slices. Lay out on a tray or plate and brush with olive oil to lightly coat. Sprinkle each slice with a pinch of flaky salt.

3. To serve, dollop tahina on top of each ta'ameya, squeeze lemon over the top, and season with flaky salt. Divide the tuna slices among the ta'ameya, then spoon the tomato-cucumber salad on top, leaving any extra liquid from the salad in the bowl. Garnish with parsley sprigs and generous pinches of Aleppo and serve immediately.

BUYING RAW TUNA

Tell the fishmonger that you plan to serve the tuna raw, and ask for a piece at least 1-inch (2.5cm) thick. If the only pieces available are thinner, you may need more slices to cover the ta'ameya. Trim away any gristle before slicing against the grain. Some fish is sold "sushi- or sashimi-grade," but all this means is that the fishmonger has deemed it safe to eat raw. It's worth having a conversation with the seller so you get what you want.

This recipe is a tribute to Egypt's love of fries. The potato is a newcomer to Egypt (relative to what the pharaohs were eating), but it has made itself at home in the country, and it's rare to see a restaurant meal that doesn't include fries, even breakfast. Egypt's fries are delicious, fluffy and creamy on the inside, crisp on the outside. To achieve this ideal texture, this recipe involves three separate steps: baking the potatoes before you slice them, then blanching them in cooler oil before freezing them and frying again. Each step forces moisture from the potato to the surface, where it cooks away. If you want to buy a little time before serving the fries, hold them in a 200°F (95°C) oven. Trios are something I am known for in my restaurants, so I offer three dip options here—pick one, a couple, or all three. The fries are even better when dusted with spices. In the photo, you'll see one of my favorites from La Boîte, a blend called Shabazi, which includes dried cilantro, green chiles, garlic, and lemon.

Serve with 1 to 3 of the following dips (serve them in small bowls like you would ketchup):
- *Bessara (page 56)*
- *Onion Labne (page 146)*
- *Mango Ketchup (page 100)*

STEAK FRIES
WITH A TRIO OF DIPS

Active Time: 30 minutes, with at least 30 minutes of downtime

Plan Ahead: The first frying step can be done several days ahead so you can keep fries in the freezer ready to fry up when friends come over. The dips can all be made a few days ahead and refrigerated until needed. If you have leftover mango chile sauce from the Kataifi-Wrapped Shrimp (page 108), add ketchup to it to make the mango ketchup.

Equipment: An instant-read thermometer for testing the temperature of the oil and a spider skimmer

SERVES 4

1 cup (128g) kosher salt

3 large russet potatoes, ideally about 5 inches (12cm) long and 12 ounces (680g) each, washed well and patted dry

2 quarts (1.8L) vegetable oil, for frying

Fine sea salt

1. Preheat the oven to 400°F (200°C). Spread a pie pan or ovenproof skillet with a layer of kosher salt and put the potatoes on top. Bake until halfway cooked, about 25 minutes. (They should give just slightly when pressed.) Let cool to a warm room temperature.

2. When cool enough to handle, halve the potatoes lengthwise and cut lengthwise into ½-inch-thick fries (leave the skins on or peel them, your call).

3. To oil-blanch the potatoes, have a spider skimmer or slotted spoon handy and line a separate sheet pan with paper towels. Heat the oil in a Dutch oven over medium-high heat until it registers about 300°F (150°C). (If you touch the tip of a fry to the surface of the oil, it should only emit a few bubbles rather than bubble vigorously.) In 3 batches (about 10 fries at a time to avoid crowding the pot), add the potatoes and fry, stirring occasionally to prevent sticking, until slightly darker but still very pale, about 3 minutes. Remove from the oil with the skimmer and scatter them on the paper towels. Check the temperature, adjusting the heat as necessary to maintain 300°F (150°C) before frying the next batch. Repeat until all the fries are blanched. Let cool to room temperature. Line a sheet pan that will fit in the freezer with parchment paper and put the fries on top in a single layer so they aren't touching. Freeze until firm, at least 2 hours or overnight (once frozen, they can be transferred to a resealable plastic bag). Let the oil cool, skimming any pieces from the surface, and save for the next step.

4. Put the dips you're using into small bowls for serving and have a plate ready for serving the fries. Line a sheet pan with fresh paper towels and place a wire rack on top. Heat the oil over medium-high heat until it reaches 375°F (190°C).

5. Take the fries from the freezer and, in 3 batches, fry, gently stirring occasionally, until deep golden brown, about 3 minutes. Remove the fries, allowing excess oil to drip off, and scatter on the rack. Generously season with fine sea salt and serve immediately with the dips.

MANGO KETCHUP

MAKES ABOUT ⅔ CUP (160ML)

2½ tablespoons diced fresh mango

2 tablespoons mango pickle (see Buying Mango Pickle and Mango Puree, page 110)

1½ tablespoons mango puree (see Buying Mango Pickle and Mango Puree, page 110)

Finely grated zest of 1 tangerine

2 tablespoons tangerine juice

½ teaspoon Aleppo pepper

⅓ cup (80ml) ketchup

1 teaspoon granulated sugar (optional)

Fine sea salt, if needed

In a blender or mini food processor, combine the fresh mango, mango pickle, mango puree, tangerine zest and juice, Aleppo pepper, and ketchup. Blend until smooth, then taste, adding the sugar and salt if needed to round out the flavor. (Some mangoes are sweeter than others, and mango pickle can vary in saltiness, so taste before seasoning.)

This is a recipe that my colleague, chef Adam Sobel, was inspired to create after visiting the Middle East: a lightly cured salmon that gives a nod to lox and bagels, which we sliced thinly and draped over bread spread with tzatziki. If it's peak summer and you have lemon cucumbers and fresh sweet peppers, slice them thinly and add them to the open-faced sandwich. Cured salmon keeps for up to five days.

ZA'ATAR-CURED SALMON
WITH TZATZIKI AND SALMON ROE

Active Time: 20 minutes

Plan Ahead: The salmon takes from 1 to 3 days to cure depending on how thick the pieces are. Do not let it go longer or it will overcure.

SERVES 8 TO 10

1 (2-pound / 908g) piece center-cut salmon fillet

⅓ cup plus 2 teaspoons (50g) kosher salt, like Diamond Crystal

¼ cup plus 2 teaspoons (30g) za'atar, divided

1 tablespoon finely grated lemon zest

2 teaspoons granulated sugar

Serve with:
Baladi Bread (page 78) or crackers

Tzatziki (page 53)

1 Persian cucumber, thinly sliced into rounds (optional)

1 or 2 red radishes, thinly sliced (optional)

Smoked salmon or smoked trout roe (optional)

1. Put the salmon skin side down in a 9- by 13-inch (23 by 33cm) baking dish. In a small bowl, mix together the salt, ¼ cup za'atar, zest, and sugar. Coat the salmon thoroughly in the salt mixture, using all of it. Cover with plastic wrap and refrigerate for at least 24 hours or up to 3 days, depending on how thick the piece of salmon is. It's done when it still feels soft to the touch but the surface of the salmon has turned a deeper pink color from the salt cure.

2. Rinse the salmon in cold water to get rid of salt, then pat dry thoroughly. Place on a cutting board and cut off the skin and any of the bloodline, if noticeable. Sprinkle the remaining 2 teaspoons za'atar on all sides and then wrap the salmon snugly in plastic wrap. Refrigerate for at least 2 hours or up to 3 days before serving.

3. To serve, use your sharpest knife to slice the salmon across the grain into thin strips. Spread baladi bread with a spoonful of tzatziki, then drape a few salmon slices over the top. Add cucumber and/or radish slices and a few pieces of roe on top (if using).

101

FAIYUM

I leave Cairo in the morning with Moustafa Elrefaey and his friends and head to Faiyum, an oasis a couple of hours southwest of the city, passing through suburbs and desert before the land turns green. Agriculture is an ancient practice here; archaeologists found grain storage bins dating 1,500 years before the pyramids were built. Way back then, this land was greener thanks to the Nile, whose annual floods fortified the farmland. We don't know exactly what these ancient people did with the grains, but the experts say it probably went into porridge, bread, or beer. When they weren't farming, they fished.

On our way to lunch, we pass the southern shore of Lake Qaroun, the green side, which looks out onto the desert. It's calm and quiet, the opposite of Cairo. Nearby is the town of Tunis, a destination for handmade ceramics. After stretching our legs from the drive, we sit on blankets around a short table and tear off pieces of flaky feteer, dipping it into a sweet golden syrup and ishta, clotted cream. It's a snack before the main meal, hamam mahshi, which will be prepared with pigeons raised on the property. The birds are stuffed with freekeh and roasted over an open fire. When they're ready, we eat them with our hands, the juice dripping down our arms.

Lake Qaroun

When my team and I were exploring how to use traditional Middle Eastern ingredients in new ways, it wasn't long before kataifi became one of my favorites. The pastry itself is made by streaming a batter through a strainer onto a hot plate that spins as it cooks, turning the batter into strands as fine as angel hair pasta. Kataifi is almost always used in desserts, but I also like it with seafood, wrapping it around prawns (pictured) or shrimp. Look for fresh or frozen kataifi at Middle Eastern grocery stores. If frozen, let it thaw according to package directions before using. Dried coconut added to the kataifi as you roll up the shrimp helps create a satisfyingly crisp texture. See Buying Mango Pickle and Mango Puree (page 110) for sourcing the right mango ingredients, and save any extra mango sauce; you can add some ketchup to it to make Mango Ketchup, a perfect dip for fries (page 98).

KATAIFI-WRAPPED SHRIMP
WITH MANGO CHILE SAUCE

Active Time: 45 minutes

Plan Ahead: Ensure the kataifi is thawed before preparing the shrimp.

Equipment: A blender

SERVES 3 TO 4

Mango Chile Sauce:

⅓ cup (50g) diced fresh mango (about ⅓ of a Manila mango)

¼ cup (50g) mango pickle

3 tablespoons mango puree

Juice (about ¼ cup / 60ml) and finely grated zest of 2 tangerines

1 teaspoon Aleppo pepper

1 tablespoon granulated sugar, if needed

Fine sea salt, if needed

Shrimp:

1 pound (454g) colossal shrimp, U12 or U16, peeled and deveined, with tails left on

Fine sea salt

8 ounces (225g) kataifi, thawed if frozen

1 cup (180g) unrefined coconut oil, melted

About 1 cup (75g) dried unsweetened coconut flakes

Vegetable oil, for frying shrimp

Basil or mint leaves, for garnish

1 lime, cut into 6 wedges

1. To make the sauce, in a blender, combine the fresh mango, mango pickle, mango puree, tangerine juice and zest, and Aleppo pepper. Blend until smooth, then taste, adding the sugar and salt if needed to round out the flavor. (Some mangoes are sweeter than others, and mango pickle can vary in saltiness, so taste before seasoning.)

2. To prepare the shrimp, pat dry, then season the shrimp on all sides with a few pinches of salt. For each shrimp, lay a strip of kataifi about 2 inches (5cm) wide and 7 to 8 inches (17 to 20cm) long on a work surface. (You will have more kataifi than you need, so sort through the strips, selecting long, unbroken strands and avoiding the short pieces.) Using a pastry brush, saturate the kataifi with the coconut oil, then sprinkle 1 tablespoon coconut flakes on top. Fold one end of the kataifi a third of the way up the strip, then place the shrimp perpendicular at the double-layer end. Roll the shrimp up snugly so that the kataifi stays in place. (It should as long as the kataifi is oiled thoroughly.) Place the wrapped shrimp on a plate seam side down and repeat with the remaining shrimp.

3. To cook the shrimp, have a plate lined with paper towels handy. Heat about ½ inch (12mm) vegetable oil in a 10-inch (25cm) skillet over medium-high heat until it shimmers. (If you put a wooden chopstick or spoon in the oil, bubbles should form immediately.) In 3 batches, cook the shrimp, basting oil over the top and turning the shrimp carefully as needed, until the kataifi is golden brown and crisp, 2 to 3 minutes. Transfer the shrimp to the paper towel–lined plate and season the tops with salt. Skim the surface of the oil to remove extra bits of kataifi and coconut in between batches, and add more vegetable oil as needed.

Continued

108

4. To serve, dollop the mango chile sauce on the plate and put the shrimp on top, serving 3 to 4 per person. Garnish with mint leaves and serve with lime wedges.

BUYING MANGO PICKLE AND MANGO PUREE

Mango pickle can be found in Indian grocery stores, some Middle Eastern stores, and occasionally the international aisle at general grocery stores. It varies widely in saltiness, so taste before adding salt to the sauce. Look for mango puree—sometimes called "mango pulp"—in the canned goods or the frozen section of an Indian or Middle Eastern grocery store. It often comes sweetened, and that's perfectly fine.

Cooking lobster has long been part of my repertoire, and I wanted to find a way to make it that paid homage to Egypt, a country with an unheralded (and amazing) variety of mangoes (see page 114). I've always thought lobster and mango work well together—they're both meaty, sweet, and decadent, so I double down here, using mango in the salad and the sauce. You can make the sauce a day or two ahead. While it makes more than you need, the extra is great on shrimp, grilled fish, or chicken, and it freezes well. The key with this salad is that the avocado, lobster, and mango should all be cut into similar-sized pieces.

LOBSTER MANGO SALAD

Active Time: 45 minutes

Plan Ahead: If working with live lobster (see Cooking a Lobster, page 113), allow enough time so the lobster is thoroughly chilled before making the salad.

Equipment: A blender

SERVES 4 GENEROUSLY

Saffron Mango Sauce:

¼ cup (60ml) freshly squeezed orange juice

2 tablespoons freshly squeezed lemon juice

2 tablespoons freshly squeezed lime juice

1 medium Manila mango, peeled, pitted, and coarsely chopped

Pinch of saffron threads

⅔ cup (160g) plain, whole-milk Greek yogurt

½ teaspoon fine sea salt

Salad:

1 tablespoon neutral oil, such as canola

1 red bell pepper, cored, seeded, and cut into 1-inch (2.5cm) chunks

¼ cup (60ml) extra-virgin olive oil

2 tablespoons freshly squeezed lemon juice

¼ teaspoon fine sea salt

Freshly ground black pepper

6 to 8 ounces (170 to 225g) cooked lobster meat (tail and claw), cut into 1-inch (2.5cm) chunks

1 medium Manila mango, peeled, pitted, and diced into 1-inch (2.5cm) chunks

1 Hass avocado, halved, pitted, skin removed, and diced into 1-inch (2.5cm) chunks

½ fennel bulb, cored and sliced very thinly (if the fennel came with fronds, save some for garnish)

Flaky sea salt, such as Maldon

1. To make the saffron mango sauce, put the citrus juices, mango, and saffron in a blender and blend on high for 2 to 3 minutes or until silky smooth and bright orange. Strain the sauce into a bowl through a fine-mesh strainer, using a rubber spatula to press the mango pulp and extract as much as possible (there may not be much pulp). Whisk in the yogurt and salt and taste, adding more salt if desired. Refrigerate until needed. If the sauce is too thick to pour when chilled, thin it with a splash of water before serving.

2. To cook the pepper for the salad, heat the neutral oil in a large skillet over medium-high heat. Add the pepper and let sear, flipping a few times, until the flesh is still crisp but no longer raw, about 2 minutes. Set aside and cool completely.

3. To make the salad, in a small bowl whisk together the olive oil, lemon juice, fine sea salt, and black pepper. In a large bowl combine the cooked lobster, red pepper, mango chunks, avocado, and fennel. Stir in enough of the olive oil vinaigrette to coat the salad lightly. Add a pinch or two of flaky salt, mix together, and taste a piece of lobster and mango, adding more vinaigrette or salt as needed. Serve the salad on a platter or in a bowl with the mango sauce poured along the edges or on the side.

Continued

111

COOKING A LOBSTER

A good fish counter often carries cooked lobster meat, but the best lobster is always the one you cook yourself. For this recipe, use a 2-pound (908g) live Maine lobster to get about 8 ounces of cooked lobster meat. Pierce the lobster between the eyes with a heavy knife, which severs the nervous system. Cooking the claws and the tail separately allows them to cook evenly, so twist off the claws, then twist the lobster head from the tail, discarding the head (or clean and save it for stock). Add water to a tall stockpot fitted with a steamer rack insert, ensuring the water isn't touching the insert. Bring the water to a boil, add the lobster, cover, and steam until cooked through, 11 minutes.

When done, the internal temperature of the lobster will read about 135°F (57° C). While the lobster steams, put ice in a large bowl and fill it with a little water. Plunge the cooked lobster in the ice water for at least 5 minutes, then drain. Crack the lobster claws and knuckles with a nutcracker, lobster cracker, or the blunt side of a knife blade. Remove the shells from the knuckles and pick off the meat. To remove the meat from the claws, pull the "thumb" of the claws off and remove the inner cartilage, then gently wiggle the meat out of the shell. Using kitchen shears, cut the shell off the tail by cutting in the center of the belly, then peel and discard. For this recipe, cut the meat into pieces the same size as the mango and avocado and ensure the meat is very cold before serving.

EGYPTIAN MANGOES

Everyone who comes from a place that grows mangoes will say that their country has the best mangoes. So indulge me when I say that Egyptian mangoes are the best. It's not only the flavor but also the variety. Chef Yasser Ramadan, who works with Moustafa Elrefaey, is a true Egyptian mango fanatic. He loves them so much that he has a refrigerator dedicated to mangoes, and every time I see him, he hands me a prized fruit.

Some varieties of mango are best for eating out of hand (like Fas, a small fruit with very little stringy fiber and a small pit); others are better for freezing and pureeing (like Zebea, which Yasser saves to make mango drinks for Ramadan). Some are endlessly versatile. (Access to different mango varieties is more limited back home, so for the recipes in this book I use Manila mangoes, which are available year-round.)

If there are mangoes at the table, Yasser will cut each into two halves, leaving the meat on the narrow sides of the pit to cut out later. With the halves, he holds one in his hand while crosshatching it with a cleaver, but he has a lot of experience cutting up mango. At home, I recommend setting the half skin side down on a cutting board, then crosshatching the meat before scooping it out to eat.

If Greek illustrations of octopus traps dating to the sixth century BC are any indication, it's likely that the Greeks perfected the technique for catching and cooking octopus before spreading their experience to other corners of the Mediterranean, including North Africa, where Bedouins once dried octopus for transport across the desert. In Greece, you find grilled octopus with beans, the charred tentacles creating a rich, meaty counterpoint to the earthy beans. Here, I've taken that inspiration and paired octopus with Ful Medames (page 60), Egypt's famous slow-cooked dried fava beans.

Most octopus from the store comes cleaned (the innards from the head, eyes, and "beak," or mouth, removed). If using frozen octopus, place it in a colander and let it defrost before cooking.

Serve with Roasted Tomatoes with Smoked Dukkah (page 273) and poached eggs.

GRILLED OCTOPUS
WITH FUL MEDAMES

Active Time: 30 minutes

Plan Ahead: Count on about 1 hour of simmering time. You can cook the octopus a day or two before grilling so it has ample time to cool before portioning and grilling.

Equipment: A gas or charcoal grill and grill brush

SERVES 4

3 tablespoons extra-virgin olive oil, divided

1 bay leaf

3 garlic cloves, peeled and lightly smashed

1 medium yellow onion, peeled and quartered through the root end

2 teaspoons black peppercorns

1 (4- to 6-pound / 1.8 to 2.7kg) octopus, thawed, if frozen, and rinsed

3 tablespoons red wine vinegar

1½ teaspoons fine sea salt, plus more if desired

Aleppo pepper

2 cups (475ml) Ful Medames (page 60)

1 tablespoon chopped flat-leaf parsley

½ lemon, cut into 4 wedges

Handful of cherry tomatoes, halved

Flaky sea salt, such as Maldon

1. In a large heavy-bottomed pot or Dutch oven, heat 2 tablespoons oil over medium heat. Add the bay leaf, garlic, onion, and peppercorns and cook, stirring occasionally, for 3 minutes or until the onion just begins to soften. Add the octopus, vinegar, and fine sea salt and stir to coat in the oil. Cover the pot and turn the heat to medium. You want a gentle simmer as the octopus starts to release water.

2. Cook for about 30 minutes, then check how much water is in the pot (the octopus should be at least partially covered in its own water; if the pot is dry for any reason, add tap water). Cook for 50 to 65 more minutes or until nearly completely cooked and tender when pierced with a knife. Let cool for 1 hour in its braising liquid. (Alternatively, cool the octopus in its braising liquid and refrigerate in the liquid overnight.)

3. Using tongs, transfer the octopus to a wire rack to cool completely, about 30 minutes. Cut the tentacles from the body and discard the head.

4. Heat a gas grill to high heat or build a fire in a charcoal grill for direct-heat cooking. When the grates are hot, clean the grill with a grill brush. Pat the tentacles dry, then brush with the remaining 1 tablespoon oil and season with a couple of pinches of fine sea salt. Place on the hottest part of the grill and cook, covered if using a gas grill, until charred, about 3 minutes per side. Sprinkle with Aleppo pepper.

5. In a small saucepan, heat up the ful medames until warm. Serve the tentacles whole or sliced into smaller pieces on a platter with the warmed ful medames. Garnish with the parsley, a few squeezes of lemon, cherry tomatoes, and pinches of flaky salt.

Night is when the streets of Cairo come alive, with people smoking shisha, playing cards in the cool evening air, or buying hawawshi from food vendors. Made with ground meat mixed with onions and peppers and cooked inside Baladi Bread (page 78), hawawshi is like a cross between a burger and a pita sandwich. For a change of pace, I use ground turkey in place of beef (turkey is cooked in Bedouin-style pit roasts in Egypt), and I incorporate spicy harissa paste into the mix. You don't have to make your own baladi bread to make hawawshi. Store-bought pita bread approximately 7 inches (17cm) in diameter works perfectly. Extra hawawshi can be cooled completely and frozen. To reheat, bake in a 400°F (200°C) oven until thawed and hot all the way through, about 12 minutes.

TURKEY HAWAWSHI

Active Time: 30 minutes

Equipment: An instant-read thermometer

SERVES 4

4 pieces whole wheat pita bread

1½ pounds (680g) ground turkey thigh and/or leg meat (dark meat preferred)

¼ cup finely chopped dried apricot

½ cup panko breadcrumbs

1 large egg

3 green onions, thinly sliced crosswise, white and green parts

2 to 3 tablespoons harissa paste, divided

1½ teaspoons fine sea salt

1 teaspoon onion powder

1 teaspoon paprika

1 teaspoon dried sage (or 2 teaspoons minced fresh sage)

½ teaspoon ground cumin

¼ teaspoon ground turmeric

4 tablespoons (45ml) extra-virgin olive oil

½ cup (118ml) mayonnaise

1. Preheat the oven to 425°F (220°C). Place a wire rack on top of a sheet pan, or line with parchment paper. Using kitchen shears or a knife, cut each flatbread into two half-moons and pry open the pockets to make room for the filling. It's okay if you tear a hole—the filling will help the bread stay together once it's cooked.

2. In a large bowl, add the turkey, apricot, panko, egg, green onions, 1 tablespoon harissa paste, salt, onion powder, paprika, sage, cumin, and turmeric. Mix with your hands, making sure to break up any pieces of apricot that are sticking together, until you can pick up the filling in one mass and lift it from the bowl, about 1 minute.

3. Divide the turkey filling between the bread pockets, filling them as much as possible (about 4 ounces / 114g per pocket). Once filled, press the bread halves so they are all an even thickness.

4. In a large skillet over medium-high heat, heat 1 tablespoon oil. When it shimmers, add two pockets and cook until they turn golden, 1 to 2 minutes. Flip over and continue to cook for 30 seconds or so, then place in a single layer on the sheet pan (it's okay if some pieces touch). Repeat with the remaining oil and bread until all sides have been griddled.

5. Bake for 15 minutes or until the bread is brown and puffed on top and the turkey is cooked through (an instant-read thermometer inserted into the center of the hawawshi should register at least 160°F / 70°C).

6. In a small bowl, stir the mayonnaise and remaining 1 to 2 tablespoons harissa paste (depending on how spicy you want it) together to make harissa mayonnaise. Serve the hawawshi warm with the mayonnaise as a dip.

Red lentil soup is part of the classic Egyptian home cooking repertoire. Red lentils are small and pink and cook quickly. As they soften and lose their shape, they also help to thicken the broth without taking over. This recipe makes an everyday red lentil soup more substantial, turning it into a satisfying, and completely plant-based, meal. For extra credit, a spoonful of pumpkin seed tahina on top gives it extra richness. In this recipe, "small diced" means small enough so that a few pieces will fit on a soup spoon, making it easy to eat.

PUMPKIN RED LENTIL SOUP

Active Time: 1½ hours

Plan Ahead: The soup is best when it has an extra 20 minutes after cooking for the flavors to meld. It tastes even better the next day.

MAKES 12 CUPS (2.8L), SERVES 6

1 small sugar or pie pumpkin

3 tablespoons extra-virgin olive oil, divided

3 teaspoons fine sea salt, divided

20 garlic cloves, peeled

3-inch (7.5cm) piece ginger, peeled

1 medium yellow onion, small diced

2 medium carrots, peeled and small diced

2 celery stalks, small diced

1½ cups small diced peeled celery root

1 medium leek, light green and white parts only, thoroughly cleaned and small diced

1 cup (200g) dried red lentils

1 small butternut squash (about 18 ounces / 520g), peeled, seeded, and small diced

8 cups (2L) Middle Eastern Vegetable Stock (page 269) or store-bought vegetable broth

2 cups chopped chard leaves without stems (half a medium bunch)

1 tablespoon thinly sliced sage

¼ cup (60ml) Pumpkin Seed Tahina (page 53), optional

1 lemon, cut into 8 wedges (optional)

1. Preheat the oven to 400°F (200°C). Line a sheet pan with aluminum foil. Halve the pumpkin, scoop out the seeds, and rub the insides with 1 tablespoon oil. Season with 1 teaspoon of the salt. Roast skin side up until tender when pierced with a knife, about 50 minutes. Let cool to room temperature, then scoop out about 2 cups (430g) cooked pumpkin pulp. Coarsely chop the pumpkin pulp and keep at room temperature. (Extra roasted pumpkin freezes well and can be used in future soups or desserts.)

2. Using a rasp grater, grate the garlic and ginger. Alternatively, coarsely chop the garlic and ginger and blend into a paste in a mini food processor. (Note that this won't work in a regular sized food processor, which won't blend the ingredients finely enough.)

3. Heat the remaining 2 tablespoons oil in a large Dutch oven or heavy pot over medium-high heat until it shimmers. Add the onion, carrots, celery, celery root, leek, and 1 teaspoon salt and cook, stirring occasionally, for 8 to 10 minutes or until the carrots are almost tender. Add the garlic and ginger and cook until aromatic, about 30 seconds.

4. Add the lentils, butternut squash, remaining 1 teaspoon salt, and the stock and bring to a boil. Lower the heat to a simmer and cook gently until the lentils and squash are soft and cooked through, about 25 minutes. Add the chard, pumpkin, and sage and simmer for another 5 minutes or until the chard is tender and the pumpkin is heated all the way through. Remove from the heat and let cool, optimally for at least 20 minutes before serving to allow the flavors to meld.

5. To serve, bring the soup back to a boil. Taste, adding more salt if desired. Divide into soup bowls and garnish with spoonfuls of pumpkin tahina (if using). Serve with lemon wedges at the table, if desired.

BUYING PUMPKINS FOR ROASTING

Look for either "sugar pumpkins" or "pie pumpkins"; you don't want to use the same kind of pumpkin you carve at Halloween. If unavailable, use small butternut or honeynut squash (about 18 ounces / 520g) and roast in step 1 just like the pumpkin.

It's been repeated over and over that the pharaohs were the first to eat foie gras, but Dr. Mennat-Allah El Dorry, an archeologist and Cairo native, isn't so sure. She thinks the story came from nineteenth-century French archeologists who found hieroglyphics showing people force-feeding birds with grains, and, being French, concluded that the ancient Egyptians ate foie gras. But Dr. Mennat, who is an expert in what the ancient Egyptians ate, says the illustrations may have depicted the process of fattening up birds for a lot of reasons, not just for the prized enlarged liver. Still, I'm coming at this story as a chef, and I like to imagine the pharaohs living large and eating foie gras. Consider this a tribute to what may (or may not have) happened during the time of Ramses the Great. To be honest, the recipe is just fine without the foie gras, too.

HUMMUS
WITH CAULIFLOWER, POMEGRANATE, AND FOIE GRAS

Active Time: 30 minutes

Plan Ahead: Make the hummus before starting this dish or use a good-quality store-bought hummus.

SERVES 4 TO 6

1 medium head cauliflower, cored

2 tablespoons vegetable oil, divided

Fine sea salt

1½ tablespoons pomegranate molasses

¼ cup chopped toasted pistachios
(see Buying and Toasting Nuts, page 267)

1½ cups (350g) Hummus (page 54),
at room temperature

10 ounces (284g) foie gras, cut into 1-inch cubes
(see Prepping and Cooking Foie Gras)

2 tablespoons pomegranate seeds

Chopped flat-leaf parsley

Pinches of za'atar

1. Cut the cauliflower into bite-sized florets no bigger than 1 inch (2.5cm), cutting away any extra core so that the florets will cook evenly. You should have about 4½ cups (1L) of florets.

2. Heat 1 tablespoon oil in a large skillet over medium-high heat. Add half the cauliflower and cook until caramelized, about 5 minutes, then transfer to a medium bowl. Repeat with the remaining 1 tablespoon oil and cauliflower, add to the same bowl, and mix in ¼ teaspoon salt and the pomegranate molasses and pistachios. Wipe out the skillet with a paper towel.

3. Spread the hummus at the base of a serving platter or bowl and spoon the cauliflower on top.

4. Heat the skillet over medium-high heat. Season the foie gras evenly with salt and add to the skillet. Sear until brown on one side, then shake the pan to release the pieces and use a spoon to turn them over to sear the other side, basting occasionally with the melted foie fat, until the cubes have a nearly melted interior, about 1 minute. Leaving the fat in the pan, spoon the cubes onto the cauliflower and scatter the pomegranate seeds and parsley on top. Sprinkle with the za'atar and serve immediately.

PREPPING AND COOKING FOIE GRAS

Have everything ready to go before cooking the foie gras, since it cooks rapidly. As an alternative to searing it in a skillet, you can skewer and grill it very briefly, turning after a few seconds just to char the exterior but before the center becomes molten. When buying foie gras, look for a nice pink color and avoid gray pieces, which means the liver has started to oxidize. When slicing it into cubes, trim away any significant veins you come across, but don't worry about the smaller ones. It's more important that the pieces are even in size so they cook in roughly the same amount of time.

SALADS AND VEGETABLES

Vegetables are an essential element of the Egyptian table, and the recipes in this chapter reflect that, leaning into the abundance of vegetables served around the Mediterranean. I kick this chapter off with salata baladi, the classic salad of diced tomatoes and cucumbers that is served year-round at every meal, before going into salads that play off other flavors from around the country and region. What ties these recipes together is the vibrant interplay of spices, herbs, and, of course, acidity.

Across the Middle East you'll find simple salads of cucumbers and tomatoes. The Egyptian version, salata baladi (*baladi* meaning "local" or "native"), is served at every meal. Especially prized are the juices left in the bowl from the tomatoes and cucumber. This "whisky," as some call it, is reserved for the guest of honor, but I like the style of the Cairo restaurant Sobhy Kaber, which offers extra shots of the juice to anyone who asks. Double or triple this salad to feed a crowd.

Serve with Grilled Lamb Kofta with Chile Labne (page 222).

SALATA BALADI

Active time: 25 minutes

SERVES 3 TO 4

2 limes, halved

½ cup finely sliced red onion

1 tablespoon minced seeded jalapeño (optional)

½ teaspoon fine sea salt, plus more if desired

¼ cup (60ml) extra-virgin olive oil

2 cups sliced ripe tomatoes (about 2 large tomatoes, a pint of cherry tomatoes, or a mix)

2 Persian cucumbers or 1 English cucumber

2 tablespoons chopped dill

Aleppo pepper (optional)

1. Squeeze the limes directly into a salad bowl (you'll have around ¼ cup / 60ml juice). Stir in the onion, jalapeño (if using), and salt. Let the onion and pepper marinate while preparing the rest of the ingredients.

2. Stir in the oil, then mix in the tomatoes, cucumber, and dill. Taste, adding more salt if needed. Sprinkle Aleppo pepper on top (if using) and serve immediately.

PREPPING CUCUMBERS

If using an English cucumber, peel it first, then halve it lengthwise. Use a spoon to scoop out the seeds. If using smaller, more tender Persian cucumbers, leave the skins and seeds in place and slice crosswise or into chunks.

Watermelon and feta salads are classics in Greece, and this salad borrows from Egypt's Mediterranean neighbors to the north, spiked with a little Urfa pepper for heat. The key in this salad is ensuring that each bite has a little of everything, so cut the Halloumi and watermelon into bite-sized pieces. If you have a FoodSaver or other vacuum sealer, consider compressing the watermelon pieces in a bag with the juice and zest from an additional lime for a more intense flavor and texture. You can mix the Halloumi with the oil and lime juice while prepping the rest of the ingredients.

HALLOUMI AND WATERMELON SALAD

Active Time: 25 minutes

Equipment (optional): See headnote above for the vacuum sealer. A mandoline, if you have one, makes easy work of shaving and slicing vegetables.

SERVES 4

3 tablespoons extra-virgin olive oil

Juice and finely grated zest of 1 lime

¼ teaspoon fine sea salt, plus more if desired

3 to 4 ounces (85 to 113g) Halloumi, cut into bite-sized (¼-inch / 2cm) pieces

2 cups watermelon cut into bite-sized pieces (about ¼ mini seedless watermelon)

1 celery stalk, thinly sliced

1 Persian cucumber, thinly sliced into rounds

3 small red radishes, sliced paper-thin

A few small purple basil or mint leaves, torn if larger than the pieces of watermelon

¼ cup toasted pistachios, coarsely chopped (see Buying and Toasting Nuts, page 267)

Pinches of Urfa pepper

In a salad bowl, mix together the oil, lime juice and zest, and salt. Add the Halloumi and mix to coat in the vinaigrette. (You can do this while prepping the other ingredients.) Add the watermelon, celery, cucumber, radishes, and basil and taste, adding more salt if desired. Sprinkle the pistachios on top and garnish with a few pinches of Urfa pepper.

Waldorf salad is the kind of classic recipe you learn in culinary school—walnuts, celery, and apple presented on a bed of lettuce. This version respects the original but adds a few Egypt-inspired twists. Tangy yogurt dressing with toasted poppy seeds anchors a mix of grapes, radishes, and celery curls on Bibb or butter lettuce while a sprinkling of dukkah provides savory flavor. Use a Y-shaped vegetable peeler on the back side of the celery stalks to make the celery strips, then soak them in ice water so they curl. For the best texture and crunch, serve the salad as soon as it's dressed, with extra dressing on the side.

MIDDLE EASTERN WALDORF

Active Time: 20 minutes

SERVES 4

Yogurt Dressing:

1½ teaspoons poppy seeds

½ cup (120ml) plain whole-milk yogurt or Greek yogurt

1 tablespoon honey

2¼ teaspoons freshly squeezed lemon juice

¼ teaspoon fine sea salt, plus more if desired

Salad:

1 large head Bibb or butter lettuce

1 large celery stalk, peeled into curls (see headnote) or sliced crosswise into ½-inch (12mm) pieces (about ½ cup)

1 large green apple, peeled, cored, and cut into ½-inch (12mm) pieces (about 2 cups)

¼ cup seedless red grapes, sliced crosswise

4 red radishes, thinly sliced (about ¼ cup)

12 walnut halves, toasted (see Buying and Toasting Nuts, page 267)

Smoked Dukkah (page 267; optional)

A handful of dill sprigs

Flaky sea salt, such as Maldon

1. To make the dressing, heat a small skillet over medium heat. Add the poppy seeds and toast for 30 seconds or until aromatic. Pour the seeds into a small bowl and let cool to room temperature. Mix in the yogurt, honey, lemon juice, and salt.

2. To make the salad, remove the core of the Bibb lettuce. Separate the leaves, then wash and dry thoroughly with a salad spinner. Arrange the leaves on a platter and top with the celery, apple, grapes, radishes, and walnuts. Spoon some of the dressing on top and season with smoked dukkah (if using). Garnish with the dill and serve immediately with flaky salt and more dressing on the side.

Okra is used extensively in Egyptian home cooking, often braised with meat or cooked in spiced tomato sauce seasoned with garlic, chiles, and lime. This recipe takes the flavors traditionally paired with okra but gives the vegetable the quick-cooked treatment so it retains a crisp texture. All you need to do is blanch the okra whole before slicing. Use fresh okra for this recipe; frozen okra will not have the same texture.

Serve with dips as part of a table spread or with Sizzling Prawns (page 170).

OKRA
WITH SHALLOTS AND CHILE

Active Time: 25 minutes

SERVES 4

1 tablespoon fine sea salt, plus more if desired

1 tablespoon all-purpose flour

1 pound (454g) fresh okra, aiming for pieces that are similar in size

2 tablespoons neutral oil, such as grapeseed

3 shallots, thinly sliced

1 small hot pepper (such as jalapeño or Anaheim), thinly sliced crosswise

½ teaspoon ground cumin

½ teaspoon ground turmeric

1 garlic clove, minced

1 lime, halved

Cilantro sprigs or blossoms (optional)

1. Fill a medium pot with water, stir in the salt, and bring to a boil. While waiting, fill a large bowl with ice water and stir in the flour (this will help even out the okra's texture after it's cooked). Once the water is boiling, add the okra and cook until just starting to soften, about 3 minutes. Transfer the okra to the ice bath and let cool completely. Once cool, drain and rinse, then trim off the stem ends and slice in half lengthwise.

2. Heat the oil in a large skillet over medium-high heat until it shimmers. Add the shallots, hot pepper, cumin, and turmeric and cook, stirring often, until the shallots have softened slightly, about 2 minutes. Stir in the garlic and cook for 30 more seconds. Add the okra to the skillet and heat through, about 2 minutes, then squeeze the lime over the top and mix it in with a few pinches of salt. Transfer to a serving plate and top with cilantro sprigs or blossoms (if using).

In my first cookbook, I paired an olive oil–poached rack of lamb with ratatouille, a French Mediterranean vegetable dish that, to me, fits in well with Egyptian meals with the addition of harissa paste. If you prefer a milder dish, cut the amount of harissa in half. Ratatouille often tastes better the day after it's made, and since it keeps in the refrigerator for a week, it's a convenient side dish to reheat with a meal. The key part is roasting the peppers, which loosens the skins. See Roasting Peppers in the Oven below if you need an alternative to the gas burner or grill indicated in the recipe.

Serve with Grilled Lamb Kofta with Chile Labne (page 222), Feta-Brined Spatchcock Chicken with Mint and Green Onions (page 208), or make a simple meal with Baladi Bread (page 78) and crumbles of a nice, punchy feta cheese.

HARISSA RATATOUILLE

Active Time: 45 minutes

Equipment: Gas burners or a gas or charcoal grill

SERVES 4 TO 6

2 red bell peppers

1 yellow bell pepper

4 tablespoons (60ml) extra-virgin olive oil, divided

1 Japanese eggplant, small diced

Fine sea salt

2 medium zucchini, small diced

½ medium red onion, finely chopped (about 1 cup)

2 garlic cloves, minced

¼ cup (60ml) tomato paste

¼ cup (60ml) harissa paste, or less for mellower heat

1 teaspoon ground cumin

1 teaspoon ground coriander

3 tablespoons chopped cilantro

1. To roast the peppers, put each pepper on a gas burner and turn the heat to medium-high. Char the peppers, turning with tongs every 2 to 3 minutes, until the skin has blackened on all sides, about 8 minutes total. (Alternatively, char the peppers on a gas or charcoal grill.)

2. Transfer to a heatproof bowl and cover with a plate or plastic wrap so the peppers steam for 10 minutes, which helps loosen their skins. Let cool for 5 to 10 minutes, then peel away the skins and remove the stem and seeds. It's okay if a bit of the skin stays in place, but wipe away any stubborn seeds. Dice the peeled peppers.

3. Heat 2 tablespoons oil in a large skillet or Dutch oven over medium-high heat until it shimmers. Add the eggplant in an even layer and cook, stirring once or twice, until lightly brown on the edges but still firm, about 4 minutes. Season with a couple of pinches of salt and transfer to the bowl with the peppers.

4. Heat 1 tablespoon oil in the skillet over medium-high heat until it shimmers. Add the zucchini in an even layer and cook, stirring once or twice, until lightly brown on the edges but still firm, 2 to 4 minutes. Season with a couple of pinches of salt and transfer to the bowl with the peppers.

5. Heat the remaining 1 tablespoon oil in the skillet over medium heat and add the onion. Cook, stirring occasionally, until it starts to soften, about 4 minutes. Stir in the garlic, tomato paste, and harissa and cook until the paste turns from bright red to brick red, about 1 minute. Stir in the roasted peppers, eggplant, and zucchini, season with the cumin, coriander, and ¼ to ½ teaspoon salt, depending on how salty the harissa is. Serve warm or at room temperature sprinkled with the cilantro.

ROASTING PEPPERS IN THE OVEN

If you don't have access to either gas burners or a charcoal or gas grill, you can roast the peppers in the oven. It doesn't achieve a smoky flavor like the other two options, but the resulting temperature is comparable. To do so, core and seed the peppers, then cut into 4 or 5 pieces, with the aim of having the pieces lie as flat as possible. Arrange an oven rack about 6 inches from the broiler and preheat to high. Line a sheet pan with aluminum foil, place the pepper pieces skin side up on the pan, and broil until the skin chars and blisters.

Cauliflower's popularity in Egypt may go back to at least the Middle Ages, when Arab botanists experimented with growing different varieties. This side dish treats cauliflower like potatoes, ricing or mashing cooked florets. The key flavor notes are the nutty, smoky dukkah and the lemon juice, which make this side work well next to rich mains, like buttery sole or braised lamb shanks. If you don't have a steamer basket for steaming vegetables, boil the cauliflower until tender, about 10 minutes.

Serve with Phyllo-Crusted Sole with Dukkah Beurre Blanc and Golden Raisins (page 195).

MASHED DUKKAH CAULIFLOWER

Active Time: 15 minutes

Equipment: A steamer basket for steaming vegetables and a food mill or potato masher

MAKES ABOUT 2 CUPS (480ML); SERVES 4

1 medium head cauliflower, cut into florets (about 5 cups)

2 tablespoons extra-virgin olive oil

1 tablespoon freshly squeezed lemon juice, plus more as needed

½ teaspoon fine sea salt, plus more as needed

¼ cup Smoked Dukkah (page 267)

1. Place a steamer basket in a pot and pour in 1½ cups (360ml) water, ensuring the water isn't higher than the steamer basket. Add the cauliflower and bring the pot to a boil over high heat. Reduce the heat to low, cover, and let the cauliflower steam until very tender when speared with a fork, 23 to 25 minutes.

2. Fit a food mill with the medium disc. Take the cauliflower out of the pot used for steaming, then drain the water from the pot. Return the pot to the stove and set the food mill over it. While still warm, pass the cauliflower through the food mill. Alternatively, put the cauliflower in the pot and mash with a potato masher. (The texture will be closer to cauliflower rice.) Stir in the oil, lemon juice, salt, and dukkah, then taste, adding more lemon juice and salt if desired. Serve warm.

Cooking with acidity is a central part of my culinary identity, even with starchy ingredients such as potatoes. It's easy enough to roast potato wedges and make them taste good with plenty of olive oil and salt but cooking the same potatoes with a lot of lemon juice is a revelation, infusing them with bright Mediterranean acidity. Serve these with any roasted or grilled meat, fish, or poultry, though they're especially good with roast chicken.

Serve with Feta-Brined Spatchcock Chicken with Mint and Green Onions (page 208) or any fish dish.

LEMON POTATOES

Active Time: 15 minutes

SERVES 4 TO 6

2½ pounds (1.2kg) large Yukon Gold potatoes (about 6)

4 garlic cloves, peeled and lightly crushed

¼ cup (60ml) water

2 tablespoons freshly squeezed lemon juice (about ½ lemon)

2 tablespoons extra-virgin olive oil

3 to 4 thyme sprigs

2¼ teaspoons fine sea salt, plus more if needed

2 tablespoons unsalted butter, cut into 8 pieces

1. Preheat the oven to 400°F (200°C). Peel the potatoes and halve lengthwise. Cut each half into 3 wedges no wider than 1 inch (2.5cm) in the thickest part. (If the potatoes are on the small side, simply cut them into wedges.)

2. In a 9- by 13-inch (23 by 33cm) baking pan, mix together the garlic, water, lemon juice, oil, thyme, and salt with a fork. Add the potatoes and mix with your hands until evenly coated. Dot the potatoes with the butter and then cover the dish with aluminum foil.

3. Roast for 40 minutes. Remove the foil, give the potatoes a stir, and return to the oven to roast until most of the liquid has evaporated and the potatoes are tender, 7 to 10 more minutes. Season with a pinch more salt before serving if desired.

Most of the time when you see dishes tinged with a yellow-gold color, it's because of turmeric. In this case, though, the color comes solely from the saffron. The key is to boil the saffron threads in water with oil and salt. The oil bonds with the saffron in a way that unleashes the color and flavor. What you end up with are potatoes delicately seasoned with saffron that are golden on the outside but still creamy white on the inside. Use a light hand when peeling fingerlings—the small potatoes have thin skins, and you don't want to whittle away too much of them. You can slice or lightly smash the potatoes to show off the color contrast, or serve them whole with a spoonful of the saffron cooking liquid on top. For some heat, drizzle on a spoonful of chile oil.

Serve with Salt-Baked Whole Fish with Zucchini and Lemon (page 188) or roast chicken.

SAFFRON FINGERLING POTATOES

Active Time: 10 minutes, not including simmering time

Plan Ahead: The potatoes can be made the day before serving; store them in their cooking liquid so they can absorb more of the saffron color and flavor.

SERVES 4

6 cups (1.4L) water

2 tablespoons extra-virgin olive oil

1 tablespoon saffron threads

2 teaspoons fine sea salt

1 pound (454g) fingerling potatoes, peeled (about 10 to 13 small potatoes)

Dill sprigs (optional)

Chile Oil (page 279, optional)

1. Bring the water, olive oil, saffron, and salt to a rolling boil in a large saucepan over high heat. Lower the heat to medium-high and let the water briskly simmer for 10 minutes to allow the flavor and color of the saffron to infuse into the oil. Add the potatoes and simmer until they are tender enough to be pierced with a fork without much resistance, 12 to 15 minutes. Remove from the heat and let the potatoes cool in the saffron water for 30 minutes so they can absorb more color and flavor.

2. To serve, bring the pot back to a brisk simmer over medium-high heat. Slice any of the larger potatoes in half lengthwise, then transfer the potatoes to a serving plate. Spoon some of the saffron-infused oil from the surface of the water on top and sprinkle with dill (if using). For extra spice, drizzle with chile oil.

In Cairo, some street vendors sell sweet potatoes roasted in a smoker and served in their skins with honey or molasses. The smoky-sweet snack tastes like dessert, but this recipe takes the idea in a savory turn, serving the potatoes with plenty of herbs and olive oil. The sweet potatoes are baked in the oven to cook through, but if you happen to be grilling the beef kebabs on page 218—which I highly recommend eating with this side— put the stuffed potatoes on the grill to reheat as the kebabs cook so they pick up a subtle smokiness. (If you're not grilling, follow the alternative broiling step below.)

Japanese sweet potatoes have dark purple skins and white flesh. They are nuttier and less sweet than their orange relatives, which is why they work better here. I like to go all out and use five fresh herbs plus lime zest to flavor them, but if you don't have five different herbs on hand, don't worry. A half-cup of any combination of herbs is all you need.

Serve with Beef Tenderloin Kebabs with Egyptian Pepper Sauce (page 218).

ROASTED WHITE SWEET POTATOES
WITH MIXED HERBS

Active time: 15 minutes

Plan Ahead: The sweet potatoes take about 1 hour to roast.

SERVES 4

4 medium Japanese (white) sweet potatoes

⅓ cup (85ml) extra-virgin olive oil, plus more as needed

½ cup loosely packed chopped mixed herbs (any combination of the following: flat-leaf parsley, dill, cilantro, mint, and/or chives)

Finely grated zest from 1 lime

Flaky sea salt, such as Maldon

1. Preheat the oven to 400°F (200°C). Scrub the outsides of the sweet potatoes well, then dry. Line a sheet pan with aluminum foil and pierce each potato a few times all over with a fork. Roast until the potatoes give slightly when pressed, like a ripe avocado, about 1 hour. When you can stick a paring knife through the center of the potato easily, it is ready to go.

2. When cool enough to handle but still warm, make a slit lengthwise down the center of each potato, stopping before you cut all the way through. Press the ends of each potato so the slit opens up, then scoop out the flesh into a medium bowl, saving the potato skin. Using a potato masher or fork, break up the cooked sweet potato and mix in the oil, herbs, zest, and 1 to 2 teaspoons flaky salt. Taste, adding more salt as desired. Once mixed and seasoned, put the filling back into the potato skins.

3. Heat a gas grill to high heat or build a fire in a charcoal grill for direct-heat cooking. When the grates are hot, clean the grill with a grill brush. Put the potatoes cut side up on a moderately hot part of the grill. Cover and grill until lightly charred, about 5 minutes. (If you'd rather skip grilling, use your oven broiler: Arrange an oven rack so it's about 6 inches away from the broiler and preheat the broiler to high. Put the potatoes on the same pan used for roasting, cut side up, and broil until the tops are lightly charred, about 3 minutes.) Sprinkle salt on top and serve.

"Mahshi" means stuffed in Arabic, and in nearly every country where Arabs traded and traveled, the practice of stuffing vegetables followed. The stuffing is often seasoned par-cooked rice, which then finishes cooking inside the vegetable. While this recipe is made with zucchini, you can definitely use the stuffing with other vegetables—Egyptians stuff everything from cabbage leaves and grape leaves to green peppers. The hardest part of the recipe is hollowing out the zucchini. Traditionalists leave only the stem end open, but hollowing out the zucchini from end to end makes filling the vegetable easier, so feel free to try either way. When leaving one end in place, I recommend using an inexpensive vegetable corer designed specifically for the task (sometimes called a zucchini corer). It looks a little like a long vegetable peeler. You plunge it into the center, twist it, and pull it out to extract the insides. Repeat a few times and you have a hollowed-out vegetable, with the skin and sides intact. If you have an apple corer, hollow out the vegetable from end to end.

Serve with Grilled Lamb Kofta with Chile Labne (page 222), Grilled Swordfish with Nigella Seeds, Preserved Lemon, and Green Onions (page 175), or Salt-Baked Whole Fish with Zucchini and Lemon (page 188).

ZUCCHINI MAHSHI

Active Time: 1 hour

Plan Ahead: You can make the stuffing a day ahead and refrigerate it before filling the zucchini. Plan on 35 minutes for simmering.

Equipment: A vegetable corer

SERVES 4 TO 6

Stuffing:
2 tablespoons vegetable oil or ghee

½ medium yellow onion, finely diced (about 1 cup)

½ teaspoon fine sea salt, divided

3 garlic cloves, minced

1 tablespoon tomato paste

1 cup (240ml) tomato puree

½ teaspoon freshly ground black pepper

½ teaspoon ground cumin

½ teaspoon ground coriander

3 tablespoons chopped flat-leaf parsley

3 tablespoons chopped cilantro

3 tablespoons chopped dill

1 cup (200g) medium-grain white rice, such as Calrose

Vegetables:
8 small zucchini (about 2 pounds / 908g)

1 tablespoon vegetable oil

1 large Roma or medium beefsteak tomato, sliced crosswise into ½-inch (12mm) thick pieces

1 garlic clove, thinly sliced

1 teaspoon Aleppo pepper

½ teaspoon fine sea salt, divided, plus more if desired

1 cup (240ml) tomato puree

1 cup (240ml) water

1. To make the stuffing, heat the oil in a saucepan over medium-high heat until it shimmers. Add the onion and ¼ teaspoon salt and cook until the onion starts to soften and turn golden around the edges, about 4 minutes. Add the garlic, lower the heat to medium, and cook 1 more minute. Stir in the tomato paste and cook, stirring constantly, until the paste turns from bright red to brick red, about 1 minute. Add the tomato puree and bring to a simmer, then add the pepper, cumin, coriander, parsley, cilantro, dill, and ¼ teaspoon salt. Stir in the rice and cook, stirring often, until the rice becomes translucent around the edges but is still raw in the center, 4 to 5 minutes. Remove from the heat and let cool to room temperature, about 45 minutes. (You will have about 1¾ cups / 420ml.)

Continued

Mahshi in Kerdasa

2. To prep the zucchini, trim off the stem ends but leave the other ends alone, then cut in half crosswise. For each half, plunge a vegetable corer into the center of the interior about three-quarters of the way in (be careful not to poke through the end), twist the corer, and then extract the insides. Repeat as needed to hollow out the zucchini so that the walls are about ¼ inch (6mm) thick. You may need to use a small spoon to scrape out the sides; just be careful not to break through the skin. (If using an apple corer, plunge it straight through—the stuffing will stay intact even if the zucchini is open-ended.) Dice the zucchini insides.

3. Rub the bottom and sides of a Dutch oven with the oil. Arrange the diced zucchini in a layer over the bottom, followed by a layer of tomato slices. Sprinkle the garlic slices and Aleppo pepper on the tomatoes and season with ¼ teaspoon salt. Season the interiors of the cored zucchini with a pinch or two of salt, then fill with the cooled rice stuffing, using about 2 tablespoons per half. Lay the zucchini on their sides in one layer over the tomatoes.

4. In a liquid measuring cup, mix together the tomato puree, water, and remaining ¼ teaspoon salt and pour the tomato water around the zucchini to nearly cover, with no rice poking out of the surface. Bring the pot to a boil over high heat, then reduce the heat to medium-low, cover, and simmer until the rice is fully cooked and the zucchini is soft, 35 to 40 minutes. Taste the cooking sauce and season with salt if desired, then serve the stuffed zucchini with the sauce.

The necks of butternut squashes can be glazed, roasted, and carved like meat for a classic fall centerpiece spiced up with Middle Eastern flavors. This dish focuses solely on the necks, which are roasted in two stages—first to cook nearly through, then peeled and glazed. At our restaurants, we juice the off-cuts, the small end pieces of the squash, to use for sauces, but at home I suggest you roast them for the pumpkin and lentil soup on page 122. Keep the onion labne in this recipe in mind for a dip with the steak fries on page 98.

ROASTED SQUASH STEAK
WITH BRUSSELS SPROUTS AND ONION LABNE

Active Time: 30 minutes

Plan Ahead: Factor in a 1-hour-plus roasting time for the squash

SERVES 4

2 butternut squash with wide, long necks between 3 to 4 inches (7.5 to 10cm) in width and length

2 tablespoons water

2 tablespoons koji or white miso paste

1 tablespoon honey

½ teaspoon Vegeta (see page 35; optional)

½ teaspoon ground cumin

¼ teaspoon dried thyme

¼ teaspoon Baharat (page 266)

Flaky sea salt, such as Maldon

Nonstick cooking spray

1 tablespoon extra-virgin olive oil, plus more as needed

5 large Brussels sprouts (about 6 ounces / 175g), trimmed into individual leaves

½ teaspoon ground sumac

2 tablespoons chopped toasted pistachios (see Buying and Toasting Nuts, page 267)

1 tablespoon finely diced or sliced candied bitter orange (optional)

Onion Labne:

½ cup (118ml) Labne (page 274) or plain whole-milk Greek yogurt

2 tablespoons grated or finely minced yellow onion

Grated zest and juice of 1 lime

Pinch of flaky sea salt, such as Maldon

1. Preheat the oven to 400°F (200°C). Line a sheet pan with aluminum foil.

2. Cut the necks away from the round ends with the seeds and reserve the ends for a separate purpose (see headnote). Place the necks on the lined pan and roast until nearly tender when pierced with a knife, about 1 hour. Remove from the oven. When cool enough to handle, about 10 minutes, peel away the skins.

3. In a small bowl, stir together the water, koji, honey, Vegeta (if using), cumin, thyme, baharat, and a couple of pinches of flaky salt.

4. Put a wire rack on the same pan used to cook the squash and coat with cooking spray. Put the squash on the rack and brush the glaze generously on all sides. Roast for 15 minutes. Brush again, using tongs to turn the pieces as needed, and bake another 15 minutes or until completely cooked through.

5. To make the onion labne, in a small bowl, stir together the labne, onion, lime zest and juice, and salt.

6. To a 10-inch (25cm) skillet over medium-high heat, add the olive oil. Saute the Brussels sprout leaves until almost tender, about 30 seconds, then remove from the heat and season with the sumac and a pinch of flaky salt.

7. Spoon labne on the serving plate. Slice the squash into 1½-inch (4cm) steaks (about two per squash neck) and place on top of the labne. Sprinkle the pistachios and candied orange (if using) on top and spoon the Brussels sprout leaves around the plate.

SOURCING KOJI

Koji is the mold that makes miso, among other things, and it's a good way to give vegetables savory depth. White miso is a fine substitute.

RICE, GRAINS, AND PASTA

If I had to pick between my two favorite comfort foods, it would be tough to choose between Ta'ameya (page 92) and Koshari (page 156), a multilayered rice and pasta extravaganza that is essentially starch on starch. Egypt takes pride in its starches, from green wheat fireek—freekeh in North America—to its medium-grain rice to its use of pasta in unexpected ways, and this chapter continues that tradition. For example, koshari, usually a filling, inexpensive workday meal in Egypt, can also be a dynamic side with seafood. It's all part of the tradition of celebrating the classics through reinterpretation.

Tabbouli is one of the more misunderstood grain salads from the Levant. We've all had versions where there's too much bulgur or the parsley has been so blitzed in a food processor that it's lost all its appeal. The real deal should be bright and refreshing. To pay homage to Egypt, I swap out bulgur for freekeh—known as fireek in Egypt—a green wheat that is coarsely cracked, partially charred, and flavorful. It's been used in Egypt for ages, especially for hamam mahshi, stuffed squab. You can find it at many Middle Eastern markets or online. As it sits, this salad gets juicy, so have some bread on hand to sop up the well-seasoned tomato and cucumber water.

Serve with Grilled Lamb Kofta with Chile Labne (page 222) or Grilled Swordfish with Nigella Seeds, Preserved Lemon, and Green Onions (page 175).

FREEKEH TABBOULI

Active Time: 30 minutes

Plan Ahead: The freekeh can be cooked ahead of making the salad and stored in the refrigerator. The salad is at its best at room temperature within an hour or so of mixing, but it will keep in the refrigerator for a few days. Taste before serving again, adding more salt and lemon juice if needed.

MAKES 4 CUPS; SERVES 4

1 cup (175g) freekeh

2 cups (480ml) water

¾ teaspoon fine sea salt, divided, plus more if desired

½ small red onion, finely diced (about ½ cup)

1 large Roma or 1 medium beefsteak tomato, finely diced (about ¼ cup)

1 Persian cucumber, finely diced (about ⅔ cup)

½ cup (26g) chopped flat-leaf parsley

¼ cup (60ml) extra-virgin olive oil

3 tablespoons freshly squeezed lemon juice, plus more if desired

1 small garlic clove, grated

1 teaspoon ground cumin

1 teaspoon ground coriander

1. In a small saucepan over medium heat, toast the freekeh until aromatic, about 2 minutes. Add the water and ½ teaspoon salt and bring to a boil over high heat. Reduce the heat to low, cover, and simmer until the freekeh is tender, 25 to 30 minutes. Uncover, then let drain in a fine-mesh strainer for 20 to 30 minutes to get rid of any excess water as it cools. Transfer to a serving bowl.

2. When the freekeh is entirely cool, stir in the onion, tomato, cucumber, and parsley. In a small bowl, whisk together the oil, lemon juice, garlic, cumin, coriander, and remaining ¼ teaspoon salt. Pour over the freekeh and stir well. Taste, adding more lemon juice or salt if desired. As the salad sits, it becomes juicy, so serve with a slotted spoon if you want to avoid the juices.

Having a box of regular (not pearled) couscous in your pantry makes it easy to create a straightforward side to go with any meal from this book. Here we take it one step more, dressing it up with saffron. Like in the fingerling potatoes on page 140, the key to unlocking saffron's flavor and color is to boil it in water and oil. If you don't have saffron, reduce the quantity of water to 1½ cups (360ml) and simply bring the water to a boil and then add the lemon olive oil or lemon zest before stirring in the couscous—no need to let it simmer for five minutes.

Serve with Tomato-Ginger Glazed Salmon (page 192) and Phyllo-Crusted Sole with Dukkah Beurre Blanc and Golden Raisins (page 195).

LEMON SAFFRON COUSCOUS

Active Time: 10 minutes, not including resting time

MAKES 3 CUPS (700ML), SERVES 2 TO 4

1¼ cups (300ml) water

2 teaspoons extra-virgin olive oil

1 teaspoon crumbled saffron threads

¾ teaspoon fine sea salt

1 teaspoon lemon olive oil or 1 teaspoon finely grated lemon zest

1 cup (185g) plain couscous

1. Bring the water, olive oil, saffron, and salt to a rolling boil in a small saucepan over high heat. Reduce the heat to medium-high and let the water briskly simmer for 5 minutes to allow the flavor and color of the saffron to infuse into the oil. Remove from the heat and stir in the lemon oil or lemon zest.

2. Stir in the couscous, cover, and let sit 15 minutes or until all the water has been absorbed and the couscous is tender. Uncover and fluff with a fork before serving. (Avoid overworking to keep the couscous fluffy and light.)

Buttery rice flecked with golden-brown bits of vermicelli noodles is part of an ensemble cast in an Egyptian meal, playing a crucial but understated role as the grain that complements bolder dishes on the table. It's also so simple that you can make it any day, any time. See Buying Vermicelli (page 158) to make sure you're using the correct style of vermicelli.

EVERYDAY EGYPTIAN RICE

Active Time: 30 minutes

MAKES 5 CUPS (1.2L) SERVES 4

1½ cups (305g) medium-grain white rice, such as Calrose

2 tablespoons ghee or unsalted butter

1 cup (90g) vermicelli pasta broken into 1-inch (2.5cm) pieces

1½ teaspoons fine sea salt, plus more if desired

2 cups (480ml) Chicken Stock (page 271) or water

1. Put the rice in a bowl and cover with cold water. Swish the rice around with your hands until the water is cloudy, then drain the rice well in a fine-mesh strainer. Repeat one or two times until the water runs clear. Let drain in the strainer while you brown the vermicelli.

2. Warm the ghee in a large saucepan or medium pot over medium-high heat. Stir in the vermicelli and cook, stirring often until the pasta turns golden, about 2 minutes. Stir in the rice and cook for 1 more minute, then stir in the salt and stock, loosening any stuck bits of rice or vermicelli from the bottom of the pot with a wooden spoon, and bring to a boil over high heat. Reduce the heat to low, cover, and cook until the rice is cooked through and all the water has been absorbed, about 20 minutes. Uncover, fluff with a fork, and taste, seasoning with more salt if desired. Cover again until ready to serve.

Spiked with black pepper, cumin, cardamom, and fresh peppers, this rice dish is associated with fishermen, and nearly always served with fish. My friend Moustafa Elrefaey taught me that it's important to cook the onion until it nearly turns black, so if your onions char a bit, just go with it. If you have a nice seafood stock, you can use it in place of the water for deeper flavor. Egyptian rice is a medium-grain variety. In the United States, white Calrose rice is the closest in texture.

Serve with Samak Singari (page 184) or any grilled or roasted fish dish.

SAYADEYA RICE

Active Time: 45 to 50 minutes

MAKES 4 CUPS (960ML), SERVES 3 TO 4

1½ cups (305g) medium-grain white rice, such as Calrose

3 tablespoons vegetable oil

1 medium yellow onion, finely diced (about 2 cups)

¼ cup (60ml) tomato paste

2 green cardamom pods, smashed

2 teaspoons ground cumin

1 teaspoon fine sea salt, plus more if desired

½ teaspoon freshly ground black pepper

2 cups (480ml) water

1 Roma tomato, halved

1 green or red hot pepper, such as serrano, jalapeño, or Fresno, halved lengthwise

1. Put the rice in a bowl and cover with cold water. Swish the rice around with your hands until the water is cloudy, then drain the rice well in a fine-mesh strainer. Repeat one or two times until the water runs clear. Let drain in the strainer while you start to cook the onion.

2. Warm the oil in a large saucepan over medium-high heat. Add the onion and cook, stirring often, until the onion is dark brown, about 8 minutes. Stir in the tomato paste and cardamom pods and cook for 1 minute more, then stir in the rice, cumin, salt, and black pepper and cook until the edges of the rice are slightly translucent, about 2 minutes.

3. Stir in the water, scraping up the brown bits from the bottom of the pan with a wooden spoon. Add the tomato and fresh pepper halves, raise the heat to high, and bring to a boil. Reduce the heat to low, cover, and cook until the rice is cooked through and all the liquid has been absorbed, 18 to 20 minutes, stirring halfway through so the rice cooks evenly. Remove the tomato, pepper, and cardamom pods. Fluff the rice with a fork, then taste, seasoning with more salt if desired. If you like, you can chop up the cooked tomato and pepper and spoon it on top before serving.

KOSHARY ABOU TAREK

Koshari (also spelled koshary and kushari) is one of the most beloved dishes in Egypt. But, until recently, it was rarely served in restaurants. You either had your mom's version or you bought it on the streets. Then came Koshary Abou Tarek.

Abou Tarek started selling koshari from a cart in the 1950s, then grew his business into an empire. He now controls an entire block in Cairo anchored by a four-story restaurant that serves one thing—koshari.

When we get there, scooter drivers wait out front to collect delivery orders while Abou Tarek sits in a comfortable chair on the sidewalk by the front door, flanked by a couple of bodyguards, watching the business. Many times during the day, people from the neighborhood stop by to pay their respects. His legendary presence continues inside, where large portraits show him in his signature pose, holding his face between the thumb and forefinger. All around us, cooks scramble to fill take-out orders, tossing lentils and chickpeas into containers with impressive precision. But it's when we take a seat upstairs that the real show starts.

A server comes to the table to assemble the dish. He tops the usual mix of lentils, pasta, and rice with a spoonful of tomato sauce, then adds garlic vinegar and a spicy chile sauce, more layers of flavor. He squeezes lime juice over the chickpeas, spoons them on top of the lentil mixture, and then sprinkles the whole dish with fried onions. The meal is a dynamic study in textures—soft, crisp, chewy—from start to finish.

The dining room at Koshary Abou Tarek

My mom made this dish all the time when I was growing up, and it's still one of my favorite things to eat. It's humble food, lentils and chickpeas served on macaroni and rice together with a tangy tomato sauce and caramelized onions. But who says humble can't be extraordinary? While there are a lot of components, many can be made ahead and you can streamline a few things based on what you have around, and how much effort you want to put in. For example, my mom skipped the macaroni to make her life a little easier, so I include it here as optional. Also, I love adding crispy fried onions for texture, but you can either skip the fried onions or buy fried onions or shallots. (They are easy to find at Asian grocery stores.) Save any extra tomato sauce to use when braising lamb shanks (page 231).

KOSHARI

Active Time: 2 hours

Plan Ahead: Make the tomato sauce and lentils a day or so ahead to make it easier to assemble. You can also make and refrigerate the caramelized onions up to 7 days ahead and store them in a sealed container in the refrigerator. Let them come to room temperature while the rice cooks.

MAKES 2½ QUARTS (2.36L); SERVES 6 TO 8

Tomato Sauce:
2 tablespoons vegetable oil, divided
1 yellow onion, finely diced (about 2 cups)
2 teaspoons fine sea salt, divided, plus more to taste
¼ cup (60ml) tomato paste
2 teaspoons ground cumin
1 teaspoon Aleppo pepper
½ teaspoon freshly ground black pepper
1 (28-ounce / 794g) can whole San Marzano tomatoes in their juices, coarsely chopped
1 cup (240ml) water
5 garlic cloves, minced
3 tablespoons distilled white vinegar

Caramelized Onions:
2 medium yellow onions, thinly sliced
½ cup (118ml) vegetable oil

Lentils and Chickpeas:
½ cup (100g) beluga lentils
2 cups (480ml) water

Fine sea salt
1 (15-ounce / 425g) can chickpeas, drained and rinsed
1 lime, halved

Vermicelli Rice:
2 tablespoons vegetable oil
½ yellow onion, finely diced
⅔ cup (60g) vermicelli pasta broken into 1-inch (2.5cm) pieces if not already broken (see Buying Vermicelli, page 158)
1½ cups (300g) Calrose rice or other medium-grain rice
1 teaspoon fine sea salt
2¼ cups (540ml) water
½ teaspoon Aleppo pepper

Optional:
1 cup (80g) elbow macaroni, cooked according to package directions (optional)

To serve:
Crispy Onions (page 278; optional)
2 tablespoons chopped flat-leaf parsley

1. To make the tomato sauce, in a large saucepan, heat 1 tablespoon oil over medium heat. Add the onion and ½ teaspoon salt and cook, stirring occasionally, until softened, about 6 minutes. Add the tomato paste, cumin, Aleppo pepper, and black pepper and cook, stirring often, until the paste changes from bright red to brick red, about 2 minutes. Increase the heat to medium-high and stir in the tomatoes, remaining 1½ teaspoons salt, and water. Bring to a brisk simmer, then lower the heat to medium and cook, stirring occasionally, until the sauce is thick enough to coat the back of a wooden spoon, about 15 minutes. You'll have slightly more than 5 cups (1.2L) sauce.

2. While the sauce is simmering, cook the garlic. In a small saucepan, heat the remaining 1 tablespoon oil over medium heat. Add the garlic and cook until golden, about 30 seconds. Right before the garlic browns, remove from the heat and pour in the vinegar (this stops the garlic from overcooking), swirling the pan to incorporate. Pour the garlic vinegar into the tomato sauce and stir to combine. (If you want the sauce smooth, use a hand blender to blend the tomato sauce.)

Continued

3. To make the caramelized onions, line a plate with paper towels. Separate the onion slices into individual pieces as much as possible. In a large skillet, heat the oil over medium-high heat, stir in the onions, then stop stirring and allow them to brown along the edges, about 3 minutes. Stir to redistribute the onions and cook, stirring occasionally, until they are dark golden brown, about 15 minutes. Transfer to the paper towels.

4. To cook the lentils and prepare the chickpeas, in a medium saucepan, combine the lentils, water, and a generous pinch of salt. Simmer over medium heat until cooked through but not completely soft, 15 to 17 minutes. Drain, then rinse well in cold water to stop the cooking. Set aside to drain again. In the same saucepan used to cook the lentils, add the chickpeas. Squeeze both lime halves on top of the chickpeas and season with a few pinches of salt, then return the lentils to the pan and warm over medium heat. Keep warm.

5. To make the vermicelli rice, heat the oil in a medium saucepan or Dutch oven over medium heat. Add the onion and cook, stirring often, until it is soft and golden brown, about 8 minutes. Add the vermicelli and cook for 3 to 4 minutes or until golden, then stir in the rice and salt and cook, letting the rice toast

slightly, about 2 minutes. Add the water and increase the heat to high. When the water is boiling, give the pot a stir, reduce the heat to low, cover, and cook until the rice is cooked through and the water has been fully absorbed, about 15 minutes. Uncover, fluff with a fork, and sprinkle the Aleppo pepper on top. Cover and keep warm.

6. To serve, put the warm lentils, chickpeas, and macaroni (if using) in a large bowl. Add the rice and stir everything together with a fork, trying as much as possible not to break up the rice pieces. Taste, adding more salt if desired.

7. Serve koshari on a rimmed platter or in individual bowls. Spoon tomato sauce along the rim as well as a few spoonfuls on top (you don't have to use all the sauce). Sprinkle the caramelized onions, crispy onions (if using), and parsley on top and serve extra sauce and onions at the table.

BUYING VERMICELLI

Vermicelli for rice pilaf and other dishes is sold already broken into small pieces and can be found in Middle Eastern or Indian markets labeled "Vermicelli" or "Vermicelli Pasta." You can also take angel-hair pasta and break it up into pieces. Avoid vermicelli noodles made with rice flour or other nonwheat starches, which are used in Vietnamese and other Southeast Asian preparations.

This recipe evolved from a Middle Eastern tasting menu at Michael Mina in San Francisco. My chefs and I played around with a ricotta gnudi, serving it with lamb meatballs. In this version, the meatballs are spiced like kofta and a sweet-tart date chutney accents the plate. The key to the ricotta dough is to let it rest overnight in a bed of semolina flour. No matter how soft it feels, the dumplings will firm up overnight, making them easy to handle. I use cake flour here to help ensure a tender dumpling. Have the water boiling for the dumplings when you put the meatballs in the oven so the meatballs and dumplings will be ready at the same time. You will likely have extra dumplings to save, or to stretch the dish to serve more people.

LAMB MEATBALLS
WITH RICOTTA DUMPLINGS AND DATE CHUTNEY

Active Time: 1 hour

Plan Ahead: Drain the ricotta 6 hours or overnight before making the dumplings, then shape the dumplings the day before cooking to give them time to firm up.

Equipment: Cheesecloth for draining the ricotta and a food processor. You may also find it helpful to have a small cookie dough scoop (with the capacity of 1½ to 2 tablespoons) for making the dumplings.

SERVES 5

Ricotta Dumplings:
2 pounds (908g) whole-milk ricotta cheese
1 cup (70g) panko breadcrumbs
⅔ cup (70g) cake flour
1 cup (30g) finely grated Parmesan cheese (using a rasp grater)
1½ teaspoons fine sea salt
2 large eggs
2 cups (335g) semolina flour
2 to 3 tablespoons extra-virgin olive oil, divided
3 lemon wedges
Flaky sea salt, such as Maldon
¾ cup (180ml) Chicken Stock (page 271), for glazing (optional)

Lamb Meatballs:
1 pound (454g) ground lamb
½ cup (35g) panko breadcrumbs
½ yellow onion, finely diced
1 large egg
1 tablespoon minced dill or flat-leaf parsley
2 teaspoons fine sea salt
1 teaspoon ground cumin
½ teaspoon ground cinnamon
½ teaspoon Aleppo pepper
½ teaspoon freshly ground black pepper

To serve:
½ cup (118ml) Date Chutney (page 279)
Dill sprigs
Finely grated zest of 1 lemon

1. To make the ricotta dumplings, layer a fine-mesh strainer with enough cheesecloth to line it twice, ensuring there's plenty of cheesecloth hanging over the rim. Place the strainer over a bowl and put the ricotta in the cheesecloth. Wrap the cheesecloth around the ricotta and tie is securely with kitchen twine. Refrigerate the bowl and strainer for 6 hours or overnight.

2. In a food processor, pulse the panko until finely ground, about 10 (1-second) pulses. Pulse in the cake flour, Parmesan, and salt for 4 pulses, then pulse in the drained ricotta and eggs briefly until evenly blended but not completely smooth, about another 10 (1-second) pulses, scraping down the sides with a rubber spatula as needed. The dough will be soft and sticky.

3. On a rimmed sheet pan, spread out the semolina flour in an even layer. Using a small cookie dough scooper or a measuring spoon, drop 1½-tablespoon-sized portions of the ricotta batter onto the semolina in a single layer. (You will have about 30 dumplings.) Refrigerate the pan, uncovered, for at least 6 hours or overnight.

Continued

4. The next day, the dumplings should be firm enough to pick up without sticking to your hands. Roll the dumplings with your hands to shape them into balls, then roll them gently in the semolina. Place back on the remaining semolina and refrigerate until needed.

5. Preheat the oven to 450°F (230°C). Line a baking sheet with parchment paper. Bring a large pot of salted water to a boil as you work on the meatballs.

6. To make the meatballs, in a large bowl, mix together all the meatball ingredients with your hands until thoroughly combined, about 1 minute. You should be able to pick up the mixture in one mass and lift it from the bowl. Roll into 16 balls and place on the parchment-lined baking sheet, spaced evenly. Roast until the tops of the meatballs start to brown, 12 to 15 minutes.

7. As the meatballs roast, cook the dumplings in boiling water in two batches until they are cooked through, 8 to 10 minutes per batch. (You can check by removing a dumpling and cutting it in half to see if the center looks cooked. Don't worry about sacrificing a dumpling to check, you will have plenty.) Transfer each batch of cooked dumplings to a large bowl and toss with 1 tablespoon oil while the dumplings are still hot so they don't stick together. Season with 2 or 3 squeezes of the lemon wedges and flaky salt. If you want to go the extra mile, heat a large skillet or Dutch oven over medium-high heat and add 1 tablespoon olive oil. When it starts to shimmer, add the dumplings and saute for a minute, then pour in the stock and cook until it lightly coats the surface of the dumplings.

8. Serve the dumplings on a platter or individual plates (about 5 per serving). Add the meatballs (about 3 per serving), dolloping each meatball with date chutney. Garnish with dill and lemon zest.

About two hours away from Cairo, the oasis of Faiyum is a haven for birds, which is why the last Egyptian king liked to come here for duck hunting. While I'm not sure how he liked his duck prepared, this is what I'd want on the table: a satisfying ragù, melding influences from southern Europe and North Africa into a comforting dish punctuated with bursts of fresh ginger and spices. This hearty one-pot wonder is equally good with ground lamb, ground beef, or even ground turkey (use leg meat, not breast meat, if using turkey). In Egypt, my friend Moustafa Elrefaey likes to pair duck confit with shareya, a wheat noodle. I took that inspiration, creating this dish with orzo, a pasta available at any supermarket. Save any of the brine from the feta to make the feta-brined chicken on page 208.

ONE-POT TOASTED ORZO
WITH DUCK RAGÙ

Active Time: 1 hour and 20 minutes

Plan Ahead: You can make the recipe the day before you serve it but leave out the peas until reheating. To reheat, stir in a splash of water and bring to a simmer over medium heat, then add the peas and simmer until cooked through.

Equipment: A food processor

SERVES 4 TO 6

2 medium carrots, peeled and coarsely chopped

1 celery stalk, coarsely chopped

½ small fennel bulb, cored and coarsely chopped

¼ medium yellow onion, coarsely chopped

½ small leek, light green and white parts only, thoroughly cleaned and coarsely chopped

10 garlic cloves, coarsely chopped

1 tablespoon coarsely chopped ginger

8 ounces (225g) orzo (about 1⅓ cups)

2 tablespoons extra-virgin olive oil, divided

2 pounds (907g) ground duck or lamb

2 teaspoons fine sea salt, divided, plus more to taste

2 teaspoons Baharat (page 266)

1 teaspoon Aleppo pepper, plus more as desired

2¼ cups (540ml) canned tomato puree

3½ cups (840ml) Chicken Stock (page 271) or water

1⅔ cups (225g) shucked peas, fresh or frozen

¼ cup (60ml) freshly squeezed lemon juice

¼ cup chopped flat-leaf parsley

Feta cheese, crumbled, for garnish

Urfa pepper, for garnish (optional)

1. In a food processor, pulse the carrots, celery, fennel, onion, and leek together 5 to 6 times, until evenly chopped. Add the garlic and ginger and pulse 5 to 6 more times, until the vegetables look like confetti (stop before they form a paste).

2. Heat a large Dutch oven or pot over medium heat. Add the orzo and toast, stirring often, until the edges just start to brown, about 4 minutes. Transfer to a bowl.

3. Heat 1 tablespoon oil in the same pot over medium-high heat. Add the duck and season with 1 teaspoon salt. Cook, breaking the meat up into pieces with a wooden spoon, until the duck is cooked and any fat has rendered out, about 8 minutes. Transfer the duck and any juices to a separate bowl from the orzo and keep warm.

4. In the same pot, heat the remaining 1 tablespoon oil over medium-high heat. Add the chopped vegetables and remaining 1 teaspoon salt and cook, stirring often, until the vegetables begin to caramelize, about 6 minutes. Return the duck and juices to the pot and mix in the baharat and Aleppo pepper. Cook briefly to draw out the spice flavors, then stir in the tomato puree and stock. Bring the pot to a boil, about 3 minutes, then reduce the heat to medium-low and gently simmer until the sauce has reduced by slightly less than half, about 15 minutes.

Continued

5. Stir in the orzo and cook over medium-low heat, stirring often to avoid sticking, until the orzo is cooked through and the ragù has thickened to the point where it stays mounded on a spoon, about 15 minutes. Stir in the peas and cook 1 minute for frozen or 3 to 4 minutes for fresh. Remove from the heat and stir in the lemon juice and parsley. Taste, adding more salt if needed. Spoon into bowls and sprinkle feta and Urfa (or more Aleppo) pepper (if using) on top.

SOURCING OR MAKING GROUND DUCK

Ground duck is sometimes available frozen at butcher shops or well-stocked grocery stores. You can also order it online from sources such as Liberty Ducks in Sonoma, California. To grind duck meat yourself, use a combination of duck breast and leg meat, skins removed. Outfit the grinder with the coarse plate and place the grinder and bowl in the freezer for 15 minutes before processing to help reduce sticking. Grind the meat directly into the chilled bowl.

Traditional macaroni béchamel is a baked pasta dish with both a white sauce and a meaty ragù-style sauce. This recipe takes the classic in a modern direction, turning the béchamel into a Mornay (cheese) sauce and shaping the noodles in a loaf pan to then slice. This recipe requires more time than any other recipe in this book. I suggest staggering the workflow: Make the mushroom Bolognese a few days ahead, then make the Mornay sauce before cooking the pasta. The sauce is a modern take on the classic, using Wondra flour (a pregelatinized, superfine flour) instead of roux to thicken it. The most time-consuming part is arranging the noodles in the loaf pan, which then needs to chill overnight. Finally, you slice the loaf and griddle the pieces to create mesmerizing crisp edges. I do this with my electric nonstick griddle. You can also work in batches to griddle the slices in a nonstick skillet. To really go over the top, shave black truffles onto the griddled slices.

MACARONI BÉCHAMEL
WITH MUSHROOM BOLOGNESE

Active Time: 2 hours

Plan Ahead: Refrigerate the terrine the day before serving so it has time to set up.

Equipment: 9- by 5-inch (23 by 12cm) loaf pan lined with plastic wrap, an electric griddle, and a food processor

MAKES ABOUT 10 CENTER SLICES, SERVES 10

Mushroom Bolognese:

1½ pounds (680g) button mushrooms, cleaned and quartered

1 medium yellow onion, coarsely chopped

½ small fennel bulb, cored and coarsely chopped

1 small leek, light green and white parts only, thoroughly cleaned and coarsely chopped

4 garlic cloves, coarsely chopped

2 tablespoons extra-virgin olive oil

¾ teaspoon fine sea salt, plus more to taste

½ teaspoon freshly ground black pepper

¼ cup (60ml) tomato paste

½ cup (118ml) dry white wine

1½ cups (360ml) Mushroom Stock (page 270) or water

Mornay Sauce:

2 cups (480ml) whole milk

2 cups (480ml) heavy cream

½ cup (65g) finely chopped yellow onion

2 thyme sprigs

1 teaspoon black peppercorns

1 small garlic clove, peeled and crushed

1 clove

1 teaspoon fine sea salt, plus more if desired

⅛ teaspoon freshly grated nutmeg

2 tablespoons Wondra flour

1¼ cups (140g) grated white mild Cheddar

1 cup (30g) finely grated Parmesan cheese (using a rasp grater)

4 wedges (78g) Laughing Cow cheese, unwrapped

Terrine:

Fine sea salt

1 pound (454g) dried pasticcio or bucatini pasta

1 cup (30g) grated Parmesan (using a rasp grater)

Extra-virgin olive oil

2 tablespoons chopped parsley

Flaky sea salt, such as Maldon

1. To make the mushroom Bolognese, in a food processor, pulse the mushrooms 10 times in 1-second pulses until evenly chopped to about the size of a pea and transfer to a large bowl. Pulse the onion, fennel, leek, and garlic 10 times in 1-second pulses until the vegetables look like confetti (stop before they form a paste). Transfer to the bowl with the mushrooms.

2. Heat the oil in a large Dutch oven or pot over medium-high heat. Add the mushroom blend, spreading it out in a single layer for even cooking. Season with the salt and pepper and cook, stirring occasionally, until the mushrooms are cooked through and starting to brown, about 6 minutes. Add the tomato paste and cook, stirring often, until the paste changes from bright red to brick red, about 2 minutes. Pour in the wine and stir to dislodge any brown bits from the bottom of the pan. Add the stock and cook until most of the liquid has evaporated, about 9 minutes. Remove from the heat, let cool, cover, and refrigerate.

Continued

Garnished with truffles and wild mushrooms

3. To make the Mornay sauce, in a medium saucepan, combine the milk, cream, onion, thyme, peppercorns, garlic, clove, salt, and nutmeg. Bring to a simmer, then turn off the heat and let steep for 20 minutes. Whisk in the Wondra flour, then bring to a simmer. Cook, stirring often to avoid scorching, for 5 minutes or until thick enough to lightly coat the back of a spoon. Whisk in the cheeses until melted, then taste, adding more salt if desired. Remove from the heat and strain through a fine-mesh strainer. You should have about 4 cups (960ml)—half to use for building the terrine, and half for serving. Return to the pan, cover, and keep warm. (Alternatively, cool, then refrigerate for up to 3 days. Rewarm gently while cooking the pasta.)

4. To shape the terrine, line a 9- by 5-inch (23 by 12cm) loaf pan with plastic wrap, leaving extra plastic wrap hanging off the two longer sides. Bring a pot of water to a boil and season it generously with salt. Cook the pasta according to the package directions, then drain. Briefly rinse with cold water to stop the cooking, then shake off the excess water and add to a large bowl. Stir in a drizzle of olive oil to keep the noodles from sticking.

5. While the noodles are still warm, stir in 2 cups (480ml) of warm Mornay sauce and ½ teaspoon sea salt. Taste a noodle and add more salt if needed. Working in layers, arrange the sauce-coated noodles in the loaf pan in straight lines with the strands running the length of the pan. Use kitchen shears to trim the extra length of the noodles so you don't have to bend the noodles to make them fit, then use the cut noodle pieces on top so all the pasta is used. Make the layers as even as possible so there are few gaps between the noodles. This will make the terrine hold its shape better and look neater when sliced and griddled. When all the pasta is used, fold the extra plastic wrap on the sides over the top of the terrine and cover. Press down to ensure the layers are stuck together. If you can, find a weight (like cans of beans) to put on top. Refrigerate overnight.

6. When ready to serve, bring the Bolognese to a simmer. In a separate pot, warm the remaining Mornay sauce.

7. Unmold the terrine and remove the plastic wrap. Slice the terrine crosswise into 10 even center slices, with two end pieces. (The end pieces may not hold up well enough to griddle; you can warm them in a saucepan and serve on the side if you'd like.) Sprinkle each piece with an even layer of Parmesan. Heat an electric nonstick griddle to the medium-high setting or a large nonstick skillet over medium heat. (If working with a skillet, preheat the oven and have a pan in the oven to transfer the griddled slices to keep them warm.) Brush the griddle with oil and sear each piece, Parmesan side down, until golden brown on one side and warm all the way through, 5 to 6 minutes.

8. Spoon a few tablespoons of warm Mornay sauce onto each serving plate. Using a spatula, flip the terrine slice seared side up and place on the Mornay. Spoon Bolognese on top and garnish with the parsley and flaky salt.

CLEANING AND COOKING WILD MUSHROOMS

If you have chanterelles or other wild mushrooms, saute them in some butter and season them simply with salt, black pepper, and a dash of sherry vinegar. To clean wild mushrooms, scrape the stems and caps gently with a paring knife.

SEAFOOD

At Aqua, the San Francisco restaurant that launched my career, I was never shy about cooking fish in bold and unexpected ways, like spooning aromatic cumin oil over spot prawns and monkfish, or dicing up raw ahi tuna for tartare in place of beef. I attribute this knack for boldness to my mom's Egyptian and Mediterranean home cooking. She went all in with big flavors, lacing her dishes with spice and punchy acidity. Egyptian chefs are the same, especially in Mediterranean cities like Alexandria and Port Said, where the catch of the day is nearly always marinated in lime juice with cumin, coriander, and black pepper before it's fried or grilled. That's the idea behind this chapter: infusing seafood meals with bold personality.

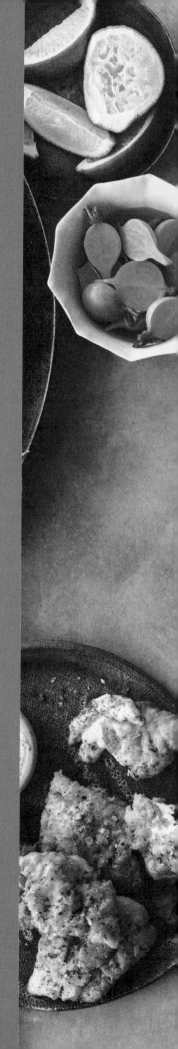

At a lunch in Alexandria with Moustafa Elrefaey, Adam Sobel, and friends, the table was already loaded with dips, pickles, and bread when out came a sizzling tinfoil package. The server opened it at the table, unleashing a puff of smoke redolent of cumin and lime. As the smoke dissipated, we saw the goodies: meaty local prawns, which we peeled and ate with our hands. This recipe is a tribute to that lunch. It mixes different kinds of onions and chiles for texture and flavor contrasts and uses shell-on prawns to maximize flavor. To re-create the sizzle, cover the Dutch oven right after putting the prawns on top of the onion mixture and bring it to the table, removing the lid in front of everyone. (Make sure you have a heatproof surface to set it on first.)

SIZZLING PRAWNS

Active Time: 30 minutes

SERVES 4 TO 6

2 pounds (908g) head-on whole prawns or colossal shrimp (about 20), unpeeled

1 teaspoon ground coriander

½ teaspoon ground cumin

½ teaspoon ground fennel

½ teaspoon ground ginger

¾ teaspoon fine sea salt

¼ teaspoon freshly ground black pepper

3 tablespoons grapeseed or other neutral oil, divided

¼ medium yellow onion, thinly sliced

¼ medium red onion, thinly sliced

3 shallots, thinly sliced

1 Fresno chile, thinly sliced crosswise

½ jalapeño, thinly sliced crosswise

Flaky sea salt, such as Maldon

1 lime, cut into 6 wedges

1. Snip the prawn shells along the back to remove the digestive tract but leave the shells in place. (If you buy your shrimp from a good fishmonger, you can ask them to do this for you.) Pat the prawns dry and place in a bowl. Season with the coriander, cumin, fennel, ginger, fine sea salt, and black pepper.

2. Cook the prawns in two batches. Heat 1 tablespoon oil in a large Dutch oven over high heat. Add half the prawns and sear, turning once or twice, until the shells turn pink and slightly charred but before the prawns are completely cooked through, about 1 minute. Transfer the first batch to a plate to keep warm and repeat with another 1 tablespoon oil and the remaining prawns.

3. Heat the remaining 1 tablespoon oil over high heat. Add the onions, shallots, and chiles all at once, stir once, then let the pan start to sizzle and smoke. Place the prawns back on top, season with a generous pinch or two of flaky salt, and cover for 1 minute (the pan should be smoking hot). Turn off the heat, uncover, and stir once or twice before serving. Serve with flaky salt and lime wedges on the side. Offer plenty of napkins so people can peel and eat the prawns with their hands.

For many Egyptians, molokhia—a rich, flavorful leafy green—is a favorite comfort food. Also called jute leaf, it develops a slippery, gelatinous texture when it cooks, as if someone crossed spinach with okra. By the tenth century, it was an entrenched favorite in Cairo, then the cultural center of the sprawling Fatimid Empire—that is, until the caliph outlawed molokhia. To get around the arbitrary molokhia law, Egyptian women began gasping to cover up the sizzle sound when hot ghee, garlic, and coriander hit the green broth. Today, the tradition of gasping lives on.

You'll see molokhia served with rabbit or chicken around Cairo and eaten with rice. But in Alexandria molokhia is served with fish. And that's where I got the idea to make molokhia like a bouillabaisse, brimming with seafood. If you can't find all the seafood ingredients listed here, improvise with what looks good at the fish counter. The recipe serves two as a main course, though molokhia is often served in small cups alongside dips, pickles, and other dishes, and over rice. I also like to sprinkle bits of fried garlic on top.

Serve with Everyday Egyptian Rice (page 152).

MOLOKHIA
BOUILLABAISSE

Active Time: 30 minutes

Equipment: A spider skimmer or slotted spoon

SERVES 2 AS A MAIN, 4 AS A SIDE

8 ounces (225g) Manila or littleneck clams (5 to 10, depending on their size)

8 ounces (225g) mussels (about 14)

10 ounces (280g) squid, bodies and tentacles

8 ounces (225g) skin-on snapper fillet

4 jumbo shrimp (U/16-20) (190g)

1½ teaspoons fine sea salt, divided, plus more if desired

3 tablespoons ghee or neutral oil

10 garlic cloves, minced

1 teaspoon crushed coriander seeds

2½ cups (600ml) Chicken Stock (page 271)

2 lemons, cut into 8 wedges each

¼ teaspoon cayenne

1 (14 oz / 400g) package frozen chopped molokhia, thawed and squeezed dry (see Sourcing and Prepping Molokhia)

2 tablespoons store-bought fried garlic (optional)

1. Scrub the clams under cold running water to get rid of grit and sand, then place in cold water while preparing the rest of the seafood. Pull the beards off the mussels (the hairy bits near the joint) if attached, then scrub well and drain, discarding any that aren't firmly closed. Halve the squid bodies lengthwise and score lightly with a crosshatch pattern, taking care not to cut all the way through. Score the skin on the snapper and cut crosswise into 4 (2-ounce / 58g) pieces. Peel and devein the shrimp, leaving the tails attached. Season the shrimp, snapper, and squid with ½ teaspoon salt. Drain the clams, discarding any sand and grit at the bottom of the bowl and removing any clams that aren't firmly closed.

2. In a medium pot, warm the ghee over medium heat until it shimmers. Add the garlic and cook until deep golden in color, about 30 seconds, then add the coriander to toast briefly, no more than 20 seconds. Pour in the stock to stop the garlic from browning further and season with ½ teaspoon salt.

3. Bring to a simmer and add the shrimp, snapper, and squid. Cook 3 minutes or until the seafood is cooked through. Using a spider skimmer or slotted spoon, transfer the seafood to a bowl and keep warm.

4. Add the clams and mussels to the pot and bring to a simmer. Cover and cook until they open, about 3 minutes. Discard any that do not open. Using the spider skimmer or slotted spoon, transfer to the bowl with the cooked seafood and season all the seafood with 2 or 3 squeezes of lemon and the cayenne. Keep warm.

Continued

5. Add the molokhia and remaining ½ teaspoon salt to the pot and simmer gently (no need to vigorously boil), stirring a couple of times, until the molokhia is completely soft, 4 to 5 minutes. If the molokhia was still somewhat frozen, cook it for a few more minutes. Taste, adding more salt if desired.

6. To serve, heat a shallow serving bowl (if serving as a side), or use 2 soup bowls for individual servings. Pour the molokhia into the bowl. Put the seafood on top and then spoon a little more molokhia on top. Garnish with fried garlic (if using) and offer lemon wedges on the side for the seafood.

SOURCING AND PREPPING MOLOKHIA

Molokhia is spelled and called different things in English. Some of its synonyms include jute leaf and Egyptian spinach. Look for frozen chopped molokhia at Middle Eastern grocery stores, where it's sold under a brand called Montana. (Avoid whole leaf molokhia.) Dried molokhia is also available under brands such as Ziyad, though it yields a darker product and needs to be boiled first to reconstitute, then chopped. (Follow the instructions on the package.)

In Alexandria, some seafood restaurants dip the tail or heads of fish in nigella seeds before frying for a nice bit of decoration. That's the inspiration here, except the black seeds are sprinkled on top just before serving to give the swordfish an earthy finish. This recipe shows off a simple restaurant trick: Brining larger finfish, such as swordfish, not only seasons the protein but also encourages even cooking. (The brine in this recipe works for halibut and salmon as well.) The preserved lemon condiment in this recipe is also versatile for a wide range of fish dishes, like Sizzling Prawns (page 170). If we have tender baby eggplant (pictured in the recipe photo), we'll also saute them to add one more element to the plate.

Serve with Smoky Baba Ghanoush (page 59) and Pickled Eggplant (page 74) or Sayadeya Rice (page 153)

GRILLED SWORDFISH
WITH NIGELLA SEEDS, PRESERVED LEMON, AND GREEN ONIONS

Active Time: 40 minutes

Plan Ahead: You can brine the swordfish the day before, then remove it from the brine after 45 minutes and refrigerate until ready to grill.

Equipment: A gas or charcoal grill and grill brush

SERVES 4

Swordfish:
4½ cups (1L) cold water
⅓ cup (50g) kosher salt (preferably Diamond Crystal)
3 garlic cloves, peeled and lightly smashed
4 swordfish steaks, about 1 inch (2.5cm) thick and 6 to 7 ounces (170 to 200g) each
2 tablespoons nigella seeds
Extra-virgin olive oil

Preserved Lemon Condiment:
¼ cup (50g) finely diced preserved lemon (both rind and flesh)
2 tablespoons extra-virgin olive oil
2 tablespoons finely chopped mint
1 tablespoon freshly squeezed lemon juice
1 teaspoon crushed pink peppercorns (optional)

To Serve:
½ cup (115g) Smoky Baba Ghanoush (page 59), warmed
4 pieces (30g) Pickled Eggplant (page 74), quartered
2 green onions, thinly sliced (about ¼ cup)
2 tablespoons chopped toasted peanuts

1. In a bowl, stir together the water, salt, and garlic until the salt has dissolved. Put the fish in an 8-inch (20cm) square baking dish or another container where they can fit in a single layer. Pour the brine on top and refrigerate for 45 minutes.

2. While the fish is brining, make the preserved lemon condiment and toast the nigella seeds. For the condiment, stir together the preserved lemon, oil, mint, lemon juice, and peppercorns (if using) in a small bowl and set aside. For the nigella seeds, toast them in a dry skillet over medium heat until you can smell their earthy aroma, about 2 minutes. Pour the seeds into a small bowl and let cool for a few minutes, then crush using a mortar and pestle or blitz briefly in a spice grinder.

3. Remove the swordfish from the brine and place on a tray. Pat dry and rub with oil.

4. Heat a gas grill to high heat or build a fire in a charcoal grill for direct-heat cooking. When the grates are hot, clean the grill with a grill brush. Add the swordfish to the grill and sear, covered if using a gas grill or uncovered if grilling with charcoal, until the fish has grill marks, about 2 minutes. Rotate the pieces 45 degrees (to create crosshatch marks) and grill for another 2 minutes. Flip over and continue to cook until grill marks form on the other side and the internal temperature of the fish is 135° to 140°F (57° to 60°C), 4 to 5 more minutes. Transfer to a clean tray, then sprinkle both sides with the crushed nigella seeds.

Continued

175

5. Spoon the baba ghanoush on the base of each plate. Place the fish on top and spoon the preserved lemon condiment around the sides. Garnish with the pickled eggplant, green onions, and peanuts.

TURNING GREEN ONIONS INTO GARNISH

Slicing green onions thinly on a sharp angle and then soaking them in ice water will cause them to curl up. It's an easy way to turn a simple ingredient into a stylish garnish. Just shake off excess water before using.

A popular way to cook fish in Alexandria is to dredge fillets in wheat bran before frying. This recipe is inspired by that technique, with a few twists, like using chickpea flour instead of bran. Any kind of mild white fish works for this recipe, like tai snapper, flounder, or cod. For the best texture, dredge the fish in the chickpea flour right before frying. While tartar sauce is not a typical Egyptian pairing with fish—Tahina (page 52) is more common—this is how I'd serve it if I had a restaurant in Alexandria.

ALEXANDRIA FISH FRY

Active Time: 45 minutes

Plan Ahead: You can make the tartar sauce a day or two ahead. Extra will keep for about a week in the refrigerator.

SERVES 4 TO 6

Egyptian Tartar Sauce:

¾ cup (170ml) mayonnaise

2 tablespoons minced cornichons

2 tablespoons minced celery

2 tablespoons finely chopped shallot

1 tablespoon minced brined capers

1 tablespoon minced preserved lemon

1 pickled hot banana pepper or peperoncini, minced (optional)

½ cup chopped herbs, preferably a combination of flat-leaf parsley, dill, and cilantro

Fish:

2 pounds (908g) boneless, skinless snapper fillets

20 garlic cloves, peeled

3-inch (7.5cm) piece ginger, peeled

2 tablespoons freshly squeezed lime juice

1 teaspoon fine sea salt, plus more as needed

¼ cup (100g) chickpea flour

1 teaspoon ground coriander

1 teaspoon ground fennel

½ teaspoon ground cumin

Vegetable oil, for frying

Flaky sea salt, such as Maldon

1. To make the tartar sauce, stir together the mayonnaise, cornichons, celery, shallot, capers, preserved lemon, banana pepper (if using), and herbs.

2. Cut the fish into 3- to 4-inch (7.5 to 10cm) pieces. Lay the fish out on a sheet pan or other rimmed baking sheet. Grate the garlic and ginger into a bowl with a rasp grater, then stir in the lime juice and salt. (You may also use a mini food processor. Pulse several times to coarsely chop the garlic and ginger, then blend to make a paste before pulsing in the lime juice and salt. A large food processor won't work.) Spread the paste evenly over the fish pieces.

3. Put the chickpea flour in a pie or baking pan and stir in the coriander, fennel, and cumin with a fork.

4. In a large, deep skillet or Dutch oven, heat 1 inch (2.5cm) of oil over medium-high heat until it reaches 375°F (190°C) and bubbles form instantly around a wooden spoon inserted in it. Line a separate sheet pan or platter with paper towels.

5. Working in two batches, press the pieces of fish in the chickpea dredge, then flip over and press again so that all sides are evenly and generously coated. Gently lower the fish into the oil and fry until golden brown on one side, about 2 minutes. Turn over and fry until golden brown on the second side and cooked through (the fish will be flaky and white in the center), about 2 more minutes. Transfer to the paper towels and drain, then season with pinches of flaky salt. Keep warm. Repeat with the remaining fish, heating another 1 inch of oil to 375°F (190°C) before frying the second batch. Serve immediately with the tartar sauce.

ALEX

Egyptians call their beloved city of Alexandria "Alex" for short. When you're in the country, people will ask if you've been to Alex or what you thought of Alex. Home to millions of Egyptians, the city is proudly set alongside the Mediterranean, situated for sunny beach days and long lunches along the water. My dad liked Alex so much that for most of my life I thought he was born there.

The fish auction in Alex starts before dawn, and fishermen haul out their local catch, selling it to the highest bidder in what can only be called organized chaos (wear waterproof shoes if you ever visit). At restaurants like Balbaa, the fish is displayed on ice so you can see how fresh it is before you order. Private clubs along the water have their own restaurants, and the good ones cook up the local catch in simple ways, marinating whole fish in lime, garlic, and cumin before throwing it on the grill. My friend Moustafa Elrefaey took us to Zephere Seafood, a prime spot near the Citadel, where the meal inspired Sizzling Prawns on page 170.

The legend goes that Alexander the Great and his army reached Naucratis, an important trading center for Egyptian papyrus and linen. He wasn't a fan, so he and his army continued to sail, landing on a shore that had fresh water, good weather, and no malaria. That was an auspicious start to a city that Egyptians—especially my dad—cherish.

Fishing off the coast of Alexandria

"Samak" in Arabic means fish, and nearly all the restaurants along the corniche in Alexandria serve fresh "samak" something. Samak singari is what Egyptians call Greek-style fish, a beautiful butterflied branzino or snapper roasted on a bed of sliced potatoes. If you can't find butterflied fish, or a whole fish to butterfly yourself, you can use two boneless fillets. A whole fish serves two people, more or less, depending on the size of the fish; for a larger dinner, double the potatoes and fish and bake everything on two sheet pans (there will be enough marinade for two fish). Ensure the bones have been removed. If tai snapper is unavailable, red snapper or branzino is a great alternate. Use a rasp grater to grate the garlic, ginger, and lemon zest.

Serve with Tomato-Braised Fennel (page 274) and Sayadeya Rice (page 153).

SAMAK SINGARI

Active Time: 30 minutes
Plan Ahead: 30 minutes for the marinating
Equipment: A box grater

SERVES 2

Tomato-Spice Marinade:
1 small Roma tomato, halved
2 tablespoons extra-virgin olive oil
1 tablespoon grated garlic (about 3 cloves)
1 tablespoon grated ginger
1 teaspoon finely grated lemon zest
2 teaspoons freshly squeezed lemon juice
2 teaspoons ground coriander
1 teaspoon fine sea salt
1 teaspoon Aleppo pepper
½ teaspoon ground cumin

Fish and Potatoes:
1 small tai snapper or branzino (about 2 pounds / 908g), butterflied, or 2 fillets
1 pound (454g) medium Yukon Gold potatoes, peeled and sliced ⅛ inch (3mm) thick crosswise
1 tablespoon extra-virgin olive oil
½ teaspoon fine sea salt, or more as needed
Freshly ground black pepper

To serve:
2 tablespoons extra-virgin olive oil
1 tablespoon freshly squeezed lemon juice, or more to taste
¼ teaspoon fine sea salt
½ small fennel bulb, fronds separated and removed (if available), and thinly sliced lengthwise
1 tablespoon chopped flat-leaf parsley (optional)
1 lemon, cut in half or in wedges (optional)

1. To make the marinade, grate the tomato with the large holes of a box grater, then discard the skin. Stir all the marinade ingredients together in a pie pan or dish large enough to fit the fish.

2. Arrange a rack on the lower third of the oven. Preheat the oven to 425°F (220°F). Line a sheet pan with parchment paper.

3. To ensure the fish lies flat, remove the head if attached. Pat the fish dry, then add to the bowl with the marinade, coating all sides evenly. Let marinate at room temperature while the oven preheats, turning once or twice, for 15 minutes. (Alternatively, refrigerate the fish in the marinade for 1 hour, taking it out 15 minutes before cooking.)

4. In a medium bowl, mix the potatoes with the oil, salt, and a few pinches of black pepper. Shingle the potatoes onto the sheet pan in 3 even rows in slightly overlapping layers. You want a flat surface for the fish to cook on, and it's okay to have pieces of potato sticking out from the fish. Bake the potatoes for 10 minutes.

5. Remove the potatoes from the oven and place the fish on top so that the skin is facing down. Spoon a little marinade on top and bake until the fish and potatoes are cooked through, about 30 minutes, depending on the size of the fish. If the fish is cooked before the potatoes, transfer the fish to a warm platter and return the potatoes to the oven.

Continued

6. Meanwhile, make the fennel salad: In a small bowl, whisk together the oil, lemon juice, and salt. Mix in the fennel and sprigs of fennel fronds if you have them and taste, adding more salt or lemon juice if needed.

7. Serve the fish directly from the sheet pan or slide the fish off the parchment and onto a serving platter. Put the fennel salad on the side. Sprinkle the fish with parsley (and fennel fronds if you have them) and offer lemon wedges on the side if desired.

Encasing fish in a crust made of whipped egg whites and salt is a classic cooking method, allowing the fish to steam gently as it absorbs the aromatics. Grape leaves do two things here: they protect the fish from absorbing too much salt, and they add delicate briny notes. The result is all about restraint: celebrating the flavor of fresh fish without a lot of interference. You can encase the fish a couple of hours before baking. To impress friends, cut away the salt crust at the table. If you have two 1-pound (454g) fish, encase and bake them on separate sheet pans (you'll need to make a second batch of salt and egg whites, too). For a decorative touch, mold the salt crust into scales. Look for egg whites sold in 16-ounce cartons. Otherwise, you will need the whites from 14 to 16 eggs. (Keep in mind that you can freeze egg whites when recipes call for yolks only and then use them up in this recipe.)

Serve with Saffron Fingerling Potatoes (page 140).

SALT-BAKED WHOLE FISH
WITH ZUCCHINI AND LEMON

Active Time: 30 minutes

Plan Ahead: You can encase the fish in the salt crust and refrigerate up to 3 hours before baking.

Equipment: A stand or handheld mixer and an instant-read thermometer

SERVES 2 TO 3

Fish:

1¼ cups (400g) egg whites, at room temperature

1 (3-pound / 1.36kg) box kosher salt (preferably Diamond Crystal)

10 large jarred grape leaves, rinsed and stems removed (you may not need all of them)

1 (1½- to 2-pound / 680 to 908kg) cleaned whole white fish, such as branzino, snapper, or sea bream

3 thinly sliced lemon rounds

Zucchini:

1 tablespoon extra-virgin olive oil

2 small zucchini, thinly sliced into rounds

1 teaspoon finely grated lemon zest

Flaky sea salt, such as Maldon

For serving:

Extra-virgin olive oil

Flaky sea salt, such as Maldon

1 tablespoon chopped flat-leaf parsley

1 lemon, cut into wedges

1. Preheat the oven to 425°F (220°C) and line a sheet pan with parchment paper.

2. In a stand mixer fitted with the whisk attachment, whisk the egg whites on medium speed until soft peaks form when you lift the whisk out of the bowl, about 2 minutes. With the mixer on low speed, gradually pour in the salt. When ready, the salt crust will feel damp but firm enough to hold a shape, not dry and sandy and not soupy.

3. Place a third of the salt crust in the center of the lined sheet pan and form into a shape a little larger than the length and diameter of the fish lying on its side. Cover the salt crust with 3 to 4 grape leaves, letting them overlap, ensuring that there's enough coverage that the fish can rest on them without touching the salt.

4. Using scissors, trim off the fish fins and discard, then pat the fish dry with paper towels. Place the fish on top of the grape leaves and tuck the lemon slices in its cavity. Leaving the head and tail exposed, cover the fish with another layer of leaves, wrapping them around the sides as best you can.

5. Leaving the head and tail exposed, cover the fish with salt crust, adding a handful at a time, until completely covered. Pat the crust to smooth it down, then use the tip of an upside-down spoon to make a pattern resembling fish scales on the crust. (If making ahead, refrigerate the fish at this point, then remove 20 minutes before baking.)

6. Bake for 25 to 30 minutes (20 minutes if using 1-pound / 454g fish) or until the crust is lightly golden around the edges and an instant-read thermometer inserted through the head or tail side reaches 125°F (52°C). (The fish will continue to cook in the salt crust after it is removed from the heat.) Remove from the oven and let it rest for about 5 minutes.

7. While the fish rests, cook the zucchini. Heat the oil in a large skillet over medium-high heat. Add the zucchini and cook, stirring occasionally, until some pieces have turned golden and are cooked through, about 5 minutes. Remove from the heat and stir in the lemon zest and a few pinches of flaky salt. Transfer to a serving platter.

8. Using a knife, cut into the side of the salt crust and remove the crust in chunks, being careful not to cut into the fish. Peel away the leaves and skin, then lift the top fillet of the fish off the bones and place on top of the zucchini. Lift the backbone from the tail and pull up toward the head to discard the bones, then add the bottom fillet to the zucchini platter. Drizzle the fish with olive oil and season with flaky salt and parsley. Offer lemon wedges and olive oil at the table for drizzling.

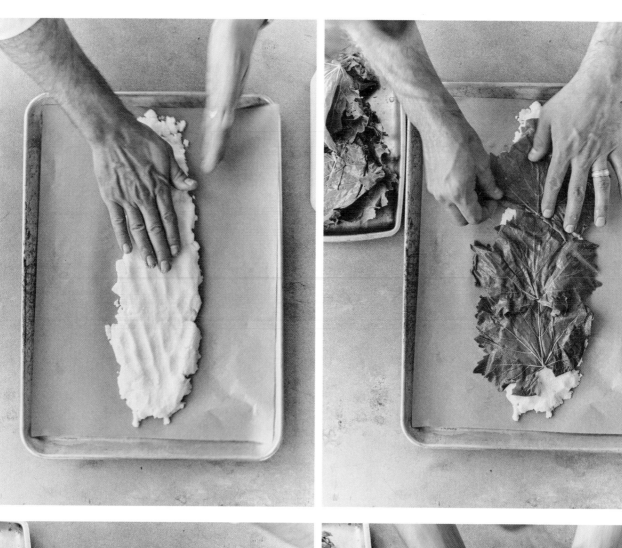

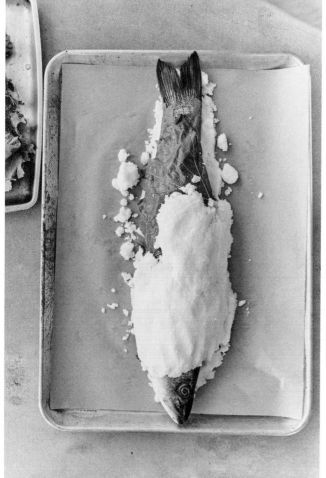

The glaze used in this recipe leverages the tangy flavors found in the Egyptian kitchen, countering the rich texture of salmon. You may make the glaze—infused with cardamom, coriander, and black pepper—a day or so before so the flavors deepen and it's ready to go when you are ready to cook the fish. The glaze makes more than you need for one recipe, but you'll be happy to have it around to glaze shrimp, chicken, carrots, or more salmon. Meanwhile, preserved lemon and herbs added at the end give the dish a bright touch. To go the extra mile, serve the salmon with Dill Yogurt Espuma (page 194).

Serve with Lemon Saffron Couscous (page 152) and Blistered Cherry Tomatoes (page 273).

TOMATO-GINGER GLAZED SALMON

Active Time: 45 minutes

Plan Ahead: Make the glaze at least a couple of hours before cooking the salmon. Extra glaze keeps, refrigerated, for 1 month.

Equipment: A pastry or basting brush for glazing the fish

SERVES 4

Tomato-Ginger Glaze:
5 green cardamom pods, crushed
1 tablespoon coriander seeds
2 teaspoons black peppercorns
2-inch (5cm) piece ginger, sliced into ¼-inch (6mm) planks
¼ cup (60ml) tomato paste
1 large Roma tomato, seeded and coarsely chopped
¼ cup plus 2 tablespoons (125g) honey
¼ cup plus 2 tablespoons (125g) light corn syrup
2 tablespoons white distilled vinegar
1 teaspoon fine sea salt

Salmon:
Nonstick cooking spray
4 center-cut portions salmon, skinned (4 ounces / 113g each)
1 teaspoon fine sea salt

2 tablespoons minced preserved lemon (optional)
2 tablespoons chopped chives
1 teaspoon crushed coriander seeds
Flaky sea salt, such as Maldon

1. To make the glaze, toast the cardamom, coriander seeds, and peppercorns in a heavy-bottomed medium saucepan over medium-high heat until aromatic, about 30 seconds. Stir in the ginger and cook until aromatic, another 30 seconds, then stir in the tomato paste and cook, stirring often, until it turns from bright red to brick red, another 30 seconds. Add the tomato, honey, corn syrup, vinegar, and salt and bring to a boil. Reduce the heat to medium-low and simmer to meld the flavors, about 15 minutes. Remove from the heat and let cool to room temperature, about 1 hour. Strain through a fine-mesh strainer, pressing against the mesh and scraping the underside to extract as much of the glaze as possible. (You will have about ¼ cup / 180ml.)

2. Arrange a rack about 6 inches from the broiler and preheat the oven to 400°F (200°C). Line a sheet pan with aluminum foil. Put a wire rack on the pan and spray with cooking spray. Place the salmon on top. Season the salmon all over with the fine sea salt and let sit for 20 minutes as the oven heats up. (This lightly cures the salmon, making it easier for the glaze to adhere.)

3. Generously brush the tops and sides of each salmon portion with the glaze (you will use about 6 tablespoons glaze total), then bake until nearly cooked through but still pink in the center, 7 to 9 minutes. Remove the salmon from the oven and preheat the broiler, then broil the salmon until the glaze begins to bubble vigorously, 2 to 4 minutes.

4. To serve, top each portion with preserved lemon (if using), chives, and crushed coriander, adding a few pinches of flaky salt if desired.

HOW TO MAKE DILL YOGURT ESPUMA

"Espuma" is a fancy word for a sauce that is aerated with the help of a whipping siphon, the same kind of canister used for whipped cream. Many kinds of sauces can be aerated with this tool—even bessara on page 56—and the key is ensuring the base has a pourable consistency. (For bessara, this means diluting it with warm water until thin enough to pour off a spoon.) For this espuma (pictured with the salmon on page 193), the base is yogurt infused with dill. Read the instructions for the whipping siphon before starting, and ensure it is for food and not for soda or drinks.

MAKES 4½ CUPS (1L)

1. Set up a small bowl with 4½ ounces (130g, or just over ½ cup) water and 1 ounce (30g) ice. Bring a saucepan of water to a boil and add 4 ounces (115g) dill sprigs. Boil for 20 seconds, then remove from the pot with a spider skimmer and plunge in the ice water. (This blanching/shocking step will help concentrate the dill's flavor and brighten its color.)

2. Transfer the water and dill to a blender and puree until very smooth. Refrigerate until cold, about 30 minutes.

3. Whisk the dill puree with 2 pounds (900g) whole-milk plain Greek yogurt, 10½ ounces (300g) heavy cream, 2 tablespoons extra-virgin olive oil, and 1 teaspoon fine sea salt. Strain through a fine-mesh strainer and then transfer to a whipping siphon. Charge with two CO_2 cartridges. To serve, apply to the plate so it appears to be a small cloud.

This is my longest-running signature dish, the oldest in the fleet, my chefs say. It's also kind of magic: Egg whites make dried-out phyllo stick to fish like scales, and when you pan-fry it all in clarified butter, the crust stays remarkably delicate and crisp. A mild, flaky fish works best for this preparation, such as petrale sole, Dover sole, or flounder. This iteration has smoked dukkah added to the usual mustard beurre blanc (see Keeping Beurre Blanc Warm, page 197), for a nutty, savory note. The golden raisins soaked in verjus add just enough acidity to cut through the richness of the sauce. This recipe makes more raisins than you need, but any extra will keep for several weeks in the refrigerator, and they're great additions to roasted cauliflower, roasted carrots, or roast chicken.

Serve with Mashed Dukkah Cauliflower (page 137) or Everyday Egyptian Rice (page 152).

PHYLLO-CRUSTED SOLE
WITH DUKKAH BEURRE BLANC AND GOLDEN RAISINS

Active Time: 1 hour

Plan Ahead: Lay out the phyllo the day before so it dries. The golden raisins can be made several days ahead.

SERVES 4

Phyllo-Crusted Sole:
10 half-sheets or 5 whole sheets phyllo (see Sourcing Phyllo, page 197)

4 (5-ounce / 140g) fillets petrale sole or flounder, no more than 1 inch (2.5cm) thick, skinned

Fine sea salt

Freshly ground black pepper

2 large egg whites (60g)

½ cup (70g) ghee or clarified butter

Golden Raisins:
½ cup (120ml) white verjus

¼ cup (60ml) dry white wine

Pinch of saffron threads (optional)

1 cup (140g) golden raisins

Beurre Blanc:
1 shallot, thinly sliced

1 thyme sprig

1 flat-leaf parsley sprig

½ bay leaf

½ teaspoon crushed coriander seeds

¼ teaspoon black peppercorns

1½ cups (360ml) dry white wine

¼ cup (60ml) champagne vinegar or white wine vinegar

½ cup (120ml) heavy cream

¼ teaspoon ground turmeric

½ pound (225g) cold unsalted butter, cut into medium dice

1 tablespoon Dijon mustard

½ teaspoon fine sea salt

For serving:
¼ cup Smoked Dukkah (page 267)

1. Separate the layers of the phyllo and lay out on the counter for a few hours (or overnight) to dry completely. Once it is brittle, break it into small pieces (about ½ inch / 12mm in size) with your hands. Spread the phyllo in a pie plate or rimmed baking sheet and set aside.

2. To make the raisins, in a small saucepan, bring the verjus, wine, and saffron (if using) to a simmer over medium heat. Simmer 5 minutes, then turn off the heat and stir in the raisins. Let cool to room temperature.

3. To make the beurre blanc, put the shallot, thyme, parsley, bay leaf, coriander seeds, and peppercorns in a small saucepan. Pour in the wine and vinegar and bring to a boil over high heat. Lower the heat to medium-high and cook until reduced to about ¼ cup, about 15 minutes. Strain into a bowl, discard the aromatics, and return the reduced liquid to the saucepan (you will have about 2 tablespoons).

4. While the wine and vinegar reduce, set up a double boiler or fashion one yourself: Fill a pot with an inch or two (2.5 to 5cm) of water and put a stainless steel bowl on top. The water should not touch the bottom of the bowl. Bring the pot to a gentle simmer.

Continued

5. To the pan with the reduced wine and vinegar, add the cream and turmeric. Cook over medium-high heat, whisking if necessary to keep the cream from boiling over, until reduced by half, 4 to 5 minutes. Turn the heat to low and gradually whisk in the butter, 3 or 4 pieces at a time. (This is the key to ensuring the butter becomes emulsified into the cream. If the butter starts to melt too fast before it has fully incorporated into the cream, pull the pan off the heat, continue to whisk, then return to the heat.) Continue until all of the butter is incorporated and the sauce is warm. Whisk in the mustard and salt, and taste, keeping in mind that the dukkah added later is also salty. Cover with a lid or plastic wrap and put the container in a warm water bath to keep warm.

6. Right before cooking, prepare the fish: season both sides with salt and pepper. In a pie dish or deep rimmed plate, whisk the egg whites until frothy. Working with one piece at a time, dip the fish into the egg whites to coat completely, letting the excess drip back into the dish, then press the fish into the pieces of phyllo, ensuring that each side is evenly and thoroughly coated.

7. Cook the fish in two batches. Heat a large nonstick skillet over medium heat. Add ¼ cup (60ml) ghee to the pan. When it begins to smoke, carefully place 2 fillets in the pan. Cook until golden brown on one side, about 2 minutes. Using a spatula, carefully turn the fish over and cook the other side until golden brown and crisp, about 2 more minutes. Remove to a plate and keep warm; repeat with the remaining 2 fillets and ¼ cup (60ml) ghee.

8. To serve, spoon the beurre blanc onto the center of 4 warm plates. Put the fish on top and scatter the dukkah over the fish and beurre blanc. Add a spoonful of golden raisins to each plate and serve the rest of the beurre blanc on the side.

SOURCING PHYLLO

Phyllo comes in either half-size (9- by 14-inch / 23 by 35.5cm) sheets or whole size (14- by 18-inch / 35.5 by 46cm) sheets. The total amount of phyllo you will use is about 3 ounces (85g), so you can buy either size package. Save extra phyllo to make the Baklava Napoleon on page 259.

KEEPING BEURRE BLANC WARM

Beurre blanc is an emulsified butter sauce made by gradually adding small cold pieces of butter into a reduction of wine and vinegar. In French, the technique is called monter au beurre, to "mount" a sauce with butter. Once mounted, a sauce is delicate: if it boils, the emulsification will break, leaving a greasy mess. This is why I add heavy cream; it's a way to help the sauce stay emulsified without babying it. Still, beurre blanc is best served as soon as possible. Keep it warm in a warm water bath (such as a double boiler removed from heat) to help prevent the sauce from breaking.

POULTRY AND MEAT

During our sprawling family gatherings when I was growing up, it was my dad's job to manage the grill. I always joke with him that he was the most consistent grill cook I'd ever seen at work. The meat was always burned on the outside and raw on the inside. But even when it's not cooked to perfection, nearly anything off the grill tastes great. Egyptians love the grill, but you'll also see a lot of other ingenious ways of cooking poultry and meat there, whether roasting it with grains or burying it in the ground for a Bedouin pit roast (see page 224). Poultry and meat are celebratory in Egypt, a way to gather people together. This collection of recipes is all about that kind of meaty, savory goodness.

Quail in grill baskets line the grills at Andrea El Mariouteya, an outdoor hilltop restaurant in New Giza, filling the air with smoky, savory aromas. I shared a meal there with Adam Sobel, and afterward gave him the green light to create a grilled quail recipe inspired by that experience. The idea is to highlight the depth of flavor that only a deep char can produce. Brushing quail with fig vinegar helps the skin blister on the grill (and if fresh figs are in season, consider roasting some to serve alongside). Semiboneless quail have had their backbones removed but their leg and wing bones are left intact. This allows them to cook quickly while still holding a recognizable shape. Most quail sold at grocery stores are semiboneless. Packs of four run 14 to 16 ounces (400 to 454g). If only available frozen, let the quail thaw completely in the refrigerator before cooking.

Serve with Vanilla-Roasted Figs (page 277).

GRILLED SESAME QUAIL
WITH BLACK TAHINA

Active Time: 30 minutes

Equipment: A gas or charcoal grill and a grill basket (see Buying and Using Grill Baskets) or 8 metal skewers

SERVES 4

Nonstick cooking spray

8 semiboneless quail, about 4 ounces (115g) each, thawed if frozen

1 teaspoon fine sea salt, plus more if desired

Freshly ground black pepper

2 tablespoons extra-virgin olive oil

2 tablespoons fig vinegar or aged balsamic vinegar

2 tablespoons white sesame seeds, plus more for garnish

2 teaspoons Aleppo pepper

½ cup (118ml) Black Tahina (page 52), at room temperature

Flaky sea salt, such as Maldon

1. Heat a gas grill to high heat or build a fire in a charcoal grill for direct-heat cooking. When the grates are hot, clean the grill with a grill brush. Spray a grill basket with cooking spray or have 8 skewers ready.

2. Pat the quail dry and arrange breast side up on a sheet pan. Tuck the wing tips behind the shoulders. Season on all sides and inside the cavity as best as you can with the salt and black pepper. Drizzle with the olive oil and vinegar and mix to coat, then lay the quail out again in an even layer and sprinkle both sides with the sesame seeds and Aleppo pepper.

3. Place the quail in a single layer in the grill basket (depending on the basket's size, you may be able to fit up to 4 quail). Close the basket. Put the quail over the hottest part of the grill and cover if using a gas grill. Cook, checking every few minutes to make sure none are burning (move the grill basket if needed to avoid flare-ups), or until the skin has blistered and charred in places and the breast is no longer pink inside, about 4 minutes per side. Set aside the cooked quail and cover with aluminum foil to keep warm while cooking the next batch. If you don't have a grill basket, use skewers: Place 2 quail side by side, then run 2 skewers through both birds perpendicularly, spearing through the torso and legs. Cook the quail, turning on either side, as you would if using a grill basket.

4. To serve, spread a layer of tahina at the base of a plate. Halve or quarter the quail and place on top. Sprinkle more sesame seeds on top if desired. Finish with pinches of flaky salt.

BUYING AND USING GRILL BASKETS

Grill baskets make cooking more than one quail at once easy: just put them in the basket, close it up, and cook. Use the handle to flip the entire basket over to cook the other side. Look for rectangular grill baskets with a handle in the center, not mesh cylinders meant for vegetables. Before using a grill basket, spray it with nonstick cooking spray.

Hamam mahshi—stuffed pigeon—is one of Egypt's most beloved food traditions. Head to the Fayoum oasis and before long you can be feasting on the birds stuffed with freekeh, tearing in with your hands, juices running down your elbows. Pigeon (often called squab in America) is found all over Egypt. On the drive from Cairo to Alexandria, houses with conical towers stick out from back-yards with round windows and wooden perches jutting out from the sides. These are borg hamam, dovecotes, where pigeons are raised specifically for food. (So no one gets confused, pet pigeons are kept in rooftop dovecotes with a different shape.) The traditional way to serve squab in Egypt is to stuff it with freekeh or other grains. This recipe borrows from that inspiration but cooks the birds on top of a mix of rice and farro instead, allowing the roasting juices to permeate the grains. Be sure to use pearled farro, as it cooks much faster than unpearled.

Serve with Smoked Beet Cream (page 55).

ROASTED SQUAB
WITH FARRO AND RICE

Active Time: 30 minutes

Plan Ahead: You can season the squab with salt the day before cooking for a deeper flavor.

Equipment: Poultry shears and a pastry or basting brush

SERVES 2 TO 4

2 squab (about 1 pound / 450g each), thawed if frozen

Fine sea salt

2 tablespoons vegetable oil

Freshly ground black pepper

2 tablespoons unsalted butter

½ yellow onion, finely diced (about 1 cup)

¼ cup (150g) pearled farro

¼ cup (150g) medium-grain white rice, such as Calrose

½ teaspoon ground cumin

½ teaspoon ground fennel

2 cups (480 ml) Chicken Stock (page 271)

1 tablespoon pomegranate or cherry molasses

¼ cup chopped toasted pistachios (see Buying and Toasting Nuts, page 267)

2 tablespoons thinly sliced chives

1. Arrange a rack in the center of the oven and preheat the oven to 400°F (200°C).

2. Pat dry each squab with paper towels and cut off the feet and head if attached. Place on a cutting board so that the back-bone faces up. Using poultry shears, snip along both sides of the backbone to remove it. (It's fine if some ribs come off as well.) Cut off the wings down to the first joint. (Save the trimmings for mak-ing poultry stock.) Snip through the breastbone to make two halves. Season all sides of the squab generously with salt.

3. Have a tray or plate handy. Heat the oil in a 10-inch (25cm) ovenproof skillet over medium-high heat. Add the squab halves breast side down and sear until lightly golden, about 2 minutes. Remove from the pan and season all sides with pepper.

4. In the same skillet, melt the butter over medium heat. Add the onion and cook, stirring often, until softened, 3 to 4 minutes. Add the farro, rice, cumin, fennel, ½ teaspoon salt, and ¼ teaspoon pepper and stir to toast the grains, about 2 minutes. Add the stock, increase the heat to medium-high, and bring to a boil, stirring once or twice, for 2 minutes. Lower the heat and simmer for 5 more minutes. Stir the farro again, add the squab skin side up, and simmer for 1 minute. Remove the pan from the heat and cover with a lid or aluminum foil. Transfer to the oven and bake until all the liquid has been absorbed and the squab breast is medium-rare, about 12 minutes.

5. Turn the oven to broil. Uncover the pan and brush the squab with the molasses. Place under the broiler until the skin deepens in color, 2 to 3 minutes. Let rest for at least 5 minutes, then sprinkle with pistachios and chives and serve.

Grapevines have been at the center of the Mediterranean agricultural and culinary landscape for at least six thousand years, with grape bunches used for eating and making wine, raisins, vinegar, and verjus, and leaves used as wrappers. Greek dolmades, Turkish dolma, and Egyptian mahshi—which means "stuffed" in Arabic—all use grape leaves to wrap around ground meat or rice. This recipe takes the idea in a different direction. Instead of rice or ground meat, I wrap yogurt-marinated, spiced chicken thighs. Grilling the chicken in the leaves gives the dish a smoky, earthy flavor. Buy more grape leaves than you need and choose leaves that are more or less the same size, discarding any that are torn or too large.

Serve with Everyday Egyptian Rice (page 152).

BAHARAT CHICKEN IN GRAPE LEAVES
WITH TANGERINE LABNE

Active Time: 1½ hours

Plan Ahead: Marinate the chicken overnight in the refrigerator—or at least 1 hour—before wrapping and skewering it. The longer the marinating time, the deeper the flavor.

Equipment: Have 12 skewers ready, and a gas or charcoal grill and grill brush. I prefer metal skewers, but you can also use wooden skewers, soaked in water for 30 minutes before using to prevent burning.

SERVES 4 TO 6

Tangerine Labne:

½ cup (100g) Labne (page 274) or plain whole-milk Greek yogurt

Finely grated zest of 2 tangerines (about 1 tablespoon)

1 tablespoon tangerine juice

Pinch of fine sea salt

Chicken:

6 large boneless, skinless chicken thighs (about 1½ pounds / 680 kg)

1 medium shallot, thinly sliced

1 large garlic clove, chopped

1 tablespoon Baharat (page 266)

1 teaspoon fine sea salt

1 teaspoon grated or crumbled dried lime (optional, see page 37)

1 tablespoon vegetable oil, plus extra for grilling

1 (16-ounce / 454g) jar grape leaves in brine

Extra-virgin olive oil, for drizzling (optional)

1. To make the tangerine labne, in a small bowl, mix together the labne, tangerine zest and juice, and salt. Refrigerate until needed.

2. Cut each thigh into 4 even pieces. In a large bowl, mix the chicken with the shallot, garlic, baharat, salt, and dried lime (if using) until the seasonings are evenly distributed. Mix in the oil to lightly coat. Refrigerate for at least 1 hour or overnight.

3. Sort through the grape leaves in the jar to find 24 intact large leaves. Rinse the leaves thoroughly and pat dry, then trim off any stems.

4. To roll each thigh piece: Place a leaf vein side up with the stem end closest to you. Put a thigh piece and a few shallot slices at the stem end. Fold the bottom left and right edges of the leaf over the chicken and then fold in the sides and roll up like a burrito. Repeat with the remaining grape leaves.

5. Heat a gas grill to high heat or build a fire in a charcoal grill for direct-heat cooking. When the grates are hot, clean the grill with a grill brush. Skewer 4 grape leaf packets together crosswise using two skewers. Repeat with the remaining packets and skewers. Rub the outside of the packets with oil, then grill over medium-high to high heat, covered if using a gas grill or uncovered if grilling with charcoal. Grill, turning the skewers once or twice, until the chicken is cooked through and parts of the grape leaves are charred, 12 to 14 minutes. Remove the skewers to a platter.

6. Give the tangerine labne a stir, adding a spoonful of water if too thick, and serve with the chicken. Drizzle the plate with olive oil to finish.

My dad didn't have much success grilling chicken in our backyard when I was growing up, but going to Egypt made me realize what he was trying to emulate: a bird with a crisp exterior that was thoroughly seasoned throughout. Here's the answer: submerging the chicken in feta brine overnight, then cooking it with the classic "under a brick" technique, which maximizes the chicken's contact with the hot surface, all but guaranteeing even cooking and crisp skin. A smaller bird (3½ to 3¾ pounds / 1.6 to 1.7 kg) is preferable to a larger bird here, because it is easier to fit into a skillet. If you have a larger chicken (4 pounds / 1.8 kg and up), it's better to cook it skin side down on a grill over a medium flame. You can put a cast-iron skillet on top to help press the bird down on the grill, ensuring it gets a crispy skin.

Serve with Lemon Potatoes (page 139).

FETA-BRINED SPATCHCOCK CHICKEN
WITH MINT AND GREEN ONIONS

Active Time: 45 minutes

Plan Ahead: Brine the chicken 8 hours or overnight in the refrigerator.

Equipment: Have a pair of poultry shears, a blender or food processor, an instant-read thermometer, and cheesecloth. Also locate a large (12-inch / 30.5cm) cast-iron skillet and another heavy, smaller skillet or Dutch oven, or something else that is heavy and oven-safe that you can put on top of the chicken as it cooks to help it stay flat.

SERVES 4 TO 6

Chicken and Brine:
1 smallish chicken (about 3½ pounds / 1.6kg)
2 ounces (57g) feta cheese
4 cups (960ml) water
5 sprigs oregano
2 garlic cloves, peeled and smashed
1 lemon, sliced ¼ inch thick
1 bay leaf
1 tablespoon black peppercorns

For Cooking and Serving:
1 tablespoon vegetable oil
2 tablespoons chopped mint, plus extra mint leaves if desired
2 tablespoons chopped flat-leaf parsley
1 Fresno chile or red jalapeño, thinly sliced crosswise, seeds removed if preferred
2 tablespoons thinly sliced green onion
1 teaspoon paprika
¼ teaspoon dried oregano
¼ cup (60ml) extra-virgin olive oil
1 lemon
¼ cup crumbled feta cheese

1. Lay the chicken breast side down. Starting at the neck, use poultry shears to cut along both sides of the spine to remove the backbone. Switch to a knife and cut out the rib cage (you can save the backbone and rib cage for stock). Flip the chicken over so it's breast side up and press down on the breastbone to crack it slightly. Next, remove the thigh bone on each leg: cut the ball joints on each end of the bone to pop them out and then cut along both sides of the bone until it is loose enough to remove. (Removing the thigh bones helps the bird lie flatter in the pan when cooking.) If you purchase your chicken from a good butcher, you can ask them to do this prep work for you.

2. In a blender or food processor, blend the feta with 2 cups (480ml) water until well blended, then blend in the remaining 2 cups (480ml) water.

3. Put the chicken skin side down in a nonreactive 9- by 13-inch (23 by 33cm) baking dish and cover with a layer of cheesecloth. Place the oregano sprigs, garlic, lemon, bay leaf, and peppercorns on top of the cheesecloth, then pour in the feta brine so the chicken is nearly submerged. Cover and refrigerate 8 hours or overnight.

Continued

4. Arrange an oven rack in the lower third of the oven and preheat the oven to 425°F (218°C). Remove the chicken from the refrigerator and discard the cheesecloth, brine, lemon, peppercorns, and herbs. Put the chicken on a tray and pat dry thoroughly with paper towels. Tuck the wing tips behind the shoulders and let air-dry breast side up for 30 to 40 minutes while the oven heats up.

5. Heat the vegetable oil in a 12-inch (30.5cm) oven-safe skillet or cast-iron pan over medium-high heat. Place the chicken skin side down, ensuring the skin on the legs is in contact with the pan. Cook until the skin begins to turn golden brown, 4 to 6 minutes. Put a smaller oven-safe skillet or Dutch oven on top of the chicken to weigh it down. Carefully transfer the pan with the weight on top to the oven and roast until an instant-read thermometer inserted in the thigh registers 170°F (77°C) and the skin is deep golden brown, about 35 minutes.

6. Remove from the oven, uncover, and gently flip the chicken over to ensure the skin hasn't stuck to the pan. If it has and begins to tear as you flip it, let it sit, skin-side down, for 1 to 2 minutes more until it releases. Transfer to a cutting board and let it rest skin side up for at least 5 minutes.

7. While the chicken rests, mix together the mint, parsley, chile, green onion, paprika, oregano, and olive oil in a small bowl. Using a rasp grater, zest the lemon directly into the bowl and stir to combine, then cut the lemon into wedges to serve with the chicken.

8. To serve the chicken, cut off the legs, then separate the drumsticks from the thighs. Cut each thigh in half. Cut the breasts off the bone and slice each one into thirds, then cut the wings off. You'll have 2 drumsticks, 4 thigh pieces, 6 breast pieces, and 2 wings. Spoon the herbs on top (or serve on the side) and scatter the feta and mint leaves around the plate. Serve with the lemon wedges.

SAVING FETA BRINE

If you habitually buy feta packed in brine, drain the cheese and freeze the brine to use for brining chicken and other kinds of poultry. In this recipe, you can use 2 cups (480ml) brine diluted with 2 cups (480ml) water.

BRINING CHICKEN

Putting cheesecloth on top of the chicken when brining ensures the bird stays covered. If you don't have cheesecloth, combine the chicken and marinade in an extra-large resealable bag, and turn a few times to coat. Seal and refrigerate, turning the bag a couple of times as the bird brines.

CAMEL LIVER IN KERDASA

Sometimes people get it in their heads that eating in Egypt means eating camel. That is not true—you are more likely to see camels walking to the Giza pyramids than on restaurant menus. But I was curious about how to prepare the meat, so Moustafa Elrefaey took me to a hole-in-the-wall place for lunch in Kerdasa, a Cairo suburb known for camel preparations.

It was fascinating to see the meal come together. The cook fired up a wegaa, a large flat wok with an indentation in the center. In there, the cook added small pieces of camel hump to render with a little oil, which happens quickly since the hump is mostly made up of fat. Once enough fat had rendered, he added onions, cooked them until soft, then shuffled them to the side of the wegaa to cook tomatoes. Once soft, they joined the onions on the side of the wegaa and he added finely sliced camel liver and heart. The cooking went quickly before everything was mixed together and seasoned thoroughly with a blend of salt, black pepper, and a proprietary blend of spices that included cumin and turmeric. The texture was chewy, though the liver meat itself was not as gamey as I was ready for, and it all was sopped up fast with baladi bread.

Not far from the corniche in Alexandria, there's El Fallah, a tiny place that only makes one thing: liver sandwiches. You say liver sandwich in Alex and people know you're talking about this spot—it's so famous that the owner has dozens of pictures of himself posing with Egyptian celebrities. The reason the sandwich works is the meat is cut paper-thin and is generously seasoned with spices. That liver sandwich inspired this recipe, which applies similar flavors to steak sliced super-thin (as in, Philly cheesesteak thin).

If you'd rather make the sandwich with beef liver instead of steak, slice the liver in half horizontally, season generously with salt and pepper, and brush with the garlic butter used in this recipe. Broil the liver for 1 to 2 minutes or until brown on the outside and slightly pink in the center. Let it cool for a couple of minutes, then slice it crosswise and add it to the bowl with the cooked shallots and other fixings.

Serve with Mixed Pickles (page 73) or Okra with Shallots and Chile (page 134).

ALEXANDRIA STEAK SANDWICHES

Active Time: 30 minutes

Plan Ahead: You can make the garlic butter ahead and refrigerate it with the garlic cloves inside. This recipe makes more garlic butter than you need, but the extra keeps, sealed in an airtight container, for a month, ready to be pulled out and used to make many other things, like garlic bread or scampi. Or take leftover Baladi Bread (page 78), brush it with garlic butter, and toast it up to make garlic crackers.

Equipment: A pastry or basting brush

SERVES 4

Garlic Butter:
¼ pound (113g) unsalted butter
5 garlic cloves, peeled and smashed
¼ teaspoon fine sea salt
Freshly ground black pepper

Sandwich:
4 soft French sandwich rolls, cut in half and toasted cut side up
2 boneless rib-eye or New York strip steaks (about 12 ounces / 340 g each)

1 teaspoon vegetable oil
Fine sea salt
Freshly ground black pepper
2 tablespoons unsalted butter
3 shallots, thinly sliced
1 small hot pepper (Anaheim or jalapeño), thinly sliced crosswise
½ teaspoon ground cumin
½ teaspoon ground turmeric
½ teaspoon paprika
1 lime, halved
1 handful cilantro sprigs

1. To make the garlic butter, in a small saucepan, melt the butter with the garlic over medium heat, about 2 minutes. Season with salt and a few pinches of pepper and let cool to a warm room temperature, about 10 minutes.

2. Using a pastry brush, lightly coat the cut side of the sandwich rolls with the garlic butter, about 1 tablespoon per roll.

3. Trim some of the fat from the steak and save to render in the pan. Cut away any gristle. Slice each steak in half crosswise, then slice thinly across the grain into 3- to 4-inch (7.5 to 10cm) long pieces (try to get as close as you can to Philly cheesesteak thinness with the slices).

4. In a large skillet over medium-high heat, render the saved beef fat for 1 minute, then remove (it's okay if not much fat comes out). Add the oil and heat for a few seconds, then add the sliced steak and sear briefly, turning the pieces once or twice and seasoning with a few pinches of salt and a generous pinch of pepper, until the beef is cooked through, about 2 minutes. Transfer the beef and any juices to a heatproof bowl and keep warm.

5. In the same skillet, melt the butter over medium heat. Add the shallots, hot pepper, cumin, turmeric, and paprika and cook until the shallots have softened slightly, about 2 minutes. Add to the bowl with the steak and stir together well. Squeeze the lime over the bowl, then mix again, adding more salt if needed.

6. Divide the steak and shallots among the sandwich rolls and finish with cilantro sprigs. Slice the sandwiches in half before serving.

There are endless varieties of kebabs made across the eastern Mediterranean and throughout the Middle East. Oftentimes the meat is lamb, but here I use a nice piece of beef tenderloin. The bell pepper sauce was inspired by the idea of au jus, the light sauce made from the natural juices of meat. But the "juices" this time come from roasted peppers and tomatoes. See Roasting Peppers in the Oven (page 136) for an alternative method.

Serve with Roasted White Sweet Potatoes and Mixed Herbs (page 142).

BEEF TENDERLOIN KEBABS
WITH EGYPTIAN PEPPER SAUCE

Active time: 40 minutes

Plan Ahead: You only need about half of the sauce; extra can be frozen. Gently reheat before using.

Equipment: Have a blender, a gas or charcoal grill and grill brush, and 16 skewers ready. I prefer metal skewers, but you can also use wooden skewers soaked in water for 30 minutes beforehand to prevent burning.

SERVES 4

Egyptian Pepper Sauce:
3 medium red bell peppers
¼ cup (60ml) extra-virgin olive oil
2 medium shallots, thinly sliced
5 garlic cloves, thinly sliced
1 large Roma tomato, diced
¼ teaspoon ground allspice
¼ teaspoon ground ginger
¼ teaspoon cayenne
1 teaspoon fine sea salt, plus more if desired
Juice of 1 lime (about 2 tablespoons)

Beef Tenderloin Kebabs:
1½ pounds (680g) beef tenderloin, cut into 1-inch (2.5cm) chunks
½ yellow onion, sliced
Extra-virgin olive oil
Flaky sea salt, such as Maldon
Freshly ground black pepper
Finely grated zest of 1 lime

1. To make the sauce, put each bell pepper on a gas burner and turn the heat to medium-high. Char the peppers, using tongs to turn every 2 to 3 minutes, until the skin has blackened on all sides, about 8 minutes total. Transfer to a heatproof bowl and cover with a plate or plastic wrap so the peppers steam for 10 minutes, which helps loosen their skins. Let cool for 5 to 10 minutes, then peel away the skins and remove the stem and seeds. It's okay if a bit of the skin stays in place, but wipe away any stubborn seeds.

2. Heat the oil in a medium saucepan over medium heat. When it begins to shimmer, add the shallots and garlic and cook, stirring often, until the shallots are tender, 1 to 2 minutes. Stir in the peppers and cook off any extra moisture, about 2 minutes. Add the tomato, spices, and salt and cook until the tomato is soft and most of its liquid has evaporated, 2 to 4 minutes. Remove from the heat and transfer to a blender. Add the lime juice and puree until smooth. Taste, adding more salt if desired. Transfer 1½ cups to a small saucepan to reheat before serving and refrigerate or freeze the rest for another use.

3. Heat a gas grill to high heat or build a fire in a charcoal grill for direct-heat cooking. When the grates are hot, clean the grill with a grill brush. Coat the meat pieces lightly in olive oil and season with a few pinches of flaky salt. Skewer 5 to 6 pieces of meat per two skewers (using two each makes the kebabs more secure and easier to turn while grilling), spacing the pieces out about ½ inch (12mm) apart with onion slices in between. Season the meat on all sides with flaky salt. Place the skewers on the hottest part of the grill and cover if using a gas grill. Cook, turning once or twice, until the meat is cooked to your liking, about 3 minutes per side. Season with black pepper.

4. Serve 2 skewers per person. Spoon a little sauce on the plate with the meat and serve the rest on the side. Season with flaky salt and sprinkle the lime zest over the top.

You don't go very far on a trip to the Middle East without eating exceptional kofta, ground beef or lamb that's well-seasoned with salt, herbs, and spices and then grilled over charcoal to infuse the meat with the flavor of char. In Cairo, the restaurant Sobhy Kaber is a three-story temple to the grilled kofta and other savory meat, and the aromas permeate the whole block. This simple, savory recipe celebrates these flavors. Serve on rice or use bread to wrap up pieces of kofta.

Serve with Salata Baladi (page 129).

GRILLED LAMB KOFTA
WITH CHILE LABNE

Active Time: 45 minutes

Equipment: A gas or charcoal grill and grill brush and an instant-read thermometer

SERVES 4

Kofta:

Vegetable oil

1 pound (454g) ground lamb

⅓ cup (45g) plain breadcrumbs

½ yellow onion, finely diced

1 large egg

2 tablespoons minced flat-leaf parsley

1 tablespoon minced dill

2 teaspoons fine sea salt

1 teaspoon ground cumin

½ teaspoon ground cinnamon

½ teaspoon freshly ground black pepper

To serve:

1 cup (240ml) Labne (page 274) or plain whole-milk Greek yogurt

2 tablespoons Chile Oil (page 279), plus more if desired

Flaky sea salt, such as Maldon (optional)

4 to 6 pieces of Baladi Bread (page 78) or store-bought pita

1. To make the kofta, oil a sheet pan or rimmed tray. In a large bowl, mix together the remaining kofta ingredients with your hands until you can pick up the mixture in one mass and lift it from the bowl, about 1 minute. Roll into 12 balls about 2 ounces (55g) each and place on the oiled pan. Press down into 2-inch (5cm) wide patties and flip over to lightly oil both sides.

2. Heat a gas grill to high heat or build a fire in a charcoal grill for direct-heat cooking. When the grates are hot, clean the grill with a grill brush. Grill the kofta over high heat, covered if using a gas grill or uncovered if grilling with charcoal, turning once or twice, until slightly charred and cooked through (no longer pink inside and an instant-read thermometer reads 155°F / 68°C), 9 to 11 minutes.

3. While the kofta is on the grill, mix together the labne and chile oil in a bowl. Sprinkle flaky salt (if using) over the kofta and serve with spoonfuls of the chile labne on the side and baladi bread.

THE PIT ROAST

I head west from the Nile to Kerdasa, a part of Greater Cairo that sits on the Giza plateau, to take part in a Bedouin-style pit roast at the farm of Moustafa Abdelrazik, a chef who works for Moustafa Elrefaey. The Pyramids of Giza sit only a few miles away, their peaks visible from the road. It's dusty and hot, and you wouldn't suspect there's a farm behind the brick wall beside me. But I walk down an alley, turn a corner, and I'm in a verdant oasis. Mango, lime, and date trees tower over rows of greens and herbs and sugarcane. One of the guys at the farm lops off a piece of sugarcane and hands it to me to chew on. Shoes off, I sit on one of the blankets spread out in the shade and sip green tea infused with marjoram and fenugreek.

Refreshed, it's time to get down to business. The shoes come back on. The first step to making a pit barbecue is starting a fire in an underground barrel, feeding the flames with mango wood. When the wood burns down, it's time to load up a tiered contraption with layers of meat. The bottom layer closest to the coals cooks the longest, so it is filled with the meat that needs the most time. Today, that's goat marinated with yellow mustard, rosemary, garlic, and onion. On the next tier goes turkey, which has a dry red pepper rub. To the final two tiers we add chicken and rabbit, both of which are marinated in black pepper and lime juice. The contraption is lowered into the barrel, then we put a lid on it and bang it shut. One of the guys covers the lid with damp towels, and then they hand me a shovel. My job, I'm told, is heaping dirt over the top, covering it completely. After I finish, they spray water on top, sealing the pit, then retreat to the shade.

Two or three hours later, it's time to eat. We dig out the lid, then four guys lift the metal contraption out of the pit. We fill a table with the meat and platters of mahshi, stuffed vegetables. Moustafa's tiny daughters join in, taking in the food and the newcomers who have come to their home. We wash up and then dig into the meal with our hands—no need for utensils, since the meat is falling off the bone. I consider whether there's a way to replicate this experience in a restaurant in North America. Maybe not with shovels and dirt, but tableside, with heated beds of salt. Then I back-burner my plan and go back for seconds.

Savory and hot, Urfa pepper is the purple-black answer to the milder Aleppo pepper. When mixed into harissa paste, it turns the paste very dark, making a simple-but-dramatic marinade for lamb chops. Frozen fava beans work very well in this dish, but if it's springtime and fresh fava beans are available, they make this dish feel even more celebratory. The marinade works for two frenched racks of lamb, or 8 to 10 individual chops, or 8 lamb T-bones.

Serve with Baladi Bread (page 78) or Everyday Egyptian Rice (page 152).

BLACK HARISSA LAMB CHOPS
WITH FAVA BEANS, PEAS, MINT, AND DRIED LIME YOGURT

Active Time: 45 minutes

Plan Ahead: You can marinate the lamb for up to 1 hour at room temperature or up to 8 hours in the refrigerator.

Equipment: A gas or charcoal grill and grill brush

SERVES 4 TO 6

2 racks of lamb (8 ribs each) or 8 lamb loin chops (about 2 pounds / 907g)

¼ cup (60ml) harissa paste

¼ cup (60ml) plus 2 tablespoons extra-virgin olive oil, divided

¼ cup Urfa pepper

2 teaspoons ground coriander

1 teaspoon freshly ground black pepper

½ teaspoon fine sea salt, plus more if desired

1 dried lime (page 37), for grating

1 cup (240ml) plain whole-milk Greek yogurt

1 cup (145g) shelled and peeled fava beans, frozen or from about 2 pounds (907g) fresh fava bean pods (see Sourcing and Prepping Fava Beans, page 56)

½ cup water

1 cup (125g) shelled sweet peas, frozen or fresh

Flaky sea salt, such as Maldon

6 green onions, kept whole with roots trimmed (optional)

Mint sprigs or pea shoots (optional)

1. If using racks of lamb, trim (french) the rack. Make a cut down the length of the top layer of fat in between the meat side and the bone side, then trim the fat off the bone side to expose the bones. Next, cut away the extra meat and fat between the bones, using a knife to scrape the bones clean. Trim away the thick layer of fat over the meat side but be careful not to cut into the meat (it's better to leave some fat in place than to trim away meat). If you purchase your lamb from a good butcher, you can ask them to do this for you. Have them remove the chine bone, too, so you can easily create chops (for more, see Buying and Prepping Lamb Chops, page 230). To portion the rack into chops, cut between the bones.

2. To make the paste, in a small bowl, stir together the harissa paste, ¼ cup (60ml) olive oil, Urfa pepper, coriander, black pepper, and fine sea salt to form a thick paste. Slather the paste on all sides of the lamb chops and leave at room temperature for at least 30 minutes or up to an hour. (Alternatively, make the marinade in a large resealable bag, then add the lamb, ensuring the marinade coats each piece before sealing. Refrigerate the bag for at least 2 hours or overnight. Remove the lamb from the refrigerator when ready to heat the grill.)

3. To make the yogurt, break the dried lime open and grate the insides with a rasp grater directly into a small bowl to get about 1 tablespoon. Stir in the yogurt and set aside.

Continued

4. Heat a gas grill to medium-high heat or build a fire in a charcoal grill. As the grill heats up, cook the fava beans and peas on the stovetop: Heat 1 tablespoon olive oil in a large skillet over medium-high heat. Stir in the fava beans and water, season with a generous pinch of salt, and bring to a brisk simmer. Cook for about 1 minute, add the peas, and cook, stirring occasionally, until the vegetables are hot all the way through and the water has evaporated, 3 to 4 minutes. (If using fresh peas instead of frozen, you may need to add a little more water and cook for a minute longer until tender.) Take the skillet off the heat and keep warm.

5. Season the chops generously with flaky salt. Grill uncovered over medium-high heat until medium rare, about 3 minutes per side for a rack of lamb chops. If cooking lamb loin chops, cook for a few minutes longer (about 11 minutes total) to ensure the meat gets hot along the center bone. (If your grill is not that hot, you may want to cover it.) Mix the green onions, if using, with the remaining 1 tablespoon olive oil. Season with a pinch of flaky salt and grill, turning once, until slightly softened, about 1 minute. Serve the chops with the green onions, favas, and peas, with the yogurt on the side. Garnish with mint sprigs or pea shoots, if desired.

BUYING AND PREPPING LAMB CHOPS

Estimate 2 to 3 chops per person if using a rack of lamb and 2 chops per person for lamb loin chops, which are meatier. A rack of lamb includes 8 ribs. If you are buying a rack of lamb that is frenched (meaning the fat has been trimmed away from the rib bones), it will weigh about 1 pound (454g). Otherwise, one rack before trimming weighs roughly 2 pounds (907g). Before cutting in between the ribs to separate the meat into chops, ensure that the rack does not have a chine bone, which is part of the backbone of the lamb and runs parallel to the meat. If it's still there, it is much more challenging to portion the chops.

At popular koshari spots like Abou Tarek (page 154), koshari is finished with a garlicky, spicy tomato sauce. That's the inspiration behind the sauce used to braise these lamb shanks. I wanted a sharp, punchy tomato flavor to counteract the richness of the braised meat. In fact, if you make koshari (see page 156 for the recipe) and have leftover tomato sauce, add it to this braise. To get the full experience, serve the shanks with the vermicelli rice and lentils prepared as you would for koshari. Or keep things simple and make Everyday Egyptian Rice (page 152) to soak up the sauce.

SPICED TOMATO-BRAISED LAMB SHANKS

Active Time: 1 hour

Plan Ahead: For the best results, season the shanks with salt the night before braising and braise them a day before serving, allowing time for the meat to soak up the flavors of the braising liquid. This also makes it easy to remove extra fat from the sauce.

Equipment: An immersion blender or blender

SERVES 4 TO 6

4 lamb shanks (about 1 to 1.3 pounds / 454 to 590g each)

1 tablespoon fine sea salt, plus more as needed

3 tablespoons vegetable oil, divided

2 teaspoons ground cumin, divided

2 teaspoons coriander seeds, crushed, divided

½ teaspoon freshly ground black pepper, plus more if desired

1 yellow onion, finely diced

4 garlic cloves, minced

1 teaspoon Aleppo pepper or ½ teaspoon red pepper flakes

¼ cup (60ml) tomato paste

¾ cup (180ml) dry white wine or ½ cup (118ml) water and either 2 tablespoons white distilled vinegar or white wine vinegar

1 (28-ounce / 794g) can whole San Marzano tomatoes in their juices, coarsely chopped

2 cups (480ml) Chicken Stock (page 271) or water

1 bay leaf (2 if small)

1 tablespoon white distilled vinegar or white wine vinegar

2 tablespoons chopped flat-leaf parsley

1 tablespoon "Dukkah" Spice (page 266; optional)

1. Season the shanks with the salt, cover, and refrigerate 8 hours or overnight.

2. Arrange an oven rack in the lower third of the oven and preheat the oven to 325°F (165°C). Remove the shanks from the refrigerator while the oven is preheating and pat dry with paper towels.

3. Heat 1 tablespoon oil in a large (6- to 7-quart / 5.7 to 6.6L) Dutch oven over medium-high heat. In two batches so the meat browns evenly, sear the shanks on all sides, about 3 minutes per side, then transfer to a tray or sheet pan. Season the shanks evenly with 1 teaspoon cumin, 1 teaspoon coriander, and the black pepper. (Adding the spices after searing prevents them from burning.)

4. In the same Dutch oven, heat the remaining 2 tablespoons oil over medium heat. Add the onion and a generous pinch of salt and cook, stirring occasionally, until softened, about 4 minutes.

5. Stir in the garlic, Aleppo pepper, and remaining 1 teaspoon each cumin and coriander and cook for 30 seconds to draw out the garlic aroma. Add the tomato paste and cook, stirring often, until the color changes from bright red to brick red, about 2 minutes. Pour in the wine, add a few more pinches of salt, and increase the heat to medium-high, stirring to dislodge any bits from the bottom of the pan. Simmer until the wine has reduced by about half, about 2 minutes. Stir in the tomatoes and stock, add the bay leaf, and bring to a simmer, then return the shanks to the pan, laying them on their side to fit in one layer (if they don't fit in one layer, don't worry, as long as they are nearly covered in the sauce). Bring to a simmer, then turn off the heat, cover, and transfer to the oven.

Continued

231

6. Braise, flipping the shanks halfway through, until the meat is tender enough to slip off the bone when prodded with a fork, 2¾ to 3 hours. Once tender, remove from the oven, uncover, and let rest for 20 minutes.

7. Remove the shanks from the braise and transfer to a sheet pan. Remove the bay leaf; skim any fat that has risen to the surface of the braising liquid with a ladle and discard. Using an immersion blender, blend the sauce directly in the pot until smooth. (If you don't have one, you can transfer the sauce to a conventional blender and blend until smooth. Work in batches if necessary, never filling the pitcher more than one-third of the way, and be sure to hold the lid in place as you blend; hot liquids are prone to blender blowouts.) Return the shanks and sauce to the pot. (At this point, you can refrigerate the shanks and sauce together to reheat later.)

8. To serve, cover the pot and bring the braise to a simmer over medium heat, 5 to 10 minutes. Add the vinegar and simmer again, flipping the shanks one or two times, until hot all the way through. Taste, adding salt if needed. Sprinkle the parsley and dukkah (if using) on top and serve the shanks with plenty of sauce.

A QUICK WAY TO PREP WHOLE CANNED TOMATOES

You don't have to use a knife to chop canned San Marzano tomatoes. Instead, using clean kitchen shears, snip the tomatoes into pieces directly in the can. You can also pour the tomatoes into a bowl and squish them with your hands to break them up.

Oxtails braised with onions and spices is classic Egyptian comfort food, a dish that's always better the day after it's made. The reason: Oxtails need to cook low and slow to become tender, but once you let them sit in their braising liquid overnight, they'll reabsorb some of the flavors from the braise. (This recipe also works well in a slow cooker; see page 236 if you want to go in that direction.) To contrast all the richness, a simple topping of shaved carrots and sliced green onions adds a little brightness and color. Crispy Chickpeas (page 70), sprinkled on top, give the braise a nice crunch, though the dish is fine without them.

Serve with Saffron Fingerling Potatoes (page 140) if you prefer to cook the potatoes separately.

BRAISED OXTAILS
WITH POTATOES AND SHAVED CARROTS

Active Time: 1 hour

Plan Ahead: For the deepest flavor, season the oxtails with salt the night before braising and cook them a day before serving.

SERVES 4 TO 5

Oxtails:

5 pounds (2.3 kg) oxtails, as many meaty, large pieces as possible

1 tablespoon fine sea salt, plus more as needed

2 tablespoons vegetable oil

2 teaspoons ground cumin

2 teaspoons coriander seeds, crushed

½ teaspoon coarsely ground black pepper

2 medium yellow onions, diced (about 4½ cups)

¼ cup (60ml) tomato paste

6 garlic cloves, coarsely chopped

1 teaspoon Aleppo pepper or
2 to 3 dried chiles de arbol

2 bay leaves

5 thyme sprigs

4 cups (960ml) water

6 fingerling potatoes, peeled, or 4 small Yukon Gold potatoes, peeled and halved lengthwise

2 tablespoons chopped flat-leaf parsley or dill

Shaved Carrots:

6 small (young) carrots, peeled and trimmed

2 green onions, green parts only

1 tablespoon distilled white vinegar

1 tablespoon extra-virgin olive oil

Fine sea salt

Crispy Chickpeas (page 70), optional

1. Season the oxtails with the salt, cover, and refrigerate 8 hours or overnight.

2. Preheat the oven to 300°F (150°C). Remove the oxtails from the refrigerator while the oven is preheating and pat dry with paper towels.

3. Heat the vegetable oil in a large (7- to 7½-quart / 6.6 to 7L) Dutch oven over medium-high heat. Sear the oxtails on all sides, about 3 minutes per side, then transfer to a tray or sheet pan. (If using a smaller cooking vessel, sear in batches to avoid crowding the pan.) Season evenly with the cumin, coriander, and black pepper. (Adding the spices after searing prevents them from burning.)

4. In the same Dutch oven, still over medium-high heat, stir in the onions and a pinch of salt and cook, stirring occasionally, until golden brown, about 8 minutes. Stir in the tomato paste, garlic, and Aleppo pepper and cook for 30 seconds to draw out the garlic aroma. Return the oxtails and any spices left on the tray to the Dutch oven and add the bay leaves, thyme, and a few pinches of salt. Pour in the water and bring to a brisk simmer over high heat. Turn off the heat, cover the Dutch oven, and transfer to the oven.

5. Braise until the meat is tender when pierced with a fork, about 4 hours, stirring in the potatoes after 2 hours. In the first 30 minutes, check the braise to make sure it isn't bubbling rapidly (a few lazy bubbles are fine). If the braise is briskly simmering, reduce the heat by 25 °F (13 °C). Once tender, remove the Dutch oven from the oven, uncover, and let the braise cool at room temperature. (Once cool, you can refrigerate it to reheat and serve later on.)

Continued

6. Skim any fat that has risen to the surface and discard. Cover and bring the braise to a simmer over medium-low heat until the oxtails are hot all the way through, 10 minutes if reheating from room temperature and 20 to 30 minutes from the refrigerator. Add the parsley and taste, adding salt if desired.

7. Using a vegetable peeler, peel and shave the carrots from the stem end and slice the green parts of the green onions very thinly at an angle with a sharp knife. (If you want the carrots and green onions to curl, put them in ice water, then drain well, shaking off excess water.) In a bowl, mix the carrots and green onions with the vinegar and olive oil and season with salt to taste. Top the braise with the seasoned carrots and green onions and sprinkle crispy chickpeas on top (if using).

COOKING OXTAILS IN A SLOW COOKER

Raj Dixit, executive chef at Michael Mina at the Bellagio in Las Vegas, made this recipe at home in a slow cooker, and the trickiest part was keeping his dog out of the kitchen because it smelled so good. To make this recipe in a slow cooker, follow the instructions up to step 4 where it says to return the oxtails to the Dutch oven. Instead, add the oxtails, along with the onions and seasonings, to the slow cooker with 2 cups of water (not 4). Then add the bay leaves, thyme, and potatoes. The potatoes won't overcook in a slow cooker like they will in the oven. Cover and cook on high for 4 hours or low for 8 hours.

DESSERTS

One of the best pastry counters in Cairo is at Mandarine Koueider, an historic sweet shop with several branches, but my favorite is on the island of Zamalek. The counter gleams with trays of basbousa, a classic sponge cake soaked in syrup, as well as baklava and many other sweets made with phyllo, kataifi, and other ingredients from around the Eastern Mediterranean and North Africa. My strategy is to load up a box of pastries to take home, though they never make it that far.

In Alexandria, El Sheikh Wafik is a shop near the water that specializes in variations of rice pudding and om ali, Egypt's answer to bread pudding, and there is always a line out the door.

When I was growing up, these were the kinds of desserts that were on the table when extended family came over. It's encouraged me to use Middle Eastern ingredients, like the thin vermicelli-like strands of kataifi, in different ways. This collection of desserts, which I developed with the Mina Group's pastry chef Veronica Arroyo, pays homage to the classics while also breaking new ground.

Italian families have biscotti, Egyptians have fayesh. They're not the same—fayesh has yeast, for example, and is more savory, like crostini—but both are baked dry, intended for long storage. This recipe comes from my mom, who used to make huge batches to last all month long. My dad is the biggest fan. He likes to dunk fayesh in black tea, which he brews extra strong and drinks with creamer.

The golden color in the dough comes from turmeric while the mild, almond-like sweetness comes from mahlab. Also called mahleb, it's made from grinding black cherry pits, though if you can't track it down, it's not a deal breaker. If your work surface is wood or another porous material, you may want to lay down a silicone baking mat, such as Fleximat, to prevent the turmeric from staining it.

MINERVA'S FAYESH

Active Time: 45 minutes

Plan Ahead: Allow 2½ hours for letting the dough rise and 1½ hours for baking.

Equipment: Have a bench scraper or kitchen knife for portioning the dough.

MAKES 62 (3-INCH / 7.5CM) FAYESH

5 tablespoons (2½ ounces / 75g) unsalted butter, divided

1 cup (240ml) whole milk

½ cup (100g) granulated sugar

½ teaspoon ground turmeric

½ teaspoon ground mahlab

1 teaspoon fine sea salt

3¼ cups (490g) all-purpose flour

1½ teaspoons instant yeast

Nonstick cooking spray

1. In a small saucepan over medium heat, melt 4 tablespoons (2 ounces / 60g) butter. Stir in the milk, sugar, turmeric, mahlab, and salt. Stir well, then heat until the milk feels like warm bathwater, about 1 minute. Don't let it boil. Remove from the heat and let sit for 5 minutes.

2. Put the flour in a large bowl and whisk in the yeast. Make a well in the center, then pour in the milk mixture. With the tips of your fingers or a rubber spatula,

mix it into the flour until a coarse dough forms, then press the dough into the base of the bowl and fold it over a few times. Place the dough on a clean, dry work surface. Knead by stretching and folding the dough over itself until smooth, glossy, and supple, about 6 minutes.

3. Wash and dry the bowl and lightly coat it with cooking spray, then put the dough back in, cover, and let rise until puffed though not quite doubled, about 2 hours.

4. Line 2 sheet pans with parchment paper. Punch down the dough to deflate it, folding the sides over to the center, then transfer to a lightly dusted counter. Using a bench scraper or a knife, divide the dough in 4 even pieces (about 8 ounces / 222g each). Pat each piece into a rectangle, patting down to deflate any fermentation bubbles, then fold the long sides into the center like a business letter. Roll each piece into a thin log about 14 inches (35.5cm) long, with an even thickness and no tapered ends. (If you've ever made baguettes before, it is the same technique, but try not to taper the ends.) Melt the remaining 1 tablespoon (½ ounce / 15g) butter. Place 2 logs on each lined pan and brush with the melted butter. Cover with plastic wrap and let rise until the dough holds an indent when pressed, about 1½ hours.

5. A half hour before baking, arrange the oven racks into thirds to fit two pans at once and preheat the oven to 350°F (180°C).

6. Press down the logs slightly so they're about 2 inches (5cm) wide. Uncover the pans and bake for 30 minutes, rotating them halfway through, or until lightly golden brown around the edges. Remove from the oven and cool for 20 minutes on the pans. Reduce the oven temperature to 200°F (95°C). Using a serrated knife, slice each log on a slight diagonal into ½-inch (12mm) thick pieces and return to the sheet pans, making sure they aren't touching. Bake 1 hour, flipping the pieces after 30 minutes, until they are dried out completely. They are ready when you can break a piece in half and the center feels dry. Store for up to 1 month at room temperature in a tightly sealed container.

Egypt makes some of the best limeade I've ever had, and this recipe turns that refresher into a tart Popsicle studded with chunks of white peach. It was inspired by a dish we served at our Middle'Terranea pop-up, where we presented a frozen square of limeade with a beautiful piece of fresh white peach. The balance between water and simple syrup is important in the freezing process, so don't skip that step.

LIME POPSICLES
WITH MINT AND WHITE PEACH

Active Time: 15 minutes

Plan Ahead: You can make the simple syrup several days ahead and refrigerate until needed. The Popsicles will take about 8 hours to freeze.

Equipment: 6 (3-ounce / 90ml) Popsicle molds and 6 sticks

MAKES 6 POPSICLES

½ cup (100g) granulated sugar

1½ cups (360ml) water, divided

1 large ripe but firm white peach

1 tablespoon sliced mint

¼ cup (60ml) freshly squeezed lime juice

1. To make the simple syrup, in a small saucepan over medium heat, bring the sugar and ½ cup (120ml) water to a boil, about 3 minutes. Remove from the heat and cool completely.

2. Peel the peach with a vegetable peeler and dice into pieces that will fit in the Popsicle molds. Add to a small bowl and mix with the mint. Divide the peaches and mint evenly among the molds.

3. In a 2-cup (480ml) liquid measuring cup, whisk together the simple syrup, lime juice, and remaining 1 cup (240ml) water. Pour over the peaches in their molds, then give a stir before adding the sticks to suspend the peaches in the limeade. Freeze until solid, at least 8 hours or overnight. To remove, run the molds quickly under hot water and gently pull out the pops.

These sweet, gently aromatic pistachios give frozen desserts—like Raspberry Rose Water Granita (page 244) and Labne Frozen Yogurt with Honey and Stone Fruits (page 247)—a bit of crunch, but they are also tasty enough to be eaten alone as a snack. If you don't have black cardamom, use two green cardamom pods instead.

CARDAMOM CANDIED PISTACHIOS

Active Time: 15 minutes

Plan Ahead: You can make and steep the simple syrup a few days ahead. The nuts keep in an airtight container at room temperature for up to 2 weeks.

MAKES 2 CUPS (250G)

1 cup (200g) granulated sugar

1 cup (240ml) water

1 black cardamom pod, crushed

2 cups (250g) shelled whole pistachios (either raw or roasted and lightly salted)

1. To make the cardamom simple syrup, combine the sugar and water in a small saucepan and bring to a boil. Remove from the heat, add the cardamom, and steep for 30 minutes. Scoop out the cardamom pod and discard.

2. While the cardamom steeps, preheat the oven to 375°F (190°C). Line a sheet pan with a silicone liner (such as a Silpat) or parchment paper.

3. Stir the pistachios into the syrup and bring the pan to a boil. Cook for 10 minutes over medium-high heat, gently swirling the pan as needed to avoid scorching (but don't stir, as this may cause the nuts to crystallize before they are fully toasted). Drain the pistachios, discarding the syrup.

4. Scatter the pistachios in one even layer on the lined pan. Bake without stirring (which will cause the sugar to crystallize) until golden, 12 to 18 minutes. Let cool thoroughly. Store in an airtight container until needed to keep the sugar coating from going soft.

The aromas of fresh raspberries and rose are natural pairings and the inspiration for this refreshing granita. It's not hard to make, just stir and scrape the granita with a fork periodically as it freezes to encourage small ice crystals to form. Rose water and orange blossom water are common in North African and Middle Eastern cooking, especially in desserts. When used correctly, they enhance a dessert, not take over. Since brands vary on potency, I recommend starting with five drops, then continuing up to ten, tasting as you go so it's not overpowering.

Serve with Cardamom Candied Pistachios (page 243).

RASPBERRY ROSE WATER GRANITA

Active Time: 20 minutes

Plan Ahead: Allow about 2½ hours for the granita to freeze. It can be scraped and stored in an airtight container a few days before serving. Before serving, chill 4 bowls or cups.

SERVES 4

Granita:

1½ pounds (680g) fresh or frozen and thawed raspberries

2 cups (480ml) water

½ cup (100g) superfine or granulated sugar

2 tablespoons freshly squeezed lemon juice

5 to 10 drops rose water

To serve:

Handful fresh raspberries (optional)

¼ cup Cardamom Candied Pistachios (page 243), slightly crushed

1. In a blender, puree the raspberries with the water, sugar, and lemon juice until thoroughly blended. Strain the mixture through a fine-mesh strainer to remove the seeds, pressing firmly down on the berries with a rubber spatula and scraping the underside of the strainer to extract as much puree as possible. (If the strainer gets clogged with seeds, give it a rinse before continuing.) Stir in the rose water, tasting as you go, starting with 5 drops and increasing up to 10 as needed.

2. Pour into a freezer-safe 9- by 13-inch (23 by 33cm) baking dish that will lie flat in the freezer. After 1 hour, the edges and surface should have started to freeze. Use a fork to scrape the surface and the edges, breaking up the slush. Freeze for 20 more minutes, then repeat the scraping step. Continue to scrape the ice with a fork every 20 minutes until completely set, about 1 hour and 20 minutes longer. Transfer to an airtight container and keep in the freezer if not serving right away.

3. To serve, add a few fresh raspberries to each bowl or cup if you like and spoon the granita on top. Sprinkle candied pistachios on top and serve immediately.

I am always looking for ways to add acidity to dishes, even at dessert. This is why I am a fan of frozen yogurt. Its creamy dairy richness, contrasted with its light acidity, makes a simple dessert feel complex. I've served this tableside, mixing in shards of sesame phyllo, honey, and toasted pistachios, but I'm also happy to scoop it into bowls and serve it with fresh fruit. The frozen yogurt becomes firm when left in the freezer overnight, so if you make it the day before, take it out of the freezer about 15 minutes before serving so it softens to a scoopable consistency.

LABNE FROZEN YOGURT
WITH STONE FRUIT

Active Time: 20 minutes

Plan Ahead: Store the ice cream machine base in the freezer overnight before using it. Allow at least 1 hour of freezing time after the yogurt has been spun before serving.

Equipment: Ice cream maker

MAKES ABOUT 5½ CUPS (1.2L), SERVES 3 TO 4

Labne Frozen Yogurt:
1½ cups (300g) granulated sugar
⅓ cup (116g) light corn syrup
¼ teaspoon fine sea salt
2⅓ cups (560ml) water
1¼ cups (300ml) plain whole-milk yogurt or whole-milk Greek yogurt
1¼ cups (300ml) Labne (page 274, or store-bought)

To serve:
Sliced fresh stone fruit, such as white or yellow peaches or nectarines, plums, pluots, or cherries

1. In a medium saucepan, combine the sugar, corn syrup, and salt. Pour in the water and whisk together. Bring the pan to a boil over high heat to dissolve the sugar, then remove from the heat and let cool completely, about 2 hours at room temperature (or chill over an ice bath).

2. In a large bowl, whisk together the yogurt and labne. Pour in the sugar syrup, whisk well to get any lumps out, then refrigerate until thoroughly chilled, at least 1 hour or up to a few days.

3. Whisk the base well before pouring into an ice cream maker, then freeze according to the manufacturer's instructions until it reaches a soft-serve consistency, 18 to 20 minutes in a regular home ice cream maker (avoid running the machine too long to avoid overchurning).

4. Transfer the frozen yogurt to a 2-quart (2L) container and store in the freezer until firm enough to scoop, about 1 hour. Remove from the freezer and scoop into bowls. Serve with fresh fruit.

I was stuck on finding a new way to create a banana split using carob ice cream and that's where the idea came to wrap bananas in kataifi. Thanks to the fine, vermicelli-like strands of kataifi, the baked bananas become a crunchy, caramelized component for my version of an ultimate banana split—but they're just as good on their own, too. The trick when working with kataifi is to carefully untangle it first, then make sure you've thoroughly coated it in clarified butter before you start to roll up the banana pieces. Look for fresh or frozen kataifi at Middle Eastern grocery stores. If frozen, let it thaw according to the package directions before using, and use leftover kataifi for Kataifi-Wrapped Shrimp (page 108). If you have small bananas, use four of them and trim the ends of each one so it's about 4 inches (10cm) long.

Serve with Carob Ice Cream (page 251).

KATAIFI-WRAPPED CARAMELIZED BANANAS

Active Time: 40 minutes

Plan Ahead: Be sure to allow enough time so the kataifi is completely thawed before starting.

SERVES 4

½ cup (100g) light brown sugar

1 vanilla bean, split lengthwise

4 ounces (115g) kataifi, thawed if necessary

½ cup (100g) clarified butter (page 38) or ghee, melted

2 bananas, peeled and halved crosswise

Pinches of flaky sea salt, such as Maldon (optional)

Powdered sugar for garnish

1. Preheat the oven to 400°F (200°C). Line a sheet pan with parchment paper.

2. Put the brown sugar on a rimmed plate. Using a spoon, scrape the vanilla bean pod halves to remove the seeds, then use your fingers to disperse the seeds into the sugar.

3. Lay out a strip of kataifi strands about 4 inches (10cm) wide and as straight as possible. (Select long, unbroken pieces and avoid the short ones. It's also important to carefully untangle the strands and make sure they are evenly distributed.) Cut the strips in half crosswise to make 2 rectangles. Using a pastry brush, saturate the kataifi with the clarified butter until fully drenched. (The more clarified butter, the better the kataifi sticks to the banana.)

4. Roll 1 banana half in the brown sugar until fully coated, then place at the short end of one of the kataifi rectangles. Roll up, ensuring the ends of the kataifi stay secured to the banana by brushing with more clarified butter if necessary. Repeat with the second banana half, then repeat step 3 with the remaining kataifi and banana until all the banana pieces are rolled up. If not serving right away, you can refrigerate them for up to 2 hours—any longer than that and the bananas will begin to turn brown.

5. Put the bananas on the lined sheet pan, brush with any remaining clarified butter, and lightly sprinkle with flaky salt (if using). Bake until the kataifi is brown and crisp, about 20 minutes. Dust with powdered sugar and serve warm.

Carob is underused in the States but popular in Egypt. Chocolaty, fruity, with a bitterness similar to unsweetened cocoa or molasses, carob comes from pods that are cooked down and turned into molasses, juice, or even alternatives to chocolate chips. On hot days in Cairo, you drink chilled carob juice. Carob molasses is a little more intense than the juice—it has a color and consistency similar to that of regular molasses but a smoother, sweeter flavor. As soon as I tried it, I knew I wanted to use it in ice cream. Look for pure carob molasses at Middle Eastern specialty stores. Any extra can be used in place of blackstrap molasses in baking.

Serve with Kataifi-Wrapped Caramelized Bananas (page 248).

CAROB ICE CREAM

Active Time: 30 minutes

Plan Ahead: Make and refrigerate the ice cream base the day before and store the ice cream machine base in the freezer overnight before using. Allow at least 1 hour of freezing time after the ice cream has been spun before serving.

Equipment: Ice cream maker and an instant-read thermometer

MAKES ABOUT 1½ QUARTS (1.4L), SERVES ABOUT 4

2 cups (480ml) whole milk

2 cups (480ml) heavy cream

1 cup (200g) granulated sugar, divided

1 teaspoon vanilla bean paste or 1 vanilla bean, split lengthwise

6 large egg yolks

¼ cup (60ml) carob molasses

1. Freeze the base of an ice cream maker according to the manufacturer's directions (overnight is a good rule of thumb). Set a fine-mesh strainer over a heatproof medium bowl and set aside.

2. In a medium saucepan, whisk together the milk, cream, ¾ cup (150g) sugar, and vanilla bean paste. Bring the mixture to a simmer and cook over medium heat, about 11 minutes, watching carefully and adjusting the heat to maintain a gentle simmer and avoid boiling over. Remove from the heat. In a large bowl whisk together the egg yolks and remaining ¼ cup (50g) sugar.

3. Slowly and gradually ladle the hot cream mixture into the egg yolks, whisking constantly as you add it so the eggs don't curdle. Return the custard to the saucepan and gently cook over medium heat, whisking constantly, until the mixture is 187°F (86°C) and thick enough to lightly coat the back of a spoon, about 2 to 3 minutes.

4. Pour the custard through the strainer. (If using a vanilla bean instead of vanilla paste, save the vanilla bean to add back to the ice cream base after mixing in the carob molasses. This will allow it to impart a little more flavor to the mix. Just remember to remove the vanilla bean before adding the mixture to the ice cream maker.) While the custard is still warm, whisk in the molasses until thoroughly combined. Set the bowl over ice water and stir occasionally until cool. Cover the bowl and refrigerate overnight.

5. Freeze in an ice cream maker according to the manufacturer's instructions until it reaches a soft-serve consistency, 15 to 20 minutes in a regular home ice cream maker (avoid running the machine too long to keep from churning the cream into butter). Transfer the ice cream into a 2-quart (2L) container and store in the freezer until firm enough to scoop, about 1 hour.

In Alexandria, the hotspot for desserts is El Sheikh Wafik. Sure, it sells ice cream. But it is best known for rice pudding, couscous cooked in sweetened milk, and om ali (see page 225). All of these local favorites can be served plain or with dried fruits and chopped nuts.

The trick to this rice pudding recipe is long, slow cooking. The pudding needs to boil (yes, bubble vigorously) for half an hour to ensure the rice is cooked and the dairy has reduced. It's not hard to make, but don't do it while multitasking—it requires vigilance and near-constant stirring as it cooks so it doesn't scorch. But it's worth the attention: the result is the most velvety rice pudding I've ever tried. This version is dressed up with fresh figs, sprinkled with sugar, and brûléed lightly with a torch, though it is also excellent on its own or with other seasonal fruit.

RICE PUDDING
WITH FIGS

Active Time: 1 hour

Plan Ahead: The pudding needs time to cool, and it tastes best when made at least a day before serving so the vanilla can permeate the rice more completely.

Equipment: Brûlée torch for the figs (optional)

MAKES 8 CUPS (2L), SERVES ABOUT 8

1¼ cups (260g) medium-grain white rice, such as Calrose

1¼ cups (250g) plus 4 teaspoons granulated sugar, divided

1 cup (240ml) water

7½ cups (1.8L) whole milk

1 (14-ounce / 398g) can sweetened condensed milk

1¼ cups (300ml) heavy cream

1 teaspoon vanilla bean paste or 1 vanilla bean, split lengthwise

8 fresh figs, stems removed, halved

Ground cinnamon, for garnish (optional)

1. Gently warm the rice, 1¼ cups (250g) sugar, and water in a Dutch oven or large heavy-bottomed pot over medium heat, stirring often, until the sugar has dissolved and the water begins to simmer, about 5 minutes. Add the milk, condensed milk, and cream and continue to stir until large bubbles start to form on the edges, about 16 minutes. Increase the heat to medium-high so the pudding is boiling and cook for another 30 to 35 minutes (no less than 30), stirring often, as though you're making risotto. As you stir, scrape the bottom of the pan to avoid scorching and adjust the heat to keep the milk from boiling over. It's done when the rice is cooked through, even if the pudding still seems thin. It will thicken as it cools.

2. Remove from the heat and stir in the vanilla, then transfer to a baking dish or heatproof bowl to let cool to room temperature, stirring occasionally, about 1 hour. Cover and refrigerate overnight so the vanilla has more time to infuse into the rice.

3. When ready to serve, place the figs cut side up on a heatproof plate and sprinkle each half with ¼ teaspoon of the remaining sugar. If using a brûlée torch, torch each fig until the sugar has started to caramelize. If you don't have a torch, heat a nonstick skillet over medium heat. Put each fig half, sugared side down, into the skillet and cook until caramelized, about 2 minutes.

4. If using the vanilla bean, remove the pod from the pudding before serving, scraping any seeds from the pod into the pudding and stirring them in. For each serving, scoop the pudding into a small bowl (an ice cream scoop works well). Sprinkle with a few pinches of cinnamon (if using). Serve with the brûléed figs on top, about 2 halves per serving.

I have heard a few origin stories about this recipe, and none of them say the same thing, so I just think of it as a nice dessert made by the mom of someone named Ali. The recipe is like bread pudding made without eggs, and it's served all over Egypt. The key for my version is using croissants that are a few days old—the drier they are, the better they'll soak up the milk and cream. Many people make this with stale puff pastry instead, and that's an option here as well. For the best texture, bake om ali in shallow cast-iron or metal pans so there is ample surface area to allow the top to get golden and crunchy. Or, you can make them in shallow individual 6-ounce (180g) vessels, as pictured. If going that route, the ideal ratio is 3½ ounces (100g) croissant to 7 ounces (200g) spiced milk base. You can also bake in a larger baking pan, a large cast-iron pan, or gratin dish. Indicators of success are crispy bits of toasted croissant on the top, with subtle traces of scalded cream.

OM ALI

Active Time: 25 minutes

Plan Ahead: This can be baked ahead and rewarmed before serving. You can also boil together the milk, condensed milk, cream, and spices, then store in the refrigerator for up to 5 days until you're ready to complete the dish.

SERVES 8

1 pound (454g) croissants (about 8), preferably a couple of days old

3 cups (700ml) whole milk

7 ounces (200g) sweetened condensed milk (about half a can, ⅔ cup)

½ cup (120ml) heavy cream, plus 2 tablespoons (30ml), divided

2 to 3 tablespoons granulated sugar

1 teaspoon vanilla bean paste or vanilla extract

½ teaspoon ground cinnamon

½ teaspoon ground cardamom

Finely grated zest of 1 orange

½ cup (80g) chopped toasted pistachios, divided (see Buying and Toasting Nuts, page 267)

½ cup (80g) coarsely chopped toasted almonds, divided (see Buying and Toasting Nuts, page 267)

½ cup (40g) toasted unsweetened dried coconut, divided

¾ cup (100g) golden raisins, chopped

1. Preheat the oven to 325°F (165°C). Cut the croissants into bite-sized pieces (you should have about 12 cups / 2.8L). Scatter on a sheet pan and bake to dry out further, 10 minutes if they are already dry and 15 to 18 if they're only a day old or less. Let cool to room temperature. Increase the oven temperature to 400°F (200°C).

2. In a medium saucepan whisk together the milk, condensed milk, ½ cup (120ml) cream, sugar, vanilla, cinnamon, cardamom, and orange zest and bring to a boil over medium heat. Remove from the heat and let steep until the croissants are cooled.

3. Transfer the cooled croissants to a 12-inch (30.5cm) cast-iron pan or a 9- by 13-inch (23 by 33cm) baking pan and stir in half of the nuts and coconut and all of the raisins. Pour the spiced milk and cream over the top, poking and prodding the croissants to ensure all pieces are coated, and let sit 15 minutes. Before baking, drizzle the remaining 2 tablespoons (30ml) cream on top.

4. Bake until tiny bubbles form on the edges, about 25 minutes. Remove from the oven and top with the remaining nuts and coconut. Serve warm.

During Ramadan, it's common to break the daily fast with a small sweet to get your stomach ready for the meal that follows, and these date-filled cookies do the trick. But ma'amoul isn't only for Muslims—everyone eats them. My family is Coptic Christian and we had variations of these cookies around to offer if relatives came over for coffee or tea. Some bakers add almonds, pistachios, or cinnamon to the date paste, and others include mahlab, a spice made from ground black cherries that my mom uses in her Fayesh (page 241). Once you have the basics down, you can experiment. The pattern comes from the wooden molds used to press and shape the cookies. You can order ma'amoul molds online, though this recipe also gives instructions for making them without a mold. Because of the variation in mold sizes, your yield may be different from mine. If the cookies are much larger or smaller in size than the ones in this recipe, adjust the baking time accordingly.

MA'AMOUL

Active Time: 40 minutes

Equipment: A stand mixer and ma'amoul molds. If you don't have access to molds, see Shaping Ma'amoul Without a Mold (page 258).

MAKES ABOUT 20 COOKIES, DEPENDING ON THE SIZE OF THE MOLD

¼ cup plus 1 tablespoon (185g) clarified butter, melted

3 tablespoons granulated sugar

2 teaspoons orange blossom water or vanilla extract

1 large egg

2 tablespoons whole milk, plus more if needed

1 cup (157g) fine semolina flour

1 cup plus 1 tablespoon (150g) all-purpose flour, plus additional for dusting

½ teaspoon fine sea salt

9 ounces (255g) date paste (see Buying and Making Date Paste, page 258)

1. In a stand mixer fitted with the whisk attachment, whisk together the clarified butter, sugar, and orange blossom water on medium speed until combined, about 1 minute, scraping down the side of the bowl with a rubber spatula as needed. Add the egg and milk and mix on medium speed to combine, about 30 seconds.

2. In a separate bowl, whisk together the flours and salt. Replace the whisk attachment on the mixer with the paddle attachment. In three batches, add the flours to the bowl on low speed, scraping down the bowl with a rubber spatula as needed, until a dough forms. Press the dough into the base of the bowl with your hands, then cover with a clean kitchen towel and let rest for about 15 minutes so the flours can fully hydrate.

3. Preheat the oven to 350°F (180°C). Line 2 sheet pans with parchment paper.

4. Uncover the bowl and pinch the dough. It should feel soft and pliable, not too dry or sticky. Ideally it should be easy to roll into a ball without sticking to your hands or crumbling. If it is sticky, mix in a tablespoon of flour. If it is too dry, mix in a tablespoon of milk.

5. If using a ma'amoul mold, dust the mold lightly with flour (if your mold is brand-new, the flour may not stick, so you may need to dampen the mold slightly). Pinch off a piece of dough slightly smaller than a golf ball (about 1¼ inches / 3cm wide and ¾ ounce / 20g) and roll into a ball. Press the ball into the mold until it fills half of the depth. Push the dough up the sides until it reaches the edges. Ideally you want ¼ inch (6mm) of dough along the base and sides of the mold.

6. Pinch a piece of date paste (just under ½ ounce / 12g) and roll into a 1-inch (2.5cm) ball, then press into a 1½-inch (4cm) wide patty. Place in the center of the mold. You want enough date paste in the center so the cookie doesn't taste dry.

Continued

7. Pinch off another piece of dough (about ⅓ ounce / 10g) and roll into a ball about 1-inch (2.5cm) wide. Press the ball into a patty and place on top of the paste. Press down on the ball to completely cover the paste and go all the way to the edges of the mold, keeping a ¼-inch (6mm) thickness between the dough and paste as much as possible. Bang the mold against the work surface to knock the cookie out, then transfer to the lined sheet pan. In between shaping each cookie, dust the mold with flour.

8. Bake the cookies for 19 to 21 minutes or until lightly browned on the bottom and at the edges. If the tops begin to crack, remove them from the oven so they don't overbake. Let cool completely on the pans. Ma'amoul keep in an airtight container for up to a week.

BUYING AND MAKING DATE PASTE

It's become a lot easier to buy date paste at grocery stores, but it's also not hard to make your own. Take 9 ounces (255g) pitted dates and blend them in a food processor. If the dates are very dry, soak them briefly in water. The exact kind of date doesn't matter, and you can use a combination of date varieties as well. If it's very sticky, consider blending in some dried coconut to make it easier to place inside the dough.

SHAPING MA'AMOUL WITHOUT A MOLD

If you do not have a traditional mold, start with the date paste. Form a 1-inch / 2.5cm (¾ ounce / 12g) ball of date paste, then flatten into a 1½-inch (4cm) wide disc. Pinch off a piece of dough (about 1 ounce / 30g) and roll into a 1½-inch (4cm) ball. Press the ball into a patty, then make an indentation in the center large enough to fit the date paste. Put the date paste in the indentation, then wrap the edges of the dough up and around the disc to completely enclose.

This dessert sums up what traditional baklava is all about—layers on layers on layers—but in a new format. Pastry chef Veronica Arroyo and I created this deconstructed baklava, making it all about crisp shards of honey-sweetened phyllo and a yogurt-white chocolate cream. For nuts, we mixed toasted walnuts with honey and cardamom. Once you have the components, it's a choose-your-own-adventure situation in how you want to serve it: Stack the phyllo neatly and use a pastry bag to pipe the cream or, to make it a little more abstract, spoon the cream on the plate and pile the phyllo shards any way you want. The recipe is generous, so make it for a crowd and let everyone assemble their own. The yogurt cream keeps its shape thanks to the use of gelatin sheets, which are also sold as leaf gelatin; look for them at specialty pastry shops or online. Powdered gelatin isn't a direct substitution.

BAKLAVA NAPOLEON

Active Time: 1 hour

Plan Ahead: The cream—a crémeux in French pastry terms—needs to be refrigerated overnight to allow the gelatin to set before it's ready to go. The phyllo is best eaten on the day it's baked, though it can be assembled and refrigerated a day before baking.

SERVES 12

Yogurt Cream:
2 sheets (5g) gelatin
1 pound (454g) white chocolate, finely chopped
1 cup (240ml) whole milk
2 tablespoons light corn syrup
1 cup (240ml) plain whole-milk Greek yogurt
⅔ cup (160ml) heavy cream
Finely grated zest of 1 orange

Layered Phyllo:
⅔ cup (115g) clarified butter, melted
15 (9- by 14-inch / 23 by 35.5cm) phyllo sheets
(6 ounces / 170g)
⅔ cup (226g) honey, warmed briefly
so it is brushable
½ cup (60g) toasted white sesame seeds

Honey Walnuts:
½ cup (60g) chopped toasted walnuts
(see Buying and Toasting Nuts, page 267)
¼ cup (60ml) honey
½ teaspoon ground cardamom

1. To make the yogurt cream, fill a 2-cup (480ml) liquid measuring cup with ice water and add the gelatin to soften. Put the white chocolate in a medium heat-proof bowl. In a small saucepan, heat the milk and corn syrup over medium-high heat until bubbles form along the edge of the pan. Remove the pan from the heat. Squeeze out the excess water from the gelatin and stir into the scalded milk until fully melted. Pour the milk-and-gelatin mixture over the white chocolate. Let sit 1 minute, then whisk until the chocolate is completely melted and creamy. Whisk in the yogurt, cream, and orange zest. Cover and refrigerate at least 24 hours before using.

2. Preheat the oven to 350°F (180°C). Line a sheet pan with parchment paper and brush with a thin layer of clarified butter. Unroll the phyllo pastry and lay flat on a clean kitchen towel. Cover with a second clean kitchen towel and ensure the stacked sheets stay covered as you work to prevent them from drying out.

3. Lay a sheet of phyllo on the lined pan and brush the top generously, corner to corner, with clarified butter (make sure no part of the phyllo is dry). Brush a layer of warmed honey over the butter, then place a second sheet of phyllo on top. Repeat the process until you have a stack of 5 phyllo sheets. Sprinkle the top layer with a third of the sesame seeds (about 3 scant tablespoons), then lay another sheet of phyllo on top. Repeat the process with the clarified butter and honey until the stack has 10 sheets total. Sprinkle with a third of the sesame seeds, then repeat the process until you have 15 stacked sheets in all. Sprinkle the remaining sesame seeds on top.

Continued

4. Bake the phyllo until deep golden brown, about 25 minutes. Let cool on the pan for 10 minutes, then transfer to a wire rack to cool completely.

5. To make the honey walnuts, in a small bowl, mix together the honey, walnuts, and cardamom. If the honey is hard to mix, set the bowl in a bowl of hot water for a minute or two to soften.

6. To serve, give the yogurt cream a good stir. Transfer it to a pastry bag or simply spoon it on the plate. Either cut the phyllo into rectangles or break it into shards to serve with the cream. Spoon the honey walnuts alongside.

SOURCING AND USING PHYLLO

Phyllo comes in either half-size or whole-size sheets. The half-size sheets are 9 by 14 inches (23 by 35.5cm) while the whole-size are 14 by 18 inches (35.5 by 46cm). You can use the whole-size sheets if they're more available; just cut them in half crosswise first. Put frozen phyllo in the refrigerator the night before using to thaw. Keep any extra phyllo for the phyllo-crusted sole on page 195.

I am a huge mango fan. At some point I got stuck on the idea of finding a way to incorporate mangoes into basbousa, a classic semolina cake I ate as a kid. And that's where this upside-down cake came from. Thin slices of mango are layered at the base of the pan and the basbousa batter poured on top. Traditionally, you pour syrup over the top of basbousa while it's still in the baking pan, but in this recipe I unmold the cake to show off all that beautiful caramelized mango, then pour the syrup on top before serving.

MANGO BASBOUSA

Active Time: 1 hour

Equipment: The best way to bake these is in 4 mini oval 9-ounce (255g) cast-iron pans because one pan fits half a sliced mango (as in the photo). But the recipe also works in a 10-inch (25cm) cast-iron skillet.

SERVES 8 TO 10

Basbousa:

Nonstick cooking spray

2 large ripe but firm mangoes
(just over 1 pound / 454g each)

2 cups (320g) fine semolina flour

½ cup (100g) granulated sugar

½ cup (40g) unsweetened shredded coconut

1½ teaspoons baking powder

¾ teaspoon fine sea salt

1 cup (200g) clarified butter, melted

½ cup plus 1 tablespoon (140ml) plain whole-fat Greek yogurt, well stirred

2 tablespoons tahini, well stirred

1 tablespoon honey

Syrup:

1 cup (200g) granulated sugar

7 ounces (200ml) water

1 tablespoon freshly squeezed lemon juice

1 tablespoon honey

Finely grated zest of 1 orange

1 to 2 teaspoons orange blossom water (optional)

1. Preheat the oven to 375°F (190°C). If using 4 mini cast-iron pans, place them on a rimmed sheet pan. Coat the pan(s) generously with cooking spray.

2. Peel the mangoes with a vegetable peeler, then cut each into halves around the pit, keeping the halves intact as much as possible. Trim the remaining meat off the pits and reserve in case it's needed. Slice the mango halves thinly crosswise (about ⅛ inch / 4mm thick), then shingle the slices at the base of the pan(s) to mimic the shape of the mango. Keep the shingles tight and avoid gaps as much as possible. Use any small pieces of mango to fill the empty spaces in the pan(s).

3. To make the batter, in a large bowl whisk together the flour, sugar, coconut, baking powder, and salt.

4. In a separate large bowl, whisk together the clarified butter, yogurt, tahini, and honey until smooth. Using a rubber spatula, add the yogurt mixture to the dry ingredients and stir until thoroughly combined. The batter will be thick.

5. Scoop the batter over the mangoes, filling nearly to the rim of the pan(s), using about ¾ cup (180ml) per pan if using the smaller pans. (The batter does not rise much.) Smooth out the surface(s) with a rubber or offset spatula and transfer to the oven. Bake small cakes for 28 to 30 minutes and a large cake for 35 to 40 minutes, or until a toothpick inserted into the center comes out clean and the edges of the cake turn golden.

6. Meanwhile, make the syrup. In a medium saucepan, bring the sugar, water, lemon juice, honey, orange zest, and orange blossom water (if using) to a boil over high heat. Lower the heat to medium-high and simmer briskly for 10 minutes. You'll have about 1⅓ cups (320ml) syrup. Keep warm.

7. Remove the cake(s) from the oven and make a few incisions in the surface (avoiding cutting into the mangoes). This will help the cake absorb the syrup. Let cool for 5 minutes. While still warm, invert the cake onto a rimmed sheet pan so the mango slices are on top. Remove the pan(s) and pour the syrup over the cake(s) and let soak for 20 to 30 minutes before serving.

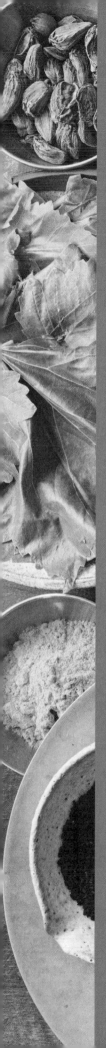

BASICS

Think of this section as the extended pantry of the book, a place to curate your own spice blends, sauces, chutneys, infused oils, stocks, and other ingredients important to my Egyptian larder. These are the kind of secret weapons that can dress up something as simple as roasted chicken in a matter of minutes. Some of these recipes are used frequently in the book (like Smoked Dukkah), others less so, but all are open to experimentation. For example, I suggest serving Tomato-Braised Fennel (page 274) with Samak Singari (page 184). But once you taste the relish, you may be inspired to serve it with all kinds of things, from poultry to steak to a vegetarian spread. Follow your imagination!

Baharat means "spice" in Arabic, but the word also connotes a spice blend made and sold all over North Africa and the Levant. There are probably a million ways to make baharat, but nearly all contain black pepper in the mix (bahār in Arabic means pepper). This version leans on warm baking spices like allspice, cinnamon, and clove. It's great for leveraging sweetness in roasted root vegetables, such as carrots and parsnips, as well as adding some zip to roasted Brussels sprouts. You can whisk it into a simple vinaigrette to dress salads.

Use in Baharat Chicken in Grape Leaves with Tangerine Labne (page 206) and Roasted Squash Steak with Brussels Sprouts and Onion Labne (page 146).

BAHARAT

Active Time: 5 minutes

MAKES A GENEROUS ¼ CUP (30G)

1 tablespoon freshly ground black pepper

2 teaspoons paprika

1 teaspoon ground coriander

1 teaspoon ground cumin

1 teaspoon ground allspice

1 teaspoon ground nutmeg

1 teaspoon ground cloves

½ teaspoon ground cinnamon

½ teaspoon ground cardamom (from green pods, if grinding from whole spices)

½ teaspoon fine sea salt

In a small bowl, whisk together the spices. Store in a glass jar away from heat for up to 1 month.

This isn't really traditional dukkah because it doesn't have any nuts (see Smoked Dukkah, page 267). But some people are allergic to nuts and some dishes are rich enough without the nuts. So that's how this blend came about. It's ideal for dusting over braised dishes like lamb shanks or roasted vegetables, adding bright contrast to the deep flavor.

Sprinkle on Spiced Tomato-Braised Lamb Shanks (page 231) or Braised Oxtails with Potatoes and Shaved Carrots (page 234).

"DUKKAH" SPICE

Active Time: 10 minutes

Equipment: A spice grinder or coffee grinder used only for spices

MAKES A SCANT 1 CUP (105G)

¼ cup fennel seeds

¼ cup cumin seeds

3 tablespoons coriander seeds

2 tablespoons dill seeds

1 tablespoon fine sea salt

1 tablespoon Aleppo pepper or red pepper flakes

1. In a large, dry skillet over medium heat, toast the fennel, cumin, coriander, and dill seeds, lowering the heat as needed to keep the spices from burning, until fragrant, about 3 minutes. Transfer to a bowl and let cool for 5 minutes. Stir in the salt and Aleppo pepper.

2. In two or three batches, depending on the size of your spice grinder, pulse the spices to a medium-ground consistency: fine enough so the spices are well blended but not so fine that they turn to powder. Store in an airtight container at room temperature for up to 1 month.

There is no one way to make this iconic Egyptian spice blend—essentially, it's unique to the creator. The key difference, like so many things in life, depends on wealth. A rich family uses a lot of nuts while a poor family may get by on using peanuts or, if things are especially scarce, using the heart of an apricot pit for a nutty flavor. With savory notes from smoked sea salt, this dukkah is dynamic with fish and poultry. If you can't find raw pistachios or if your hazelnuts are already toasted and skinned, add them in the last 5 minutes of toasting the almonds to warm through.

Sprinkle on Phyllo-Crusted Sole with Dukkah Beurre Blanc and Golden Raisins (page 195), Dukkah Flatbread (page 84), Middle Eastern Waldorf (page 133), and Roasted Tomatoes with Smoked Dukkah (page 273).

SMOKED DUKKAH

Active Time: 15 minutes
Equipment: A food processor

MAKES ABOUT 2½ CUPS (300G)

½ cup raw sliced almonds

½ cup raw shelled pistachios

½ cup raw hazelnuts

⅓ cup white sesame seeds

¼ cup fennel seeds

Generous ¼ cup coriander seeds

¼ cup smoked sea salt, such as Maldon

1. Preheat the oven to 300°F (150°C). Put the almonds and pistachios on one side of a sheet pan and the hazelnuts on the other side. Toast, stirring once, until the nuts are aromatic and the sliced almonds have turned a light golden color, about 15 minutes. While still warm, fold the toasted hazelnuts into a clean kitchen towel and rub to loosen and dislodge the skins. (It's okay if some of the skins are too stubborn to remove.) Let all the nuts cool to room temperature, then transfer to a food processor. Pulse until the largest hazelnut pieces are no bigger than half a hazelnut, about 10 (1-second) pulses.

2. Meanwhile, in a large skillet over medium heat, toast the sesame seeds, fennel seeds, and coriander seeds, lowering the heat as needed to keep the spices from burning, until fragrant, 3 to 4 minutes. The sesame seeds should be lightly golden in color. Transfer to a small heatproof bowl and let cool for 5 minutes, then pulse in a spice grinder until coarsely ground, about 3 (1-second) pulses.

3. Add the ground sesame and spices and the smoked salt to the food processor and pulse about 5 times to incorporate, then let cool completely. Store in an airtight container at room temperature for 1 week or freeze for up to 1 month, retoasting the mix in a dry skillet to draw out the aromas before using.

BUYING AND TOASTING NUTS

Buy nuts close to when you plan to use them or store in the freezer. This prevents them from turning rancid. Toast nuts between 300°F (150°C) and 350°F (180°C); the lower temperature is gentler while the higher temperature gets the job done faster, but you have to watch the oven more carefully to ensure the nuts don't burn. Use a timer to check after the first 10 minutes, giving them a stir and baking for 2 to 8 more minutes or until golden in color in the center (raw nuts with skins, like unblanched almonds, may take longer). Test a nut by piercing it in the center with the tip of a paring knife. Keep in mind that nuts with skins will continue to toast once removed from the oven.

Ginger, chile, and spices give always versatile vegetable stock a memorable twist while navel orange (peel and all) gives a sweet-bitter note. Use this for vegetarian and vegan soups, or for cooking freekeh and rice. Starting the stock with cold water allows the flavors to come together gently as the pot heats up. (If you cooked dried chickpeas for Hummus (page 54), you can use the chickpea cooking liquid in place of half the water for a more full-bodied texture.) For an even more savory flavor, add a spoonful of Vegeta, a seasoning blend from Croatia that's popular in the Middle East.

Use in Pumpkin Red Lentil Soup (page 122).

MIDDLE EASTERN VEGETABLE STOCK

Active Time: 30 minutes

Plan Ahead: The stock needs to simmer for 1 hour

MAKES 3 QUARTS (3L)

2 cups (180g) coarsely chopped leeks, both white and green parts, washed well

½ medium yellow onion, chopped

1 large carrot, peeled and chopped

½ navel orange, cut into wedges with peel

½ Granny Smith apple, cored and cut into chunks

2 celery stalks, chopped

5 garlic cloves, peeled and crushed

2-inch (5cm) piece ginger, peeled and sliced into planks lengthwise

1 Fresno chile or jalapeño, halved lengthwise

3 thyme sprigs

1 bay leaf

2 tablespoons black peppercorns

2 tablespoons Vegeta (see page 35; optional)

1 tablespoon coriander seeds

1 teaspoon fine sea salt

½ teaspoon ground turmeric

½ teaspoon paprika

4 quarts (3.8L) cold water

1. Combine the ingredients in a large pot over medium-high heat. Cover the pot and bring to a boil. Once boiling, remove the lid, reduce the heat to medium-low, and simmer gently for 1 hour or until the liquid has reduced by about a third.

2. Using a fine-mesh strainer, strain the stock, discarding the solids. Cool to room temperature, then cover and refrigerate for up to 5 days or freeze for up to 2 months.

This stock is a good back-pocket recipe to keep in mind, not only when cooking from this book but any time you need a savory vegetarian stock. The key ingredient is kombu, a mineral-rich seaweed. Used in Japanese dashi, kombu gives the broth a deep, savory flavor. Look for it at the grocery store where seaweed snacks and ingredients for sushi are sold.

Use in Mushroom Bolognese for Macaroni Béchamel (page 165).

MUSHROOM STOCK

Active Time: 20 minutes

Plan Ahead: The stock needs to simmer for 45 minutes and steep for another 45 minutes.

Equipment: A food processor

MAKES ABOUT 2 QUARTS (2L)

1 pound (454g) button mushrooms, cleaned and trimmed, halved, or quartered if large

1 pound (454g) cremini mushrooms, cleaned and trimmed, halved, or quartered if large

2 tablespoons (30ml) grapeseed or other neutral oil

1 teaspoon fine sea salt

3 quarts (2.8L) water

8-inch (20cm) long piece kombu, wiped clean

1 small leek, light green and white parts only, thoroughly cleaned and coarsely chopped

2 thyme sprigs

½ bay leaf

1. Using a food processor, pulse the mushrooms in two batches until evenly chopped to about the size of chickpeas, 8 to 10 (1-second) pulses.

2. Heat the oil in a large pot over medium-high heat. Add the mushrooms and salt and cook, stirring occasionally, until the mushrooms have shrunk in volume by about half, about 6 minutes. Add the water, cover the pot, and bring to a boil. Once boiling, remove the lid and simmer gently for 45 minutes or until the liquid has reduced by about a third.

3. Turn off the heat and add the kombu, leek, thyme, and bay leaf. Let sit for 45 minutes. Using a fine-mesh strainer, strain the stock, discarding the solids. Cool to room temperature, then cover and refrigerate for up to 5 days or freeze for up to 2 months.

This chicken stock has a clean, light flavor profile, making it versatile enough to use in a range of recipes. There are two reasons for the clean flavor: First, you boil the chicken bones in water, then strain them, then return them to the pot with clean water. The second is that the stock is simmered for 2 hours, not any longer, so the flavors stay bright. Chicken feet are light on flavor, but add rich texture, giving the broth more body. You can often find them in Asian supermarkets. If chicken feet are unavailable fresh, ask if the butcher keeps any frozen.

CHICKEN STOCK

Active Time: 30 minutes

Plan Ahead: The stock simmers for 2 hours, then has 1 hour of rest time before it is strained and ready to use

Equipment: To fit all the bones and water comfortably, you need a large stockpot (with at least 10-quart / 10L capacity)

MAKES ABOUT 4 QUARTS (3.8L)

4 pounds (1.8kg) mixed chicken bones (necks, backs, wings, and ribs)

4 ounces (113g) chicken feet (optional)

1 medium yellow onion, peeled

1 clove

1 large carrot, peeled and cut into chunks

1 large celery stalk, cut into chunks

1 tablespoon coriander seeds

1 tablespoon black peppercorns

5 flat-leaf parsley sprigs, stems and leaves

5 thyme sprigs

5 quarts (4.7L) water

1. Put the chicken bones and feet (if using) in a 10-quart (10L) stockpot. Cover with enough water to cover the bones (this is not the water listed in the ingredients; it will be discarded) and place over high heat. Bring to a boil, then remove from the heat, drain, and rinse. (This gets rid of impurities.) When cool enough to handle, wash out the pot, then put the chicken back in it.

2. Stud the onion with the clove. Put the onion, carrot, celery, coriander seeds, peppercorns, parsley, and thyme in the pot. Add the water, cover the pot, and bring to a brisk simmer. Once boiling, remove the lid, reduce the heat to medium-low, and simmer gently for 2 hours. Turn off the heat and let the stock steep with the bones and aromatics for 1 hour.

3. Using a fine-mesh strainer, strain the stock, discarding the solids. Cool to room temperature, then cover and refrigerate for up to 5 days or freeze for up to 2 months.

271

Slow roasting tomatoes concentrates their flavor while also giving them a longer shelf life. The resulting texture is something halfway between a dried and fresh tomato. Here, I push the flavor one step further, adding dukkah at the end for a nutty, smoky finish (though you can leave it out for more direct tomato flavor). Serve these tomatoes as a room-temperature side for grilled fish or poultry, or serve with any of the dips in the Setting the Table chapter, page 50.

ROASTED TOMATOES
WITH SMOKED DUKKAH

Active Time: 10 minutes

MAKES ABOUT 2½ CUPS (600ML)

6 large, ripe tomatoes, either Romas or a collection of varieties

¼ teaspoon fine sea salt

½ teaspoon ground cumin

½ teaspoon Aleppo pepper

¼ cup (60ml) extra-virgin olive oil

¼ cup Smoked Dukkah (page 267)

1. Preheat the oven to 350°F (180°C). Line a sheet pan with parchment paper.

2. Cut off the stem end of each tomato with a paring knife, then slice crosswise into ½-inch (1.25cm) rounds. In a bowl, mix the tomatoes with the salt, cumin, and Aleppo pepper.

3. Lay the tomatoes on the parchment paper in one layer. Roast until the tomatoes have shrunk by a third of their original size but are still soft inside, about 30 minutes. Let cool completely on the pan.

4. When cool, toss the tomatoes with the oil and dukkah to coat. Taste, adding more salt if desired. Serve at room temperature or refrigerate for up to 7 days.

When cherry tomatoes are in season, they make a satisfying condiment in a matter of seconds. It's dead simple, too: Get a pan nice and hot with some oil, add the cherry tomatoes, and you're there. Spoon the blistered tomatoes on top of fish, chicken, vegetables, or anything that would benefit from a sweet-tart summer accent. Ensure you pat the tomatoes dry—they will always splatter some when they first hit the oil, but removing as much water as possible from their exteriors keeps the splatter at a minimum.

Serve with Tomato-Ginger Glazed Salmon (page 192).

BLISTERED CHERRY TOMATOES

Active Time: 5 minutes

MAKES ABOUT 1 PINT (300G)

1 pint (300g) cherry tomatoes, stemmed if necessary but left whole

3 tablespoons grapeseed or other neutral oil

Pinch of flaky sea salt, such as Maldon

Pat the tomatoes dry with a kitchen towel. Heat the oil in a large saucepan over high heat until it shimmers and is nearly smoking. Add the tomatoes carefully; they will pop on contact with the oil, so be aware of any oil splattering up. Shake or stir the pan until the skins of the tomatoes start to split, 20 to 30 seconds. Once all the skins have popped open, season with flaky salt and eat right away, or allow to cool, then transfer to an airtight container, and use within a week.

Fresh fennel isn't that common in Egypt (they're more likely to use dried fennel seeds), but when cooked in tomato sauce, fennel becomes a sweet-tart relish that pairs well with fish and poultry. Here, the sweetness of fennel is emphasized with golden raisins, while garlic, ginger, and Aleppo add pungency and heat. If you have extra fennel, you can roast wedges of the bulb in a 400°F (200°C) oven for 20 minutes or until caramelized for a simple side dish.

Serve with whole fish, like Samak Singari (page 184).

TOMATO-BRAISED FENNEL

Active Time: 40 minutes

SERVES 4

3 tablespoons extra-virgin olive oil

1 medium yellow onion, finely diced

1 large fennel bulb, cored and diced (about 2 cups)

½ teaspoon fine sea salt, plus more as needed

2 garlic cloves, minced

1 tablespoon minced ginger

1 teaspoon Aleppo pepper

2 large heirloom or 4 Roma tomatoes, cored and diced (about 3 cups)

¼ cup golden raisins

5 Kalamata olives, pitted and coarsely chopped

½ cup (113ml) water

1. Heat the oil in a large saucepan over medium-high heat. Add the onion and fennel and cook, stirring often, until the onion starts to soften, about 4 minutes. Stir in the salt, garlic, ginger, and Aleppo pepper and cook until the garlic is fragrant, about 30 seconds.

2. Add the tomatoes, raisins, olives, and water and simmer until the fennel is soft, the tomato pieces have fallen apart, and most of the liquid has been cooked off, about 10 minutes. Serve warm or cool completely and refrigerate for up to 1 week. To reheat, gently warm in a pan on the stove with a splash of water.

Thicker, creamier, and tangier than yogurt, labne has become a go-to ingredient for when I need a quick and simple dip or sauce for a dish. These days, you can buy good labne in the dairy section of Middle Eastern grocery stores and many general grocery stores, too. If you can't buy labne, there are two options: use plain whole-milk Greek yogurt or make it yourself. All it takes is draining out the whey from plain yogurt with the help of some cheesecloth. Consider using this as the base of Tangerine Labne (page 206), Onion Labne (page 146), or Chile Labne (page 222).

LABNE

Active Time: 10 minutes

Plan Ahead: The labne needs to drain for 6 hours

Equipment: Enough cheesecloth to line a strainer in two layers and kitchen twine. The finer the cheesecloth, the easier it is to scrape the labne out after draining.

MAKES ABOUT 2½ CUPS (600ML)

1 quart (908g) plain whole-milk yogurt

Layer a fine-mesh strainer with a double thickness of cheesecloth, ensuring there's plenty of cheesecloth hanging over the rim of the strainer. Place the strainer over a bowl and spoon the yogurt into the cheesecloth. Tie the cheesecloth closed with kitchen twine so the yogurt is covered, then refrigerate the bowl and strainer for 6 hours or overnight. Uncover and transfer to a storage container. Labne generally keeps in the refrigerator as long as yogurt.

This recipe can work with savory or sweet preparations, from grilled quail to ice cream. Baking the figs in the fig leaves gives the fruit a subtle almond flavor while the vanilla provides a lovely floral fragrance. We make vanilla oil at the restaurants by scraping the seeds from one vanilla bean and adding them to 1 cup grapeseed oil. Then we put the vanilla bean, seeds, and oil in a bottle so that, over time, the oil gets infused with more vanilla flavor. If you love vanilla and like to find uses beyond desserts, make the oil and store it in a mason jar. Here, since we only need a little oil for the figs, we're making only a small amount of oil.

Serve with Grilled Sesame Quail with Black Tahina (page 200).

VANILLA-ROASTED FIGS

Active Time: 15 minutes

Equipment: 4 (3-inch / 7.5cm) ring molds or 3 (4-inch / 10cm) ring molds and toothpicks, or parchment paper. If using 3-inch molds, you will need 4 fresh fig leaves. If using 4-inch ring molds, you will need 3 leaves. If using parchment, no fig leaves are necessary.

MAKES 1 CUP

3 to 4 large fresh fig leaves (optional, see Equipment note above)

2 tablespoons grapeseed oil

¾ teaspoon vanilla bean paste or seeds from a split vanilla bean

12 fresh Mission or green figs, stemmed and halved through the stem end

1. Preheat the oven to 400°F (204°C). Put 3 to 4 (3- or 4-inch / 7.5 or 10cm) ring molds on a sheet pan. For each ring mold, press a fig leaf into the mold so that the surface of the sheet pan at the base and sides of the mold is covered. If you don't have a ring mold, cut two 16- by 12-inch (40.5 by 30.5cm) pieces of parchment paper.

2. In a medium bowl, stir together the oil and vanilla bean paste. Add the figs and mix to coat in the oil. Divide the figs between 3 to 4 ring molds. Cover the figs with the leaf ends, then secure closed as best as you can with a few toothpicks. If using parchment paper, fold each piece in half crosswise, then open and lay flat. Center half the figs on one side of each piece of parchment. Fold the opposite side over, then fold up the sides a few times to make a secure packet, enclosing the figs inside.

3. Bake until the figs are soft in the center, about 15 minutes. Let cool completely in the packets so they can absorb the aromas of the leaves (if using) and the vanilla.

I am a big fan of caramelized onions, but sometimes I want onions with a little more texture, especially for topping dishes that benefit from extra texture, like Koshari (page 156). Onions in Egypt tend to be drier than what we have in the United States, so they fry up crisp. In America, the most reliable way to get onions to fry up crisp is coat them in flour first. I do one more step here, first soaking the onions in buttermilk to remove some of their pungency and making them taste sweeter while ensuring the flour clings to the slices.

Serve with Koshari (page 156), Fresh Fava Bean Bessara (page 56), or on any braise.

CRISPY ONIONS

Active Time: 20 minutes

Plan Ahead: You can make the onions a day or two ahead and keep them in the refrigerator. Before using, crisp up in a nonstick skillet until hot.

MAKES A SCANT 2 CUPS (200G)

1 small yellow onion

¼ cup (60ml) buttermilk

1 cup (140g) all-purpose flour

1 teaspoon paprika

½ teaspoon cayenne pepper

Fine sea salt

1½ cups (360ml) vegetable oil

1. Slice the onion as thinly as possible into half-moons. Place in a bowl and add the buttermilk. Toss the onions in the buttermilk with your hands, separating the onion slices, until coated. Let sit 15 minutes or up to 30 minutes (any longer and the acid from the buttermilk will overly soften the onions). Drain the onions.

2. In a medium bowl, whisk together the flour, paprika, cayenne, and a generous pinch or two of salt. Add the onions a handful at a time and toss to coat, then shake off the extra flour and lay the onions in an even layer (where they don't overlap too much) in a large pie plate or baking pan.

3. Have a tray lined with paper towels ready. Heat the oil in a large skillet over medium-high heat until bubbles form rapidly around a wooden spoon placed in the oil and the oil reaches about 350°F (180°C). Add half the onions and fry, stirring occasionally, until they are deep golden brown all over, 3 to 4 minutes. Using a slotted spoon, scoop the onions out of the pan and scatter on the paper towels to absorb excess oil, then repeat with the remaining onions. While still warm, season the onions with a couple of pinches of salt. Extra onions can be refrigerated for up to 5 days.

Dates have long been associated with North Africa and the Gulf States, where there are many varieties. One of the most prized is medjool, which is large, meaty, and sweet. Contrast its jammy flavors with onion and wine, and you have a complex chutney to serve with cheese, chicken salad sandwiches, or—in the case of this book—meatballs. Vadouvan, a fenugreek-spiked curry blend, is especially good here. If you don't have Vadouvan, add a pinch of ground sumac.

Serve with Lamb Meatballs with Ricotta Dumplings and Date Chutney (page 159).

DATE CHUTNEY

Active Time: 15 minutes

MAKES ABOUT 1¼ CUPS (300ML)

1 tablespoon extra-virgin olive oil

½ small red onion or 2 shallots, finely diced

8 ounces (225g) dried dates (preferably medjool), pitted and coarsely chopped

½ cup (120ml) dry white wine or ½ cup (120ml) and 1 tablespoon (15ml) distilled white vinegar

1 teaspoon Vadouvan curry powder

1 teaspoon freshly squeezed lemon juice

1 teaspoon finely grated lemon zest

¼ teaspoon fine sea salt, plus more if desired

Heat the oil in a medium skillet over medium heat. Add the onion and sweat until softened, about 4 minutes. Stir in the dates, wine, and curry powder, increase the heat to medium-high, and cook until most of the wine has evaporated, about 3 minutes. Stir in the lemon juice, zest, and salt and taste, adding more salt if desired. Date chutney keeps in the refrigerator for 2 months.

The bright taste of Aleppo pepper in this infused oil can dress up nearly everything, from plain rice or potatoes to grilled fish and meat. And if you like your Koshari (page 156) on the spicy side, leave the chile oil at the table so you can add some as you eat.

CHILE OIL

Active Time: 10 minutes

Equipment: A heatproof glass pint jar, instant-read thermometer

MAKES A SCANT ½ CUP (118ML)

2 tablespoons Aleppo pepper or red pepper flakes

1 tablespoon minced garlic

½ teaspoon fine sea salt

½ cup (118ml) vegetable oil

Put the Aleppo pepper, garlic, and salt in a heatproof glass pint jar. In a small saucepan over medium heat, warm the oil until it shimmers (when an instant-read thermometer registers 350°F / 177°C). Pour the oil slowly into the jar (it will bubble up vigorously) and stir to combine. Let cool at room temperature, then store in the refrigerator for up to a month.

ACKNOWLEDGMENTS

The life of a chef is built on meeting and learning from others, from mentors to friends and colleagues. Writing this book opened up my world even more as I made new connections through my travels. Words alone don't go far enough to thank everyone who helped bring this book to life.

I would like to thank the chefs I've had the privilege of getting to know in Egypt, where I've shared some of the most memorable dining experiences of my life. First and foremost is Moustafa Elrefaey, who opened Egypt up to me and introduced me to the following culinary talents: Yasser Ramadan, Shady Elshalkany, Moustafa Abdelrazik, Omar Kerdasa, Hady Ahmed, "Kory" (Mohamed Mahmoud), Shermeen Moaanis, Emad Refaat, Amer Gouda, Hussien Bahary, Ahmed Fahmy, Mohamed Salah, and Kareem Abdelrahman. Thanks to you all.

This book would never have happened without the support and expertise of the MINA Group. A special thanks to Adam Sobel, whose culinary passion is second to none, and who not only traveled with me in Egypt but also used the experience to craft dishes destined to become classics. To Veronica Arroyo, who helped create the desserts, and to Gerald Chin, Alex Griffiths, Raj Dixit, and Harrison Chernick for everything from recipe development, to prep and execution during the photo shoot. (Thank you all for your attention to detail.) To Leah Smith for liaising the project between the book team and our chef teams, and to Ashley Keeney, for keeping us moving forward and managing our schedules. Thank you, team.

Since no book writes (or photographs or designs) itself, thanks to the book team led by writer Kate Leahy. To John Lee, who captured the spirit of modern-day Egypt, Alice Chau for expert art direction and graphic design, Christine Gallary for testing recipes to make sure they worked for home cooks, Daniela Vergara and the Ornos team for recipe testing support, Lillian Kang for food styling, Glenn Jenkins for prop styling, and Leslie Jonath for assembling the team. Stunning work, everyone. In Egypt, thanks to Khalid Alazem and Abo Obaida Alazem for traveling with John Lee, and to Dr. Mennat Eldorry for fielding Egyptian history questions.

Big thanks to Michael Szczerban, whose patience is unparalleled and whose thorough, thoughtful feedback shaped the book into something I am immensely proud of. Also thanks to Tucker Shaw for sharpening the story, Pam Kingsley for copyediting, Christine Corcoran Cox and Katherine Isaacs for proofreading, and Elizabeth Parson for indexing. At Little, Brown, gratitude also goes to Arik Hardin, Ben Allen, Lucy Kim, Thea Diklich-Newell, Nyamekye Waliyaya, Gianella Rojas, and Lauren Ortiz for all that you do behind the scenes. Thanks also to Janis Donnaud for agenting the book.

Finally, I would especially like to thank my parents, Minerva and Ezzat, who sacrificed everything to bring our family to the United States and kept our family's Egyptian roots alive at home. Thanks also to my brother, Magid, and sister, Mennel, for supporting me. And to my wife, Diane, and sons, Sammy and Anthony, who are my world. Thank you for your unwavering love and support, no matter how many days I spend on the road. This book is for you.

INDEX

Note: Page references in *italics* indicate photographs.

A

acid and citrus, 37
Ahi Crudo on Ta'ameya, *96*, 97
Aleppo pepper, 37
   Chile Oil, *141*, 279
   "Dukkah" Spice, 266
   Tangerine Carrot Juice with
      Aleppo Sugar, 46, *47*
Alexandria ("Alex"), 180
almonds
   Om Ali, *254*, 255
   Smoked Dukkah, 267
appetizers, list of, 20
apples
   Middle Eastern Waldorf, *132*, 133
arugula, 40

B

Baba Ghanoush, Smoky, *58*, 59
baharat
   Baharat, 266
   Baharat Chicken in Grape
      Leaves with Tangerine
      Labne, 206, *207*
Baklava Napoleon, 259–61, *260*
baladi bread
   about, 42
   Baladi Bread, 78–79, *82*
Bananas, Kataifi-Wrapped
   Caramelized, 248, *249*
Basbousa, Mango, 262, *263*
beans. *See* chickpeas; fava beans
beef
   Alexandria Steak Sandwiches,
      216, 217
   Beef Tenderloin Kebabs with
      Egyptian Pepper Sauce,
      218, *219*
   Braised Oxtails with Potatoes
      and Shaved Carrots,
      234–36, *235*
Beet Cream, Smoked, *51*, 55
bessara
   about, 42
   Fresh Fava Bean Bessara,
      56, *57*
Beurre Blanc, Dukkah, 195–97, *196*
Black Tahina, *50*, 52
Bouillabaisse, Molokhia,
   172–74, *173*
breads
   Baladi Bread, 78–79, *82*
   baladi bread, about, 42
   Dukkah Flatbread, 84–85, *86*
   feteer, about, 42
   Feteer with Ishta, 87–88, *89*
Brussels Sprouts and Onion
   Labne, Roasted Squash Steak
   with, 146, *147*

butter
   clarifying, 38
   Garlic Butter, 217

C

camel liver in Kerdasa, 212
Cardamom Candied Pistachios,
   243, *245*
carob molasses
   about, 41
   Carob Ice Cream, *250*, 251
carrots
   Braised Oxtails with Potatoes
      and Shaved Carrots, 234–36,
      235
   Mixed Pickles, *72*, 73
   Tangerine Carrot Juice with
      Aleppo Sugar, 46, *47*
cashews, 40
cauliflower
   Hummus with Cauliflower,
      Pomegranate, and Foie Gras,
      124, 125
   Mashed Dukkah Cauliflower, 137
   Mixed Pickles, *72*, 73
cheese, 38
   Feta-Brined Spatchcock
      Chicken with Mint and
      Green Onions, 208–10, *209*
   Feteer with Ishta, 87–88, *89*
   Halloumi and Watermelon
      Salad, 130, *131*
   Lamb Meatballs with Ricotta
      Dumplings and Date
      Chutney, 159–61, *160*
   Macaroni Béchamel with
      Mushroom Bolognese,
      165–67, *166*
   saving feta brine, 210
chicken
   Baharat Chicken in Grape
      Leaves with Tangerine
      Labne, 206, *207*
   brining, 210
   Chicken Stock, 271
   Feta-Brined Spatchcock
      Chicken with Mint and
      Green Onions, 208–10, *209*
chickpeas, 40
   Crispy Chickpeas, 70, *71*
   Hummus, *51*, 54
   Koshari, 156–58, *157*
chiles/red peppers, 37. *See also*
   Aleppo pepper
   Chile Oil, *141*, 279
   "Dukkah" Spice, 266
   Okra with Shallots and Chile,
      134, *135*
Chutney, Date, *160*, 279

coconut
   Kataifi-Wrapped Shrimp
      with Mango Chile Sauce,
      108–10, *109*
   Mango Basbousa, 262, *263*
   Om Ali, *254*, 255
coriander
   "Dukkah" Spice, 266
   Smoked Dukkah, 267
   Ta'ameya, 92, *93*
couscous, 40
   Lemon Saffron Couscous,
      152, *193*
cream
   Baklava Napoleon, 259–61, *260*
   Smoked Beet Cream, *51*, 55
croissants
   Om Ali, *254*, 255
cucumbers
   Ahi Crudo on Ta'ameya, *96*, 97
   Cucumber Honeydew Juice,
      47, 49
   Freekeh Tabbouli, 150, *151*
   prepping, 129
   Salata Baladi, *128*, 129
   Tzatziki, *51*, 53

D

dairy, 38
dates, 41
   buying and making date
      paste, 258
   Date Chutney, *160*, 279
   Ma'amoul, 256–58, *257*
desserts, list of, 21
Dill Yogurt Espuma, *193*, 194
dips and sauces. *See also* tahina
   Dill Yogurt Espuma, *193*, 194
   Dukkah Beurre Blanc, 195–97,
      196
   Egyptian Pepper Sauce, 218, *219*
   Egyptian Tartar Sauce, 178, *179*
   Fresh Fava Bean Bessara, 56, *57*
   Ful Medames, 60, *61*
   Hummus, *51*, 54
   Hummus with Cauliflower,
      Pomegranate, and Foie Gras,
      124, 125
   Mango Chile Sauce, 108, *109*
   Mango Ketchup, *99*, 100
   Onion Labne, 146
   Saffron Mango Sauce, 111, *112*
   Smoked Beet Cream, *51*, 55
   Smoky Baba Ghanoush, *58*, 59
   Tzatziki, *51*, 53
drinks
   Cucumber Honeydew Juice,
      47, 49
   Hibiscus Pomegranate Juice,
      47, 48

Limeade, 46
Tangerine Carrot Juice with Aleppo Sugar, 46, *47*
duck
ground, sourcing or making, 164
One-Pot Toasted Orzo with Duck Ragù, 162–64, *163*
dukkah
Dukkah Beurre Blanc, 195–97, *196*
Dukkah Flatbread, 84–85, *86*
Mashed Dukkah Cauliflower, 137
Roasted Tomatoes with Smoked Dukkah, *272, 273*
Smoked Dukkah, 267
"Dukkah" Spice, 266
Dumplings, Ricotta, and Date Chutney, Lamb Meatballs with, 159–61, *160*

E
edible flowers, 37
eggplant
Harissa Ratatouille, 136
Pickled Eggplant, 74, *75*
Smoky Baba Ghanoush, *58, 59*
Egyptian classic dishes, 42
Elrefaey, Moustafa, 22, 26, 28, 30, *31,* 56, 80, 92, 104, 114, 153, 162, 170, 180, 212, 224, 281
El Sheikh Wafik, 238
equipment, 41

F
Faiyum, 104
Farro and Rice, Roasted Squab with, *202, 203*
fats, cooking, 37–38
fava beans
about, 38–40
Black Harissa Lamb Chops with Fava Beans, Peas, Mint, and Dried Lime Yogurt, 228–30, *229*
canned vs. fresh, 61
Fresh Fava Bean Bessara, 56, *57*
Ful Medames, 60, *61*
Ta'ameya, 92, *93*
Fayesh, Minerva's, *240,* 241
felucca ride, 66
fennel
"Dukkah" Spice, 266
Smoked Dukkah, 267
Tomato-Braised Fennel, *185,* 274
feteer
about, 42
Feteer with Ishta, 87–88, *89*
figs
Rice Pudding with Figs, 252, *253*
Vanilla-Roasted Figs, *201,* 277
fish
Ahi Crudo on Ta'ameya, *96,* 97
Alexandria Fish Fry, 178, *179*
buying raw tuna, 97

Grilled Octopus with Ful Medames, 118, *119*
Grilled Swordfish with Nigella Seeds, Preserved Lemon, and Green Onions, 175–77, *176*
Molokhia Bouillabaisse, 172–74, *173*
Phyllo-Crusted Sole with Dukkah Beurre Blanc and Golden Raisins, 195–97, *196*
Salt-Baked Whole Fish with Zucchini and Lemon, 188–91, *189*
Samak Singari, 184–87, *185*
Tomato-Ginger Glazed Salmon, 192, *193*
flour, 40
flower waters, 37
foie gras
Hummus with Cauliflower, Pomegranate, and Foie Gras, *124,* 125
prepping and cooking, 125
freekeh, 40
Freekeh Tabbouli, 150, *151*
fruit molasses, 41
fruits. *See also specific fruits*
citrus, 37
Labne Frozen Yogurt with Stone Fruit, *246,* 247
ful medames
about, 42
Ful Medames, 60, *61*
Grilled Octopus with Ful Medames, 118, *119*

G
garlic, 40
Chile Oil, *141,* 279
Garlic Butter, 217
ghee and clarified butter, 38
Ginger-Tomato Glazed Salmon, 192, *193*
grains, 40. *See also specific grains*
Granita, Raspberry Rose Water, 244, *245*
Grape Leaves, Baharat Chicken in, with Tangerine Labne, 206, *207*
grill baskets, buying and using, 200
ground red pepper, 37

H
Halloumi and Watermelon Salad, 130, *131*
hamam mahshi, about, 42
harissa, 37
Black Harissa Lamb Chops with Fava Beans, Peas, Mint, and Dried Lime Yogurt, 228–30, *229*
Harissa Ratatouille, 136
Hawawshi, Turkey, *120,* 121
hazelnuts
about, 40
Smoked Dukkah, 267

herbs, 40
Egyptian Tartar Sauce, 178, *179*
Roasted White Sweet Potatoes with Mixed Herbs, 142, *219*
Hibiscus Pomegranate Juice, *47,* 48
honey
Baklava Napoleon, 259–61, *260*
Honeydew Cucumber Juice, *47,* 49
Hummus, *51,* 54
Hummus with Cauliflower, Pomegranate, and Foie Gras, *124,* 125

I
Ice Cream, Carob, *250,* 251
ishta, about, 38
Ishta, Feteer with, 87–88, *89*

K
Kafr El Dawwar, 80
Kataifi-Wrapped Caramelized Bananas, 248, *249*
Kataifi-Wrapped Shrimp with Mango Chile Sauce, 108–10, *109*
Ketchup, Mango, *99,* 100
koji, about, 146
koshari
about, 42
Koshari, 156–58, *157*
Koshary Abou Tarek, 154

L
labne, 38
Grilled Lamb Kofte with Chile Labne, 222, *223*
Labne, 274, *275*
Labne Frozen Yogurt with Stone Fruit, *246,* 247
Onion Labne, 146
Tangerine Labne, 206, *207*
lamb
Black Harissa Lamb Chops with Fava Beans, Peas, Mint, and Dried Lime Yogurt, 228–30, *229*
chops, buying and prepping, 230
Grilled Lamb Kofte with Chile Labne, 222, *223*
Lamb Meatballs with Ricotta Dumplings and Date Chutney, 159–61, *160*
Spiced Tomato-Braised Lamb Shanks, 231–33, *232*
lemon olive oil, 38
lemons, 37
Lemon Potatoes, *138,* 139
Lemon Saffron Couscous, 152, *193*
Preserved Onion Condiment, 175
Salt-Baked Whole Fish with Zucchini and Lemon, 188–91, *189*

lentils, 38
  Ful Medames, 60, *61*
  Koshari, 156–58, *157*
  Pumpkin Red Lentil Soup, 122, *123*
limes, 37
  dried, about, 37
  Limeade, 46
  Lime Popsicles with Mint and White Peach, *242,* 243
lobster
  cooking lobster, 113
  Lobster Mango Salad, 111–13, *112*

M

Ma'amoul, 256–58, *257*
macaroni
  Koshari, 156–58, *157*
  macaroni béchamel, about, 42
  Macaroni Béchamel with Mushroom Bolognese, 165–67, *166*
mahlab
  Minerva's Fayesh, *240,* 241
Mandarine Koueider, 238
mangos
  buying mango pickle and mango puree, 110
  Egyptian, about, 114
  Lobster Mango Salad, 111–13, *112*
  Mango Basbousa, 262, *263*
  Mango Chile Sauce, 108, *109*
  Mango Ketchup, *99,* 100
  Saffron Mango Sauce, 111, *112*
Meatballs, Lamb, with Ricotta Dumplings and Date Chutney, 159–61, *160*
Mint and White Peach, Lime Popsicles with, *242,* 243
molokhia
  about, 42
  Molokhia Bouillabaisse, 172–74, *173*
  sourcing and prepping, 174
mushrooms
  Macaroni Béchamel with Mushroom Bolognese, 165–67, *166*
  Mushroom Stock, 270
  wild, cleaning and cooking, 167

N

Nile River, 66
nuts, 40. *See also specific nuts*
  buying and toasting, 267

O

Octopus, Grilled, with Ful Medames, 118, *119*
oils
  Chile Oil, *141,* 279
  for cooking, 37–38
Okra with Shallots and Chile, 134, *135*

olive oil, 38
om ali
  about, 42
  Om Ali, *254,* 255
onions, 40
  Crispy Onions, 278
  green, turning into garnish, 177
  Koshari, 156–58, *157*
  Onion Labne, 146
  Sayadeya Rice, 153
  Sizzling Prawns, 170, *171*
Ossol Al Tahey (Fundamentals of Cooking), 43
Oxtails, Braised, with Potatoes and Shaved Carrots, 234–36, *235*

P

pantry items, 35–41
paprika
  Baharat, 266
pasta, 40. *See also* couscous; vermicelli
  Koshari, 156–58, *157*
  Macaroni Béchamel with Mushroom Bolognese, 165–67, *166*
  One-Pot Toasted Orzo with Duck Ragù, 162–64, *163*
peanuts, 40
peppers. *See also* chiles/red peppers
  Egyptian Pepper Sauce, 218, *219*
  Harissa Ratatouille, 136
  roasting peppers in the oven, 136
phyllo
  Baklava Napoleon, 259–61, *260*
  Phyllo-Crusted Sole with Dukkah Beurre Blanc and Golden Raisins, 195–97, *196*
  sourcing, 197
  sourcing and using, 261
Pickled Eggplant, 74, *75*
pickles
  making quick pickles, 74
  Mixed Pickles, *72,* 73
pistachios
  Cardamom Candied Pistachios, 243, *245*
  Om Ali, *254,* 255
  Smoked Dukkah, 267
the pit roast, 224
pomegranate
  Hibiscus Pomegranate Juice, *47,* 48
  Hummus with Cauliflower, Pomegranate, and Foie Gras, *124,* 125
  pomegranate molasses, about, 41
Popsicles, Lime, with Mint and White Peach, *242,* 243

potatoes
  Braised Oxtails with Potatoes and Shaved Carrots, 234–36, *235*
  Lemon Potatoes, *138,* 139
  Roasted White Sweet Potatoes with Mixed Herbs, 142, *219*
  Saffron Fingerling Potatoes, 140, *141*
  Samak Singari, 184–87, *185*
  Steak Fries with a Trio of Dips, 98, *99*
Prawns, Sizzling, 170, *171*
preserved citrus, 37
pudding
  Om Ali, *254,* 255
  Rice Pudding with Figs, 252, *253*
pumpkin
  buying pumpkin for roasting, 122
  Pumpkin Red Lentil Soup, 122, *123*
  Pumpkin Seed Tahina, *51,* 53

Q

Quail, Grilled Sesame, with Black Tahina, 200, *201*

R

raisins
  Om Ali, *254,* 255
  Phyllo-Crusted Sole with Dukkah Beurre Blanc and Golden Raisins, 195–97, *196*
  Tomato-Braised Fennel, *185,* 274
Raspberry Rose Water Granita, 244, *245*
Ratatouille, Harissa, 136
rice, 40
  Everyday Egyptian Rice, 152
  Koshari, 156–58, *157*
  Rice Pudding with Figs, 252, *253*
  Roasted Squab with Farro and Rice, *202,* 203
  Sayadeya Rice, 153
  Zucchini Mahshi, 143–45, *144*
Rose Water Raspberry Granita, 244, *245*

S

saffron
  Lemon Saffron Couscous, 152, *193*
  Saffron Fingerling Potatoes, 140, *141*
  Saffron Mango Sauce, 111, *112*
salads
  Freekeh Tabbouli, 150, *151*
  Halloumi and Watermelon Salad, 130, *131*
  Lobster Mango Salad, 111–13, *112*
  Middle Eastern Waldorf, *132,* 133
  Salata Baladi, *128,* 129

salmon
Tomato-Ginger Glazed Salmon, 192, *193*
Za'atar-Cured Salmon with Tzatziki and Salmon Roe, 101, *102, 103*
salt, 35
Salt-Baked Whole Fish with Zucchini and Lemon, 188–91, *189*
Samak Singari, 184–87, *185*
Sandwiches, Alexandria Steak, *216,* 217
sauces. *See* dips and sauces
Sayadeya Rice, 153
seasonings, 35–37
seeds, 40. *See also* Pumpkin Seed; sesame seeds
sesame seeds, 40
Baklava Napoleon, 259–61, *260*
Grilled Sesame Quail with Black Tahina, 200, *201*
Smoked Dukkah, 267
Ta'ameya, 92, *93*
Shallots and Chile, Okra with, 134, *135*
shellfish
cooking lobster, 113
Kataifi-Wrapped Shrimp with Mango Chile Sauce, 108–10, *109*
Lobster Mango Salad, 111–13, *112*
Molokhia Bouillabaisse, 172–74, *173*
Sizzling Prawns, 170, *171*
shrimp
Kataifi-Wrapped Shrimp with Mango Chile Sauce, 108–10, *109*
Molokhia Bouillabaisse, 172–74, *173*
Simple Syrup, 49
snapper
Alexandria Fish Fry, 178, *179*
Molokhia Bouillabaisse, 172–74, *173*
Samak Singari, 184–87, *185, 186*
Sole, Phyllo-Crusted, with Dukkah Beurre Blanc and Golden Raisins, 195–97, *196*
Soup, Pumpkin Red Lentil, 122, *123*
spice blends
Baharat, 266
"Dukkah" Spice, 266
Smoked Dukkah, 267
spices
cooking with, 34
list of, 35–37
toasting, grinding, and storing, 37
squab
hamam mahshi, about, 42
Roasted Squab with Farro and Rice, *202,* 203

squash
buying pumpkin for roasting, 122
Harissa Ratatouille, 136
Pumpkin Red Lentil Soup, 122, *123*
Roasted Squash Steak with Brussels Sprouts and Onion Labne, 146, *147*
Salt-Baked Whole Fish with Zucchini and Lemon, 188–91, *189*
Zucchini Mahshi, 143–45, *144*
stocks
Chicken Stock, 271
Middle Eastern Vegetable Stock, 269
Mushroom Stock, 270
sweeteners, 41
Sweet Potatoes, Roasted White, with Mixed Herbs, 142, *219*
Swordfish, Grilled, with Nigella Seeds, Preserved Lemon, and Green Onions, 175–77, *176*

T
ta'ameya
about, 42
Ahi Crudo on Ta'ameya, *96,* 97
Ta'ameya, 92, *93*
Tabbouli, Freekeh, 150, *151*
tahina
about, 41
Black Tahina, *50, 52*
Grilled Sesame Quail with Black Tahina, 200, *201*
Pumpkin Seed Tahina, *51, 53*
Tahina, *51, 52*
tahini paste. *See also* tahina
about, 40–41
Hummus, *51,* 54
Smoky Baba Ghanoush, *58,* 59
tangerines
Mango Chile Sauce, 108, *109*
Tangerine Carrot Juice with Aleppo Sugar, 46, *47*
Tangerine Labne, 206, *207*
Tarek, Abou, 154
Tartar Sauce, Egyptian, 178, *179*
tomatoes
Ahi Crudo on Ta'ameya, *96,* 97
Blistered Cherry Tomatoes, *193,* 273
Freekeh Tabbouli, 150, *151*
Koshari, 156–58, *157*
One-Pot Toasted Orzo with Duck Ragù, 162–64, *163*
Roasted Tomatoes with Smoked Dukkah, *272,* 273
Salata Baladi, *128,* 129
Spiced Tomato-Braised Lamb Shanks, 231–33, *232*
Tomato-Braised Fennel, *185,* 274

Tomato-Ginger Glazed Salmon, 192, *193*
whole canned, prepping, 233
Zucchini Mahshi, 143–45, *144*
tuna
Ahi Crudo on Ta'ameya, *96,* 97
buying raw tuna, 97
Turkey Hawawshi, *120,* 121
Tzatziki, *51, 53*

V
Vanilla-Roasted Figs, *201,* 277
vegeta (seasoning mix), 35
vegetables. *See also specific vegetables*
making quick pickles with, 74
Middle Eastern Vegetable Stock, 269
verjus, 37
vermicelli
buying, 158
Everyday Egyptian Rice, 152
Koshari, 156–58, *157*
vinegar, 37

W
Waldorf, Middle Eastern, *132,* 133
walnuts
Baklava Napoleon, 259–61, *260*
Middle Eastern Waldorf, *132,* 133
Watermelon and Halloumi Salad, 130, *131*
wheat berries, 40
white chocolate
Baklava Napoleon, 259–61, *260*
White Peach and Mint, Lime Popsicles with, *242,* 243

Y
yogurt. *See also* labne
Baklava Napoleon, 259–61, *260*
Black Harissa Lamb Chops with Fava Beans, Peas, Mint, and Dried Lime Yogurt, 228–30, *229*
Dill Yogurt Espuma, *193,* 194
Labne Frozen Yogurt with Stone Fruit, *246,* 247
Middle Eastern Waldorf, *132,* 133
Tzatziki, *51, 53*

Z
Za'atar-Cured Salmon with Tzatziki and Salmon Roe, 101, *102, 103*
Zooba, 30
zucchini
Harissa Ratatouille, 136
Salt-Baked Whole Fish with Zucchini and Lemon, 188–91, *189*
Zucchini Mahshi, 143–45, *144*

ABOUT THE AUTHORS

Born in Cairo and raised in Ellensburg, Washington, **Michael Mina** is the chef, founder, and executive chairman of the MINA Group, which owns and operates more than thirty restaurants around the world.

Chef Mina began his epicurean journey at the Culinary Institute of America in New York, where he spent weekends working in Chef Charlie Palmer's restaurant Aureole in New York City. Early in his career, Mina was presented with a rare opportunity to develop an upscale seafood restaurant in San Francisco with Chef George Morrone. Unfazed by the 1989 earthquake that rocked San Francisco on his second day in the city, he worked developing the concept for two years as chef de cuisine, opening Aqua with Morrone to national acclaim in 1991. Two years later, he became Aqua's executive chef. Over the course of his time at the restaurant, he garnered two James Beard Awards, including Rising Star Chef and Best Chef: California.

Chef Mina's culinary and business vision led to the founding of the MINA Group in 2002, creating restaurants that have received numerous accolades, including a Michelin star for his eponymous San Francisco restaurant, Michael Mina, the subject of his first cookbook. His restaurants have been featured on the Food Network and *Today* and in *Bon Appétit*, *Food & Wine*, *TIME*, *Robb Report*, *Travel + Leisure*, and *Wine Spectator*, and he has cooked for presidents Bill Clinton, George W. Bush, and Barack Obama. In 2013, he was inducted into the James Beard Foundation's Who's Who of Food & Beverage in America.

Adam Sobel is a television personality and chef/partner of the MINA Group. Sobel earned early acclaim in Las Vegas as chef de cuisine at Guy Savoy before serving as executive chef at MINA Group restaurants Bourbon Steak in Washington, DC, and, later, executive chef and partner at RN74 in San Francisco. He develops menus and trains chefs across the MINA Group portfolio and has appeared on popular shows such as Guy Fieri's *Tournament of Champions*.

Kate Leahy is a San Francisco–based writer who has collaborated on more than a dozen books on food and wine.